AN OPEN BOOK

Also by MICHAEL DIRDA

Readings: Essays and Literary Entertainments

AN OPEN BOOK

Coming of Age in the Heartland

MICHAEL DIRDA

W. W. Norton & Company
New York   London

For information about permission to reproduce selections from this book,
write to Permissions, W. W. Norton & Company, Inc., 500 Fifth Avenue,
New York, NY 10110

Manufacturing by Quebecor World, Fairfield
Book design by Blue Shoe Studio
Production manager: Amanda Morrison

LIBRARY OF CONGRESS CATALOGING-IN-PUBLICATION DATA

Dirda, Michael.
An open book : coming of age in the heartland / by Michael Dirda.—
1st ed.
p. cm.
ISBN 0-393-05756-9 (hardcover)
1. Dirda, Michael. 2. Journalists—United States—Biography.
3. Critics—United States—Biography. I. Title.
PN4874.D475A3 2003
809—dc21

2003011413

W. W. Norton & Company, Inc., 500 Fifth Avenue, New York, N.Y. 10110
www.wwnorton.com

W. W. Norton & Company Ltd.
Castle House, 75/76 Wells Street, London W1T 3QT

1 2 3 4 5 6 7 8 9 0

For Chris, Mike and Nate

The thought of our past years in me doth breed
Perpetual benediction. . . .

—*Wordsworth*

Contents

Preface   13

PART ONE   Learning to Read

Chapter One   21

Chapter Two   48

Chapter Three   70

Chapter Four   90

PART TWO   Turning the Pages

Chapter Five   107

Chapter Six   126

Chapter Seven   147

PART THREE   Adult Material

Chapter Eight   157

Chapter Nine   176

Chapter Ten   186

Chapter Eleven   202

Chapter Twelve   220

Chapter Thirteen   228

PART FOUR A Liberal Education

Chapter Fourteen   243

Chapter Fifteen   254

Chapter Sixteen   261

Chapter Seventeen   268

Chapter Eighteen   278

Chapter Nineteen   285

Chapter Twenty   295

Chapter Twenty-one   305

Epilogue   319

Michael Dirda's Book List   323

Acknowledgments   327

Index   329

Preface

Back in the mid-1990s *The Washington Post* awarded me a fellowship to study for three weeks at Duke University. But instead of spending my days auditing classes or attending lectures, I started to write a memoir about my childhood. Mine has always been a wistful, retrospective nature, veering between genuine melancholy and a kind of humorous self-deprecating playfulness. It's not at all the character I should have preferred, and had the gods of nature or nurture consulted me I would have opted for a sunny, swashbuckling disposition, supported by a certain debonair suavity: Errol Flynn, with touches of Cary Grant. Still, in midlife, I began wondering about this ironic, moody self of mine and decided to explore its origins a little. The more I thought, the more I grew convinced that my story was also one about books and reading.

In a good autobiography the chaos of life's experience (truth) must be given some kind of order or pattern (design). St. Augustine's *Confessions*, for instance, charts the progress of a soul toward conversion to Christianity—probably the most popular template for writing about the self, though now the acceptance of God is usually replaced by the discovery of an artistic vocation or the resolution to embark on a "new life" of some more secular sort. In a less programmatic way in the *Life of Henry Brulard* Stendhal meanders through his childhood and youth, disclosing a recurrent pattern of heightened expectation followed by disappointment: After every anticipated event, whether a battle or a love affair, the novelist's reaction is a bemused, "Is that all there is?" But no matter whether you pick up Cellini's *Memoirs* or Rousseau's *Confessions* or *The Education of Henry Adams* or Eudora Welty's *One Writer's Beginnings*, all these books are thematically the same: Here is how I became who I am.

Unlike the childhoods of other writers, my early life wasn't filled with obvious violence, heartbreak or dislocation. But neither was it particularly idyllic. What I proffer here, then, are reminiscences about books, family and school, an evocation of the 1950s and 1960s in a midwestern steel town and, tangentially, a little guidance toward good reading for young people. Most of all, I wanted these pages to celebrate the joy that books brought to my young self and to record how I discovered them, what I felt, and how they shaped my character and dreams.

Mine, it now seems, may be the last generation to value the traditional bound book as the engine of education, culture and personal advancement. The future belongs to screens and keyboards. Though that may sound direly elegiac, I know people will always need stories and that any era's external packaging of them hardly matters: Oral formulas, scrolls, codices, paperbacks, e-texts—they all get the narrative job done. Nonetheless, what follows may often appear a kind of memorial, a minor monument to a time of softly turned pages, when the young entered libraries hungry for books to devour rather than information to download, when printed matter still mattered and kids daydreamed more often of writing The Great American Novel than of working on their websites.

Some readers may wonder if I discovered any unexpected truths or insights in working on *An Open Book*. Perhaps only, as Chekhov once observed, that it takes a god to distinguish between our successes and failures in life. Still, one can at least chart some of the forces at work and recall a few of the turning points.

MICHAEL DIRDA, Washington, D.C.,
January 25, 2003

NOTE: Although I touch on many books in the following pages, I seldom discuss any title for more than a few sentences, if that. Longer, more expansive pieces on books and their authors will be found in a forthcoming collection and, to some extent, in the already published *Readings: Essays and Literary Entertainments*.

For *An Open Book* I have changed a few names, in particular those of nearly all the young women I was sweet on after eighth grade. Who knows if all—or any—of them would want our association remembered? I've also adapted a few autobiographical passages from *Readings*.

AN OPEN BOOK

Part One

LEARNING
TO READ

Chapter One

The spirit afterwards, but first the touch.
—*Charlotte Mew*

Daydreaming is my only hobby. Like many people, I have now and again tried to imagine the perfect environment, the ideal conditions for reading: A worn leather armchair on a rainy night? A hammock in a freshly mowed backyard? A verandah overlooking some summer sea? Good choices, every one. But I have no doubt that they are all merely displacements, sentimental attempts to replicate the warmth and snugness of my mother's lap.

Even now I can close my eyes and again she sits, Indian-style, on the floor in a corner of our family's dining room. Leaning against the steel-ribbed vents of the heat register, she wraps the chenille housecoat tight against her body and awaits the periodic exhalations of warm, dry air. Like any picture-book hatchling or newborn, I burrow against the softness of her breast. From a small blond bookcase, she selects one of a dozen or so worn Golden Books shelved there next to the cookie tin of broken crayons and the stack of torn coloring books. Her fingers are wrinkled, puckered from the hot water of the now-drying dinner dishes.

My mother begins to explain the bright pictures to me: "Look, Michael. See the little duck! Isn't it cute? Ooh, look at the puppy!" She laughs contentedly while cradling her four-year-old son.

Do I "really and truly" remember a story about a duck? Certainly I can still summon up vague memories of ravenous tigers whizzing ever more quickly around a palm tree and gradually turning into butter: *Little Black Sambo*, which was still widely read in those days. Mostly, of course, I recall the restful security of my mother's embrace, as we would "read" together after supper, when I was all washed up like a big boy and ready for bed in my pajamas. That feeling of animal satisfaction—of a full belly and soft cotton—has ever since been high among the myriad pleasures of a life spent reading.

We lived in Lorain, Ohio—a blue-collar industrial town of sixty-five thousand on the shores of Lake Erie, thirty miles west of Cleveland and home to the largest steel pipe mill in the world. I had been born on November 6, 1948, just a few years after my father, Michael Dirda, Sr., had been honorably discharged from the Navy, with thirteen battle stars, a deep tan and just enough money to buy some new "civvies." On October 25, 1947, at the age of thirty, the second-generation Russian had married Christine Burcl, a blond, shapely Slovak beauty of not quite twenty-five. In family mythology my father had first glimpsed my mother as a young girl: She was slowly feeding a long piece of string baited with a chunk of raw chicken into a crayfish hole. There was a Band-Aid on her knee. I picture a sunshiny July afternoon as the ten-year-old crouched on the bank of the so-called County Ditch, impatient for a twitch upon her line. My father I envisage as a scrawny teenager, leaning rakishly across the handlebars of his artfully cobbled-together bicycle.

One of ten children in an impoverished widow's family, my mother grew up near the railroad tracks in South Lorain, with chickens, geese and a cow named Rosie. As kids, she and her siblings would scavenge along the rails for bits of coal for winter heat, beg for odd jobs to supplement the family's meager resources and every Sunday devoutly attend mass at St. Vitus. After Pearl Harbor, Mom contributed to the war effort by working in Elyria, eight miles from Lorain, operating a drill press that turned out screws and bolts. It was said that no one was faster or more efficient than she—and years later, when I watched her load up peck baskets with strawberries, not so much picking as threshing the sun-parched rows, I knew it had to be true.

My father's father—a Cossack who back in Russia spent more money on his horse than on his family, fought for the Czar and emigated around the time of the Revolution—died at the age of fifty-two, forcing his son to quit school to support a mother, a half-brother and two sisters. The sixteen-year-old ultimately settled for a job in "the mill," the National Tube division of U.S. Steel, and returned to it following his service in the South Pacific on the heavy cruiser *Pensacola*. Alas, the dream-burdened young man, like Miniver Cheevy in Edwin Arlington Robinson's poem, hated his lot in life with every particle of his moody, dissatisfied soul. Nonetheless, for more than four gloomy decades he walked (a forty-minute trek), then later drove to the No. 4 seamless pipe division, working shifts (seven to three one week, three to eleven the next and eleven to seven—the bone-wearying "nights"—on the third). Hardly a day went by when Dad didn't curse his fate, with loud disgust, and blame his father for dying on him.

Not surprisingly, my parents' marriage proved tense and difficult, largely because of my father's persistent sense of failure. Burdened with inchoate ambition, he lacked the will or confidence to do more than take an occasional night-school class in, say, How to Buy Stocks—and then discover that he couldn't afford to risk his hard-earned savings on what always seemed an overly volatile market. Given to long after-dinner silences, to staring into the middle distance while compulsively drumming his fingers against the arms of any easy chair he sat in, he would finally erupt into anger over some trivial domestic matter—"You're all just leeches, sucking the blood out of me"—or just as suddenly stump up to bed without a word. My mother would call him "hon" and attempt to placate these outbursts of choleric self-pity, but he would rage all the louder, troubling deaf heaven and his frightened children with his bootless cries. "I don't give a care," he would spit, and push away any would-be comforter.

Of my earliest years I know very little. For a while the newlyweds lived with my grandmother Anna Burcl (née Pittinik), on a gravel road, with open ditches—swarming with tadpoles and cattails—along its side. I was once given a toy drum, which I carefully placed on the ground, climbed up on and noisily stamped with my feet until it broke and I cried. Perhaps this was my first recognition that no pleasure lasts for very long.

Sometime when I was two we moved from run-down South Lorain—traditional home to the city's newest immigrants, whether East European "DPs," Puerto Ricans or southern blacks—across town to a simple, wooden house at 1031 West 29th Street. It was an anniversary surprise for my mother, who always regretted that she'd had no input into its design. Not that much could have been done with so modest a structure: an unfinished basement (where, in years to come, my friends and I would roller-skate on rainy Saturdays around the furnace and workbench), a small living room, a dining room with just enough space for a table, a linoleumed kitchen. The upstairs held one bathroom and two bedrooms—one for the parents, one for the children.

With no money left over for furniture, come evening my parents would shift the wooden dining room chairs into the living room and perch, stiff-backed, next to the big upright Philco radio/record player and listen to Glenn Miller's big-band swing or adventure serials. I vaguely recall the chill of low sinister voices—"Who knows what evil lurks in the hearts of men? The Shadow knows"—and the glow of the radio's illuminated dial, which I liked to twirl when nobody was looking.

By the time I was four I was sharing my parents' attention with two sisters, Sandra, the "little mother," and Pamela, the vixen and troublemaker. The three of us liked to race along in our stocking feet, then slide as far as we could on the waxed floors of our then sparsely furnished house. A few years later Linda would suddenly appear in a bassinet and become my father's indulged favorite. For as long as I can remember my three sisters were always referred to as "the girls."

Because she usually needed to stay with her babies at home, my mother carefully taught her little boy exactly how to walk the quarter mile to Garfield Elementary School, a veritable expedition for a four-year-old. I would march straight and tall to the corner of 29th and Washington Avenue, methodically look both ways before crossing, then saunter for two more blocks to Central Park, go halfway around its leafy circumference, then lollygag for another two long blocks to a stern red-brick building that was even then dilapidated.

During this long trek to school I regularly paused for a few minutes to drop big gray stones between the rusty grates of the park's storm sewers. The resulting *kerplop* and prismatic ripples of the oil-slicked water soothed me almost hypnotically, awakening an amniotic peacefulness in my young heart. Indeed, throughout my life the sound of sloshing or of running water has regularly lulled me into a meditative, "zoned-out" state. Perhaps this aqueous tropism explains why one wind-lashed autumn afternoon, during recess, I bravely lay down in a pool of rainwater on the Garfield playground, then kicked my trousered legs as I swam—or rather dragged myself—across the pebbly blacktop toward a leafless tree, rising at the pool's center like a solitary palm on an atoll in a miniature Pacific ocean. My mom later brought fresh, dry clothes to the principal's office, where I was seated on the edge of a counter, shivering in a scrap of blanket.

On yet another occasion, a tornado alert sounded, and all the schoolchildren were sent scurrying home. Having left my sisters with a neighbor, Mom pulled a babushka around her head and rushed breathlessly to Garfield to hurry her eldest to the safety of our fruit cellar. I was, naturally, the last kid out the double doors, hands in my pockets, nonchalant, an inquisitive look on my face: Where was this famous tornado everyone kept talking about? "It's coming, Mikey, it's coming this time, I know it. We have to run home as fast as we can." And so we raced, mother and son, down the street as big raindrops wet our faces and the trees swayed back and forth as if shaken by invisible giants.

Oh, my poor, worried mother. Nature's violence terrified her. During thunderstorms she would unplug everything in the house, convinced that electrical appliances could draw down lightning. I believed her. Hadn't my father told me the story of how he'd been working on a farm once when a storm kicked up and the farmer's wife was struck and killed instantly out in the open cornfield? You couldn't be too careful. During tornado alerts my mother herded her children into the cold basement, where we crouched next to the Mason jars of homemade strawberry jam and the cans of peas, corn and tuna fish, while our eyes grew wide and wider as she described the destruction of the Palace Theater when a big twister touched down in 1924, killing nineteen people. "Can you imagine? One minute you're watching Hopalong Cassidy hopping along and the next minute the whole roof comes crashing down on your head. And that's it. No more movies for you, 'cause You Are Dead."

During this prelapsarian era I must have been read to at school, perhaps when we curled up fetally on our little rag rugs for the afternoon's fifteen minutes of quiet time. Yet by second or third grade, I found myself relegated to the Red Robins or the Blue Jays or whatever the teacher was calling the middle reading group that year. How could I have failed to soar with the Golden Eagles or Peregrine Falcons? As a four-year-old hadn't I figured out—in some forgotten moment of epiphany—that the squiggly marks in Golden Books were words?

In those days, a second- or third-grade teacher, like the elderly, fragile-looking Mrs. Landon, would ask one pupil after another to read aloud to the class. "Althea, please begin on page twenty-seven." She would enunciate these words with gravity, as if her personal happiness depended on the reading ability of a little black girl in a polka-dot dress. (Perhaps it did.) Then up and down the rows she'd go. More often than not, when my turn arrived I hesitated and stammered because I had been looking ahead at other pages of the picture book and had consequently lost my place. Then, as now, I was fascinated by plot and hungry to discover how an action-packed story turned out: Did the Little Engine ever make it over that mountain? Would the slow and steady Tortoise somehow outrace the boasting Hare? How tedious to listen to my classmates struggle through five-word sentences, sounding out the syllables, and guessing at meanings: "What does 'curious' mean, Mrs. Landon?"

Most Americans past forty probably recall those early grade school primers, devoted to simple animal fables, nursery classics and emotion-laden tales of Dick and Jane and their crispy-clean friends, the two-legged equivalents of a poky little puppy or cute yellow duckling. Oh, those mini-dramas of lost toys and muddy pinafores! So many domestic tragedies narrowly averted by a friendly mailman or police officer! I did, nonetheless, admire one series' exuberant cocker spaniel and the starkly laconic caption: "See Jip run." And, indeed, what pleasure to glance up to the picture and actually see Jip joyously frolic across the green grass, in hot pursuit of a bouncing red rubber ball.

Slowly, our class would machete its way through such lush, complex pages to arrive, late in the school year, at real stories that just might interest an actual breathing child. For instance, I have never forgotten the thrilling, and for the era surprisingly exotic, account of a South American ten-year-old who meticulously constructs a homemade fighting kite. In particular, we boys carefully noted how Juan mixed together ground glass and hot wax, then ran his kite string through the sticky compound to sharpen the thin line to a deadly razor's edge. In the fiesta's epic sky battle contestants would dive-bomb their flying machines at one another's strings, hoping to slash through them. At the heart-stopping climax, our hero's hands are raw, bleeding—his thin gloves have been cut to strips by the drag and play of his own line—but he makes one last, risky swoop and is elated to see his enemy's kite float up and away. For years I thought about constructing such a combat windhover, so that I could wreak havoc out on the open fields of Central Park on gusty Saturdays.

Throughout those first years of elementary school my grades proved exceptional only in their mediocrity. My natural instinct for reverie and my general inattention during classroom activities led to worries, then seemingly well-founded suspicions that I might be "retarded." My distraught parents were regularly commanded to at least check my hearing and eyesight; guidance counselors tentatively urged that I might be "happier" in a special institution for slow learners. In fact, I did pay little heed to the bustling world around me, preferring to play alone in a corner while conversing excitedly with myself. I already needed glasses by third grade, but my mother, out of fierce maternal pride in her child's supposed good looks, refused to believe that her sonny boy couldn't see. I'd be intently coloring at the dining room table, weighing the merits of turquoise and blue-green for the lake upon which the sailboat gaily floated, when she'd look up from ironing and casually say, "Mikey, do you see the clock?" That meant the wall clock in the kitchen above the sink where she washed dishes. "Yes, Mommy." "Then what time is it?" I would squint hard and guess, sometimes correctly. "See, he doesn't need glasses."

Inevitably, as my nearsightedness worsened, she had to submit to the genetically inevitable. I can still remember the trip down to South Lorain, to Pearl Road, to the optometrist's second-floor, wood-paneled office—worn chairs in the waiting room, a side table piled with old issues of *Life* and *Look*, *Coronet*, *Reader's Digest*. Might there have been copies of *Highlights for Children*, and even *Screen Gems* or *Modern Romance*? My nervous mother, who feared all doctors, sat there with a handkerchief in her hands, twisting and untwisting its scalloped edges.

After the confusing examination ("Is it clearer now?" Pause. Click. "Or now?"), soft-spoken Dr. Gradisek recommended a special hardened glass for my new specs. To prove its strength, he suddenly pitched the sample lens onto the blue linoleum floor with all his might. It didn't shatter and my mother, sisters and I looked up, duly impressed. The good doctor neglected to mention, however, that it took scarcely any effort at all to break a plastic earpiece or snap the nose bridge—especially when playing touch football or basketball or, once, even an energetic game of freeze tag.

Having grown into a pudgy, introspective eight-year-old misfit, I soon found myself further alienated from my fellows by pathetic ineptitude at all contact sports. If I played a game of touch football without my glasses, I couldn't see well enough to catch a pass. If I wore my heavy black-framed lenses, I needed to be so careful that I proved almost useless to my rough-housing team. And yet no matter how cautious my blocking or how loudly I might cry out, "Watch my glasses," I did eventually hear a sickening crack, almost always on the nose bridge—"Not again!"—which could never be glued even with epoxy. Then, after I blindly stumbled home, my mother would remind me, with a worn-out voice worthy of a particularly tired Ma Joad, just how much glasses cost and did I think, young man, that twenty-dollar bills grew on trees? A steelworker's family, with four young children, had no pennies to waste (and, in fact, kept a big jar just for pennies). As a result, I'd end up with a skin-irritating wad of electrical tape above my nose to keep my skewed glasses loosely together while I waited for the new frames to come in from the warehouse.

Not merely fat, purblind and timorous, as well as academically lackluster and the last chosen for games, I also suffered from a blatant physical deformity: severely bowed legs. Here, no doubt, my Cossack genes had asserted themselves in tibia and fibula molded to grip some Black Stallion's rippling flanks as I swept across the plains of the Caucasus with a bright saber in my upraised fist. Still, my father couldn't stand to look at this imperfection in his only son, so my Buster Browns and P.F. Flyers were fitted with cheap heel inserts, and I was repeatedly instructed to walk straight or, better yet, with my toes pointed inward. All to no avail. So Dad took to employing mockery in the hope that snide comment might embarrass me into a better stride. "You walk like a drunken sailor," he would shout to me from the front porch as I waddled up the driveway on my way home from school.

This ridicule stung, for I felt deeply ashamed of my gait even though I could do next to nothing about it. Yet I recognized that my father's cruelty somehow grew out of his fierce love for me. Ravaged by discontent, prey to both righteous and outrageous indignation, he already yearned for his namesake to accomplish great things in the world, so that one fine day I'd own "a big house on a hill" and drive a shark-finned silver Cadillac. For as far back as I can remember, he constantly urged me to better myself. I should sell newspapers door-to-door. Or Christmas cards, chocolate bars, soda pop. I should definitely invest my "savings." "McDonnell Douglas looks good. Should go up and make you a bundle." I was eight or nine.

Money or, more precisely, its lack formed the repeated leitmotif of all Dad's conversation. One winter's day we drove to Januzzi's to buy a new pair of shoes for me. Dad proudly carried a crisp new twenty-dollar bill in his pocket. Or was it in his hand? No, and not in his wallet, either. The big-shot swagger vanished. "Look all around, look under your seat." Where could the money have gone? The gray afternoon was blustery. Could it have blown away when we got out of the car? It must still be close by. "Oh, God, God." Where, where could it be? I will never forget the tears streaking down my father's face as he ran desperately, despairingly over snow-covered lawns, searching, fruitlessly searching, for that lost twenty-dollar bill.

Money. Never enough money. My parents were careful never to go into debt: Neither ever opened a checking account or carried a credit card. Dirdas paid cash or, if need be, used money orders. As my sisters and I grew older, we would land weekend and part-time jobs, but most of what we earned—at first our dimes and quarters from Kool-Aid stands and door-to-door candy sales, later our weekly paychecks—was dutifully passed on to our mother, who recorded the amounts in First Federal passbooks with each of our names on the cover. Savings for college, for the future. We received no regular allowance. Instead my father preferred us to approach him obsequiously and plead for pocket change. At such times, he could be Czar Nicholas or Daddy Warbucks, dispensing largesse: "Here's a dime, kid. Don't spend it all in one place." Similarly, when Dad one day announced that he would award me a dollar for every A on my report card, he also insisted that he be able to dock me fifty cents for a B and a dollar for a C. Unsurprisingly, I seldom made any money, poor arithmetic grades often dragging me down seriously into the red. In those days, only subtraction made sense—it was obvious that people would take away your apples or your marbles, but highly improbable that you would ever be given any.

"Your Dad's hard to be around sometimes," Mom would occasionally admit to her children. Or she'd just murmur, with resignation, as if it were an axiomatic Euclidean truth: "Dad's Dad." But I couldn't help but love this difficult, self-tormented man. Sometimes, when my mother was upstairs tucking the girls into bed, Dad would read to me about animals or ancient history from a volume of *Pictured Knowledge: The Full-Color Illustrated Encyclopedia for the Family*. One evening I wedged myself next to him—we lounged in our new cream-colored recliner (with built-in "magic fingers")—while he slowly turned the eight pages of a drastically condensed précis, with blurry, washed-out illustrations, of *Don Quixote*. Mostly I now recall how close to him I felt that night, as he described the misadventures of the deluded knight. Perhaps I already suspected that this unhappy soul, troubled by a burning but unfocused desire for material success, had much of Don Quixote in him: He never ceased wanting the world, his children and his own life to be better than they were or were ever likely to be.

While my mother made reading a sensual transport, a *plaisir du texte* that I have yearned to feel each time I pick up a book, my father introduced me to the beauty and evocative power of words. Picture a late fall afternoon. I have been sick all day, feeling headachy, and am lying under a *dhuna*—a down-filled coverlet—on our living room couch. Suddenly the family breadwinner arrives home from the mill and, learning of my illness, rushes over to his prostrate son. He strokes my hot brow and unexpectedly begins to recite: " 'Twas many and many a year ago/ In a kingdom by the sea/ That a maiden there lived/ Whom you may know/ By the name of Annabel Lee." He may have gone on to mumble something about her being a child or even about a love that was more than love, but without really knowing any more of the poem than that, not even that its author was Edgar Allan Poe. Still, I shivered with feverish pleasure at the mellifluous sonorities that my father took pains to bring out. For me they represented, to borrow Wallace Stevens's beautiful phrase, "heavenly labials in a world of gutturals."

This was also the era when he would half sing, half speak the lyrics to a Hit Parade ditty about Marianne "down by the seashore sifting sand." "Even little children love Marianne," he would repeat to himself, "down by the seashore sifting sand." As we chugged down nearby Oberlin Avenue in our green slope-roofed Chevy, past the soon-to-vanish farmhouses where we sometimes bought fresh eggs, a basket of tomatoes or a live turkey for Thanksgiving, he would often break into mournful song: "Old Dan and I our throats are dry/ For the taste of water/ Cool, clear water." In fact, crooner Frankie Laine whispered only, in a raspy voice, "cool water," but my dad always preferred "cool, clear water." The extra adjective made the dying cowboy's thirst a little more heart-wrenching.

I, however, most loved to hear the mock-heroic tale of Abdul Abulbul Emir and Ivan Skavinsky Skavar, even then a half-forgotten barroom ballad. Now I can only vaguely summon up the dramatic opening and a few later fragments of this Casey-with-a-sword folk epic: "The sons of the prophet are brave men and true/ And quite unaccustomed to fear/ But the bravest by far in the ranks of the Shah/ Was Abdul Abulbul Emir." Both Abdul and Ivan are noble warriors, and when Abdul trods, without apology, on the toe of Ivan (or was it vice versa?), this insult naturally leads to a challenge and duel. "They fought all that night 'neath the pale yellow moon/ The din it was heard of afar/ Great multitudes came so great was the fame/ of Abdul and Ivan Skavar." Eventually, both heroes perish, leaving broken-hearted comrades and a bereft Circassian sweetheart.

What I particularly relished in this poem—my father again chanted the quatrains like opera recitative—was the tall-tale exaggeration, tinged with genuine wistfulness and related in an irresistible rhythm. The sound supported, and sometimes neatly undercut, the sense. As with toys, I was beginning to realize, one could play with words.

Though years later he would be appalled at my bookishness, Dad himself introduced me to the public library. For some reason, we traveled to a small, dark branch on Pearl Road in South Lorain. Could it have been the very library my father might have visited in his own school days during the Depression, when he would "buy a loaf of bread and a jar of jelly and have enough for sandwiches all week"? The single big room was narrow, cramped with desks, tables and shelves, more like a used bookstore than today's fluorescent-bright multimedia centers. I looked around the children's section and eventually stacked up some adventurous-sounding titles, only to be informed by the pinched-faced, but no doubt well-meaning librarian that these particular works were "too difficult, far too difficult" for a little boy. She made me carefully replace them on the low-slung shelves and then proceeded to load me down with Curious George albums, *Mike Mulligan and His Steam Shovel* and comparably simple stuff. I felt angry, frustrated and helpless. Meanwhile, my father spent all this time restively browsing among the nature books, then solemnly studying an illustrated version of *Moby-Dick*, probably Rockwell Kent's. He was crazy about sailing vessels—"in those days" he would say, "there were iron men and wooden ships, nowadays we have iron ships and wooden men." But no matter how attentively he turned the pages of a nautical volume—"Red sky at morning, sailors take warning./ Red sky at night, sailors' delight"—he never checked out a single one, but always went home from the library empty-handed.

For neither of my parents read books, even though Dad built two substantial bookcases in our dining room. Each extended from floor to ceiling and framed a side window overlooking the driveway. Thinking ahead to his children's schooling, Dad gradually stocked the varnished shelves with novels, nonfiction and works of ready-reference. Sometimes he picked up department store remainders (like the 1954 first American edition of *Lord of the Flies*, for which he paid thirty-nine cents—"could have bought two dozen of them," he lamented years later when I informed him that the book was then worth a couple of hundred bucks). Other times he'd trundle in through the back door with a carton of old textbooks and ICS correspondence school volumes from a house auction, then slowly unpack *The Steel Square Handbook*, the poems of Edgar Guest ("It takes a heap of livin' to make a house a home"), a couple of *Popular Science* handyman guides, *How to Make More Money* by Marvin Small and some battered book club editions of novels by Mazo de la Roche, Frank G. Slaughter and Frances Parkinson Keyes.

Yet over the years I was to recognize that serendipity had, in fact, furnished the Dirda household with a number of surprisingly good books. I would study their titles as I sat spooning up my Rice Krispies: Samuel Shellabarger's *Captain from Castile*, *Sisler on Baseball*, Cellini's cloak-and-rapier memoirs, an omnibus of Captain Horatio Hornblower adventures, Lowell Thomas's *With Lawrence in Arabia*, a collection of classic stories called *The Golden Argosy*, *Five Tragedies of Shakespeare*, a pocket-sized selection of Keats's poems and even Ivy Compton-Burnett's *A Father and His Fate*. My dad would occasionally murmur this last title aloud to himself, in a plangent tone that hovered between the sententious and self-pitying. "A father and his . . . fate."

We also owned two encyclopedias: the dreary Funk & Wagnall's *Universal Standard*, closely printed on pulpy paper and probably acquired through weekly purchase at the local A&P, and the aforementioned "illustrated encyclopedia" that provided a hodgepodge of simple-minded articles and stories. Neither ever helped my sisters or me in writing our term papers. Our mother had other ways to be sure that her children could undertake thorough "research."

When the girls and I trotted off to elementary school, Mom naturally regaled us with advice: "Wait till the patrol says you can cross the street, then walk, don't run. You'll just trip and fall," "Wear your cap and keep the earflaps down. You don't want to get an earache." Most of these maternal counsels we duly ignored. But one request was taken to heart: "When the time comes to write reports, in geography or English or social studies, make sure your subject starts with the letter A." Why? Because our bookcases contained the first volumes of seven or eight encylopedias and similar alphabetical references. My mother would purchase volume one of, say, *Compton's* or *The World Book Encyclopedia*, at the special introductory price of fifty-nine cents and then, exercising her advertised right ("You may cancel at any time"), would promptly discontinue her order. Who would pay $9.99 for each of the subsequent twenty-five volumes? "That's just ridiculous," she would snort. "They must think the world is filled with millionaires." Still, the Dirda family soon abounded with information about topics beginning with A. And so we kids composed our classroom papers on Alaska and Antarctica, artichokes, aardvarks and asteroids. Teachers were generally quite impressed with the breadth and depth of our apparent expertise.

After all, school mattered, at least somewhat, for our entire household actually revolved around my father's moods. All of us kowtowed to his labile emotional states—"Dad's on the warpath," "Dad's in a good mood"—and we stayed alert to his departures and arrivals. When the wounded Fisher King was home, we kids had to be absolutely quiet. "No jumping on the couch. You'll wake up your father," "Turn off that TV. Your father's sleeping." Mom would rush to set a roast in a 350-degree oven, while barking, "Quit your jumping. You kids'll knock the mirror off the wall." She'd order us to the dining room table: "Just sit there and finish your homework. I've got to hurry up and run the sweeper before your father gets home." There could be no vacuuming, no mowing, no *Mickey Mouse Club* or *Sgt. Bilko* without his express permission. "Now go practice your accordion before your father gets back from Willow Hardware. . . . Sandra Christine, put those dolls away and straighten up the living room right this minute. You help her, Pamela. You too, Linda."

As we finished our cleaning, lessons and chores, Dad would pull up and park the car out front on the street, then tread heavily up the driveway to the back door, a grimace of existential pain on his face, like Prometheus remembering a trying day with a new eagle. Mom would give a cheery "Hi, hon," and Dad would stoically endure a peck on the cheek. After dropping his sack of dirty clothes on the steps to the cellar, he would open the icebox and lift out a beer and a bottle of Seagram's 7, then sit down at his place at the head of the dining room table. Following a sip of Stroh's, he'd pour himself a shot and neatly knock it back. Only then would he begin to eat, with great deliberation, the hot meal my mother had prepared for him: Breaded perch with scalloped potatoes. A well-done steak. Stuffed cabbage. Pork chops, maybe. Almost always a lettuce, tomato and cucumber salad. Sometimes there'd be a piece of nut roll or a hunk of blackberry pie for dessert. Dad would hardly lift his eyes from the newspaper folded beside his squarish yellow Corelle plastic plate. Our own meals would be simpler—frozen fish sticks and french fries, hot dogs and beans, sometimes my sisters' favorite, the meatless cutlets of fried breading we called Dibs. As a treat the four of us might see a cream horn or Twinkie cut into quarters.

In the summer Dad would frequently heave himself up after eating and, with a section of the *Journal* gripped in his fist, amble out back to relax under the oak trees in one of the wooden Adirondack chairs he had built and painted white. These moments may have been the happiest of his life, at ease in the cool shade, either digesting a good meal or, on weekends, waiting for Sandy or Pam to call him in to watch Rocky Colavito smack out home runs for the Cleveland Indians. Sometimes he would chew on a toothpick while folding and unfolding the paper, which he somehow managed to make last for an hour or more. Often he would just drift into reverie, watching the squirrels scamper for acorns or staring at the trellised rosebushes my mother carefully tended. Occasionally he'd order me to sit next to him. Then we would carry on a halting conversation, highlighted by either his swashbuckling tales of boyhood—many of them about swimming in the Black River and hanging out with his gang, the River Rats—or by the aphorisms, some original, that he liked to solemnly quote at me:

"Remember, kid, a thing is worth just so much time," "He travels fastest who travels alone," "Study long, study wrong," "I had the blues because I had no shoes/ Until upon the street/ I met a man who had no feet," "I may not always be right, but I'm never wrong."

Occasionally, he would chat with neighbors over the white corrallike fence with which he had edged and demarcated our backyard. But there were always one or two with whom he was feuding over property lines, noise or an offensive lifestyle. "I think the two of them just watch, waiting until I come sit out here. Then she tells the old man to start cutting grass with that damn power mower. What do they need a power mower for? I don't want you kids going over their house anymore. . . ."

Dad's favorite neighbor, Max Misley, repaired cars for a living, and I would periodically be ordered next door "to learn something useful." Max's garage acted as a club room for middle-aged good ol' boys, who would stop by to sip beer and escape their wives for an hour. "Women. Can't live with 'em, can't live without 'em." Over the years the happy-go-lucky Max taught me how to clean carburetors, set the dwell on new spark plugs and adjust the engine's timing—once he even allowed me to repack wheel bearings. When vexed over the refusal of some balky Caddie or Chevy to submit to his ministrations, Max would cheerfully curse that he was going to "fix it, or fix it so that nobody else can fix it." For all the kindness of this master mechanic, I never felt at ease under a hood, being fully convinced that I would make some critical misjudgment that would result in ruining a transmission or blowing the engine. Still, years later, I did manage to replace the clutch on our family's aging '58 Ford. Mostly, though, I found my eyes drawn away from oily engine blocks to the sexy Ridge Tool calendars on the wall—smiling Daisy Maes in scanties, posing with jackhammers and power drills.

In those evenings under the trees, my father particularly liked to hear his children playing quietly nearby, to listen to the groans and glee of a game of basketball or sidewalk tennis conducted on the concrete driveway he had himself poured. "It was out, the ball was clearly out." "No, it was on the line. Takeover." "No fair, you always want takeovers." Even more, he enjoyed watching my sisters and me perform simple household tasks like washing and waxing the car, weeding the vegetable garden behind the garage, unpegging dry clothes from the line. Now and again, he and I would play catch. "Throwing the ball hard is less important than throwing it straight," he would tell me.

Having grown up in the Depression and been on his own since adolescence, my father deemed it both an extravagance and an embarrassment to ask anyone for help. "I'm not begging anyone for anything." So he fixed furnaces, refrigerators, stoves, sewing machines, cars, lawn mowers, bicycles. If drainpipes clogged, he would ream them out, sometimes dismantling quite substantial lengths of plumbing. He almost single-handedly built an addition—my bedroom, with a small attached bath. Every few years he scraped, primed and painted our one-car garage or our wooden house (until, during my late adolescence, my friend Ed Partyka and I installed aluminum siding and storm windows—it took us all summer). Because of the ambitiousness of many of these domestic projects and repairs, Dad would often grow frustrated—by his ignorance or by his need for a special wrench or by the "pure stupidity" of those Detroit engineers—and before long he would break out into a sweat, his thin cotton shirt soon sticking to his back, and he would begin to curse himself, his wife and, especially, his lazy, ignorant, good-for-nothing son.

"Turn, dammit, turn," he would shout at some balky nut or bolt. "You should be doing this, not me. . . . What do they teach you kids in school?"

"I'm sorry, Dad. Let me try it."

"Get away. You don't know what the hell you're doing. You'll just strip the threads."

I would stand there helplessly. The veins on his forehead and neck would bulge out as he struggled. "I just don't have the strength."

Though my father had encouraged early reading by taking me to the library, he never wanted a bookworm in the family. Instead he envisioned a Super Son, adept with every known hand tool and eager to transform 1031 West 29th Street into an edifice that even Frank Lloyd Wright might envy or, alternately, a son so financially savvy that he would be hired at age eleven to manage J. Paul Getty's investments. Having read a news story about Michael Rockefeller's disappearance in Borneo, he commanded me to write to the Rockefeller family and offer myself as a replacement son. He wasn't kidding. Not a bit.

Whenever I actually inaugurated a project of my own, such as constructing a model blast furnace for the school science fair, he would insist on "helping," then grow annoyed that I was gripping the saw improperly or using nails when it was obvious to any idiot that I should be using screws.

"Get away from there. If you're going to do something, at least do it right. And next time pick a simpler project. You can hardly put together a plastic airplane. Think a little, just once in your life. Sometimes I don't know if you're helpless or hopeless."

In those days, I used to tremble with anxiety when my mother would whisper, as I tentatively came through the back door from school or the playground, "You'd better go change into your old clothes. Your father's down the basement." I'd creep downstairs and say, with assumed heartiness, "Hi, Dad!" and he would look up from his workbench and glare. "Get your hands out of your pockets. Where have you been? How do you expect to learn anything if you're never around when the work's being done?"

And so I would hold the board while he sawed away, or spend tortured hours standing by as he sweated in some tight corner upstairs, occasionally handing him the Vise-Grips or scurrying off to fetch a three-quarter-inch socket, a coping saw or needlenose pliers. I was supposed to observe what he did, but usually saw nothing more than a grown man suffering. Sometimes he would break down and openly weep with frustration as a delicate part broke off or he found himself incapable of manipulating some minute spring into just the right place in the carburetor.

If matters grew too awful, Dad, red in the face, shirt matted with perspiration, arms aching, might just get up from where he was kneeling—all his jobs seemed to require the skills of a contortionist—and throw down his Phillips-head screwdriver or Sears crescent wrench, thoroughly disgusted. "Why do I have to do everything around here? Other people hire plumbers, electricians, trained professionals with the right kind of tools who do this kind of thing every day. . . . I have to be at work in two hours, while you and your mother just stay here and lounge around like lizards, not a care in the world." Eventually, my dad's rage would subside, and Mom would shyly say, "It's okay, hon," and for a second he would look heartbroken and genuinely tragic, before pushing her away. He was a titan brought low by pygmies. At such dark moments, Mom would telephone my Uncle Henry for help.

Uncle Henry possessed all the skills my father lacked, along with a seemingly preternatural understanding of complex machinery, a courtly, almost debonair manner, a close-cropped brush haircut and a cheerful heart. Never on time for any appointment—"Henry'll be late for his own funeral"—my smiling uncle finally would drive up in some junkheap, sporting an old sweatshirt with the hood pulled up to the bill of a faded baseball cap. "Hey, Ike, what seems to be the problem?" He'd peer curiously into the engine block, wirebrush the battery terminals, maybe spray some aerosol sealant around the distributor and then ask his nephew to turn the key. The motor would immediately roar back into booming life, then settle into a smooth purr; he would make a few other minor adjustments and, with a showman's flourish, slam down the hood. "Well, that wasn't so bad. You might want to set the idle a little hotter. That way it won't die on you when you're at a stoplight." Afterward, Dad, relieved that that which was broken had been made whole, would invite his brother-in-law to sip a cold Stroh's beer and the pair would "chew the fat" about Thew Shovel, the Indians, hunting (my uncle's passion) and the sorrowful vagaries of life.

Eventually, Dad, embarrassed over his earlier anger, would sheepishly try to make amends—he would sooner have died than say he was sorry—either by taking his family out to Home Dairy for an ice-cream cone (vanilla for Dad, black raspberry for Mom, cherry vanilla for the kids) or by allowing his helper to stay up later than usual to watch, say, a special TV dramatization of *Huckleberry Finn*. After all, until we were teenagers my sisters and I were compelled to be in bed at seventy-thirty during the school year and at nine o'clock in the summer. Well do I remember August evenings lying in the baking heat, listening to the Delmonico or DeAngelis kids playing kickball, shooting squirt guns or chasing lightning bugs in the twilight.

On those weeks my father worked three to eleven, the household would grow almost cheery, even madcap. My mother, in looks and personality, resembled the zany Lucille Ball of *I Love Lucy*. Sometimes, while she ironed piles of laundry, Mom would regale her four mesmerized offspring with ancient family history. "I met your father at a Saturday night dance. Back then he was really tanned from being out in the Pacific, and with that black curly hair he looked just like a Puerto Rican. I almost died when he asked me to dance. . . ." No one could spin better tales, especially scary stories that she half acted out, delighting in our childish fear.

One night, for instance, Mom stood washing dishes while my sisters and I were finishing homework at the dining room table. Suddenly I heard a splash as a plate fell noisily back into the soapy water. I looked up to see our beloved mother unexpectedly drop to her knees, turn toward her children with a crazed look in her eyes and start to emit unearthly guttural noises. She growled and slavered, then began crawling slowly toward us on all fours.

My sisters and I screamed and ran with fast-beating hearts up to our bedroom, where we slammed and locked the door. For a moment there was silence. Then we could just make out the soft heavy padding of someone or some Thing laboriously climbing the steps. On hands and knees. The girls and I cowered beneath our covers. Soon, from outside the locked room came scratching sounds, and hungry whimpers, as the Creature who had been our mother tried to get through to devour us. Then further silence, followed by the metallic click of a hall cupboard being opened. We listened intently.

Had It gone away? All at once we detected, with renewed hysteria, the soft jangle of a key being stealthily inserted into the lock, followed by our sanctuary's door being flung open as the ravenous, drooling Monster rushed into the room, laughing with insidious joy, scooping us into her arms and kissing us and telling us that she loved us and that we were all such suckers. Brazenly, we told her that we knew it was a joke all along.

My mother was never a sucker. Once I hesitantly shelled out a dollar, nearly all my savings, for a bow-and-arrow set from a yard sale. When I got home, Mom took one look at my purchase and snorted, "Boy, they saw you coming." That taught me a lesson, but not the one my mother intended: Henceforth, I would keep certain things to myself. In fact, neither of my parents trusted anyone who wasn't family. Though they occasionally spoke fondly of childhood friends, none ever came to our house.

Well before her children started school, Mom made sure that we all learned to write our names, address and telephone number. For it was my mother's practice to take us with her grocery shopping. Once arrived at Meyer Goldberg's or Fisher's, she would deposit her offspring next to the store's raffle box. Then, while she picked up bread and milk and hunted for bargains on hard salami or Dutch loaf, Sandy, Pammy, Linda and I would fill out as many coupons as possible, as fast as we could, dropping them into the silver-foiled contest box, hoping to win hams or bags of groceries or money. And we did. Again and again.

My mother was fanatically serious about winning. For instance, the Dirdas always triumphed in coloring contests. After dinner, Mom would clear the table, then plop us down with the official Halloween or Christmas scene. "All right. I want each of you to color just the sky. Nothing else. Do you hear me, Pamela? Just the sky. Take your time. Spend at least fifteen minutes on it, and then call me when you're done." At this rate, we might spend two weeks on a picture, but when finished, it was perfect. Vermeer himself would envy our Easter bunnies, Poussin sigh before our angels and Wise Men. We carried off prize after prize—train sets, watches, dolls, cowboy guns, cameras, but never books.

Still, my mother herself reigned as the undisputed champion of all contests. As my sisters grew older, she one day decided that each of them would require a sewing machine. Every spring a local appliance store ran a contest that challenged people to generate as many words as possible using any combination of letters from, say, "disconsolate." The main prize? A portable sewing machine. Each year my mother would take out our unabridged Webster's dictionary and scan its columns, page by page, laboriously checking every single entry against the contest phrase. She took home the grand prize three years in a row, always finding hundreds more words than the runners-up. If Mrs. Dirda had had a dozen daughters she would certainly have kept winning sewing machines until each of her girls had been provided for.

Still, my favorite memory of those early years starts with the grand opening of the Lorain Plaza Shopping Center, at the nearby intersection of Meister Road and Oberlin Avenue. Already this latter thoroughfare was beginning the rapid surrender of its farmyards and streetside produce stands (BERRIES—25 CENTS A QUART) to block after block of dental offices, gas stations and convenience stores, as well as to the vast fiefdom of St. Peter's Church and to the huge parking lot and slender strip of shops that made up the new Plaza. Now, in those days an opening couldn't be grand without "Door Buster" sales, which advertised a handful of expensive items marked down far below their normal selling prices. When the Plaza officially opened for business, my mom made sure we were all at the W. T. Grant Department Store bright and early, bunched together at the front of the line. Like commandos, the girls and I each had orders and tactical objectives.

"When the manager unlocks the doors at nine, I want you kids to run into the store. Don't trip anybody. Michael. It says in this paper that they have boys' winter coats, regularly thirty dollars each, for only five. Today only, while supplies last. Bring me the medium, whatever color they have, I don't care. Sandy, you take Linda with you and hurry over to skirts. . . . Pamela, see if you can find your father a new . . . I'll meet you kids in men's wear. Dad needs some khakis. . . ."

And so at nine A.M. we would push our way through the crowd, then fan out across the sales floor, hurriedly grabbing coats, skirts, jeans, what have you, before reporting back to our general, who would finger the merchandise and pronounce whether it would do for her family.

At this particular grand opening the shopping center also hosted a fair in its parking lot. On the way back to our car we passed a booth—"Step right up"—where people were carefully throwing darts at small balloons. "You there, madam. Break a balloon and win a prize from one of the Plaza's new stores." I don't remember how much the darts cost, but Mom tried once, missed like everyone else and then packed up her kids and purchases and drove slowly home.

I thought no more about the matter, but my mother clearly did. Her spies leaked the intelligence that this same carnival would be returning the following May. That fall Mom acquired half a dozen darts and an old target that she hung up on the gray wooden door of the fruit cellar. For the next six months, whenever she was in the basement sorting or washing clothes (laundry tub, washboard), she would also practice with her darts. Upstairs we kids would hear the soft *thonk, thonk, thonk* as the darts hit the target. We were not allowed to play with them; they were like our father's tools—special and holy.

The next May the Plaza hosted its fair again and a seemingly ordinary housewife strolled over to the contest booth. She solemnly paid for her darts and innocently proceeded to burst balloons until they wouldn't let her play any longer. Typically, my mom didn't think it right that they should stop her from winning every prize in the place.

Chapter Two

We learned from you so much about so many things
But never what we were; and yet you made us that.
                                        —Randall Jarrell

Though my father was manfully devoted to the entire news-paper, my mother hardly ever read anything except Ann Landers—and the comics. I have seldom seen anybody derive such uncomplicated delight from a bit of black-and-white drawing and a few sentences. Mom would crumple the paper as she held it close to her face, peer at the captions and not merely smile or chuckle but actually laugh aloud. Then she would smooth out the page on the table and reflect on the cornpone antics of *Li'l Abner* and the idiocy of husband Dagwood in *Blondie*, before moving on to some more soap-opera-like strip such as *Brenda Starr* or *Mary Worth*, over which she would scowl, comment and groan. Shaking her head, she would sometimes offer advice to the hapless and often naive heroine. "Don't trust that chippy! Watch out for that bum!"

I was intrigued by my mother's reactions—what precisely was a chippy?—but my first interaction with the comics took a more prac-tical turn: My sisters and I would press down on an image with a wad of Silly Putty, then use the rubbery clay, which had absorbed some of the printer's ink, to stamp the picture onto a clean sheet of paper. I can visualize Sandy and me hunched on the kitchen floor, the blue-green speckled linoleum all around us, while my ponytailed sister Pamela tosses out her jacks and scoops them up: "Onesies, twosies, threesies . . ."

Dennis the Menace actually started me on reading the comics: Each day Hank Ketcham would run single-panel cartoons of the towheaded imp's antics. "Hello, Mr. Wilson!" Amused by these, I eventually bought several collections of Dennis cartoons. This was also the era—circa age eight—when I acquired joke books, collections of puns and a compilation of funny rhymes entitled *Yours Till Niagara Falls*. "Roses are red/ Violets are blue/ You look like a monkey/ And smell like one too." These inevitably led to a brief vogue for belting out the mouthwatering playground ditty: "Great green gobs of greasy grimy gopher guts,/ Mutilated monkey meat,/ Tiny baby birdies' feet," which builds to the heart-rending *cri du coeur*: "And me without a spoon."

From *Dennis* I progressed to narrative strips like *The Phantom*. I particularly favored the story about the origin of the centuries-old Ghost Who Walks and of his two nifty rings: One would blight villains with a skull mark, the other, the much-desired "Good Mark" of the Phantom, would protect its wearer anyplace in the world, for all malefactors instantly quailed before its dread power. Just below the Phantom I lingered over the adventures of Flash Gordon and the galactic rangerette Dale Arden, whose body-stocking space garb sweetly troubled my nights. Eventually, I also came to enjoy the satiric *Li'l Abner*, especially the strips about the plague of shmoos, those all-purpose creatures whose only goal is to please and who can make themselves taste like the food you most desire. The Amazonian Moonbeam McSwine's half-unbuttoned peasant blouse scarcely contained her bountiful endowments and further awakened inchoate sexual feelings. Alas, the angular art and rather pathetic criminals such as Half Face put me off *Dick Tracy*, one of my mother's other favorites. For some reason I never read *Terry and the Pirates* and couldn't find an entrance into the ongoing narratives in *Prince Valiant*.

Across from the regular comics, the *Journal* published a special section set aside for somewhat more adult pictorials: *Ripley's Believe It Or Not*, *There Oughta Be a Law* and Rube Goldberg's drawings of elaborate contraptions for brewing a pot of coffee or waking sleepyheads. These last I studied closely, always astonished by Goldberg's ingenuity and sometimes convinced that the improbably intricate assembly of weights, springs, dropping balls and hungry parakeets might actually work as an alarm clock. Ripley, however, I found disturbing: His anomalies and freaks hinted strongly that uncanny, even malevolent forces lurked on the edges of the known universe. I certainly didn't want rains of frogs or black snow falling in my backyard. Such monstrosities shook the settled order of things. A fretful, nervous child, I preferred God in His Heaven and all right with the world.

Not least, though, the comics pages also offered A. Leokum's "Why, Daddy?" column, later reslugged "Tell Me Why" at about the time its author's first initial was revealed to stand for the clearly un-American name Arkady. Kids would mail in "scientific" questions such as, "Why does the earth go around the sun?" and Leokum would explain in the simplest possible English. My father, less an actual than a would-be autodidact, judged this feature inordinately fascinating and frequently shared its revelations aloud at the dinner table. "So that's what blue whales eat." As we grew older he urged his inquisitive brood to send in questions, partly for the glory of seeing our names in the paper (if our letters were lucky enough to be chosen), but also for the award of various educational prizes. In due course, the Dirdas received several collegiate dictionaries, an atlas and, eventually, when we'd already outgrown it, a *Junior Encyclopedia Britannica.*

In those days the *Lorain Journal* featured Bennett Cerf's "Try and Stop Me" joke column in the bottom-left corner of its editorial page. By the late 1950s, Cerf's syndicated quips already seemed anachronistic and toastmasterish, but I turned to his "sophisticated" humor faithfully even when slightly puzzled by it. In one illustrated anecdote a sozzled drinker is swaying home from the liquor store with a paper sack, which he accidentally drops. A bottle clearly breaks, and he heartbreakingly whimpers, "Please, God, let it be the wash." Years passed before I understood a little more about the pathos of alcoholism—several uncles suffered from its depredations—and that "wash" was the ginger ale added to mixed drinks. Throughout my childhood, no father ever drank anything but beer or "highballs"— usually Seagram's 7 and Seven-Up—and mothers never drank publicly at all. Besides jokes, the urbane Cerf would often relate amusing "true" stories, like the one about the writer—perhaps the young P. G. Wodehouse—who simply tossed his stamped mail out his window onto the Manhattan pavement. He claimed that in a dozen years no letter had ever failed to be picked up by a passerby and dropped into a mailbox.

One Christmas season the paper, starting early in December, carried a special holiday serial about Santa. Some toy crisis—lost reindeer? striking elves?—threatened the distribution of presents on Christmas Eve. Each day the *Journal* published a new chapter in this suspenseful cliffhanger and I didn't miss a one. I was almost sad when December twenty-fourth arrived and the story ended. In that era too the paper would announce, in a box wreathed with holly and ivy, that twelve, then ten, then only four shopping days remained until Christmas. On one of these our family would descend on the O'Neil-Sheffield Shopping Center, its parking lot edged with ragged hillocks of dirty plowed snow and ice, and my mother invariably exclaiming, "*Yoishes Mahdia!* The cars." (However spelled, "*Yoishes Mahdia*" was Slovak for "Jesus, Mary" and was my mother's strongest oath.) After we'd finally found a place to park, we'd all traipse excitedly along the covered walkways, shopping lists in hand, stopping to ooh and aah over the holiday window displays—mannequins that actually moved!—and to confess our yuletide yearnings to the improbable talking Christmas tree.

Nowadays, papers print serious news, gossip and opinion. But back then, the *Journal* carried occasional columns such as Frank Edwards's "Stranger than Science," tales of unaccountable, terrifying "true" events something like those reported by the more famous Charles Fort in *The Book of the Damned*. When I foolishly bought a collection of these pieces, also titled *Stranger than Science*, I found them so distressing that I couldn't sleep for several nights. No mere writing before the discovery of H. P. Lovecraft ever frightened me so much. I recall one article about a southern businessman sauntering across his front lawn and vanishing into thin air before the very eyes of his wife, children and neighbors. A rip in the fabric of time? Or something worse? A circular patch of brown appeared in the grass where the unfortunate had been last glimpsed stepping along. No amount of watering or fertilizer could make it green. Finally, a year to the day after their father's uncanny disappearance, the family's children were playing near the scorched earth when they heard his pitiful voice sobbing, ever so faintly, "Help me, help me." As they listened, the cries gradually faded away. The next day the damned spot began to turn green. But neither the father nor his voice was ever heard from again. The poetic melancholy of this story haunted me for years. But there was also something deeply attractive about just disappearing from one's ordinary life. Perhaps great adventures awaited?

By the age of eight or nine I had grown addicted to, if not addled by, cereal box advertisements (decoder rings! Davy Crockett lunch boxes!), jingles, comics and jokes, not to mention stories and books. Now, a child in thrall to the typeset word will discover enchantment everywhere—even in a town without bookstores. Whenever I'd stop by the house of a friend or relative, I'd surreptitiously cruise the downstairs, the basement, parental bedrooms, even broom closets, searching for a shelf of magazines or kids' books, hoping to find something good to read. "Hey, Aunt Mary, can I borrow some of these old *Reader's Digests*?" On one visit to my Uncle Henry's I discovered that my cousin Marlene, five or six years my senior, treasured a small cache of what were called Big Little Books. After considerable cajoling, she allowed me to take home a couple of them.

Big Little Books flourished in the late 1930s and 1940s: In format they were thick, squat volumes, about three inches square, with a full-page picture on the recto and text on the verso. They thus inhabited an unlikely publishing niche, midway between the comic strip and the juvenile adventure novel. Mini-boxes of delight, they offered significant pictorial razzle-dazzle—if simple block prints can be so decribed—while supporting a relatively complex narrative. Tarzan, Red Ryder, the Phantom, even Shirley Temple appeared in Big Little Books (or their presumed rival Better Little Books). Marlene only owned a handful, but one title, *Little Orphan Annie and the Ancient Treasure of Am*, provided an early instance of my favorite kind of story: the antiquarian romance. We all recognize the elements—a mysterious and vastly powerful millionaire, a silent dark-skinned servant of immense strength, an otherworldly realm, secret treasure, an ancient wise man, supernatural monsters, suavely evil villains, advanced technology, lots of magic. The tale of Am begins in classic fashion:

Little Orphan Annie and Daddy Warbucks, with the help of Daddy's faithful servant, the Asp, had just completed their escape from Boris Sirob's gang of international thieves, who had designs on Daddy's ten-billion-dollar fortune in gems. They had outwitted the gang, and the three were coasting down a tropical river into the heart of the jungle, thousands of miles from their starting place. As the green fastnesses of the jungle closed about the stream, with no signs of human habitation, Annie began to worry. . . .

How I marveled at the palindromic cleverness of Boris Sirob and mouthed over and over that dictionary-word "fastnesses"! For years after, I searched for other Big Little Books, but by the time I found any, I also found myself an adult—and as relatively expensive collectors' items, they no longer emanated the same irresistible sorcery. But in our beginnings lie our ends, so when I later daydreamed over Alexandre Dumas' *The Count of Monte Cristo*, Sax Rohmer's *The Insidious Dr. Fu Manchu*, Umberto Eco's *Foucault's Pendulum* and John Crowley's *Little, Big*, I couldn't help but remember *The Ancient Treasure of Am*.

Inevitably, my liking for the funnies and Big Little Books soon led to a burning passion for comics. As a youngster I naturally preferred the humorous adventures of Donald Duck, chubby Little Lotta, Richie Rich, Casper the Friendly Ghost, the hapless inventor Gyro Gearloose, overgrown Baby Huey and others of that silly, lighthearted ilk. Being so poor, I particularly envied Uncle Scrooge as he frolicked joyfully, in a 1920s bathing costume, in his gigantic money bin.

When I grew a tad older I would occasionally read Archie comics, though never with much avidity. Somehow they struck me as girlish; probably due to their tiresome focus on teenage romance. I was shocked to learn from a high school cousin that rich Veronica and oily Reggie didn't pronounce their unfamiliar names Vair-oh-neye-kuh and Ree-gee. Occasionally I would hesitantly peer into an EC horror comic, such as *Tales from the Crypt*, but seldom without subsequent misgivings: I had learned early on about my propensity for nightmares. However, I do recall first shuddering through "Mars is Heaven," a Ray Bradbury story from *The Martian Chronicles*, retold as an EC shocker. Its moral: Never trust appearances, especially on the Red Planet—even your own brother may be a ravenous alien in human drag.

No, at day's end hand me a mailed fistful of superhero adventures and I was happy for as long as the supply held out. Batman and Superman, of course, but also Flash, Wonder Woman, Aquaman, Green Arrow, the entire Justice League of America. Of Green Lantern—whose puissance could be hampered only by the color yellow—no praise is suffient: Kids back then would regularly chant Hal Jordan's invocation to his power lamp: "In brightest day, in darkest night" it began and ended with the fearsome warning to all malefactors: "Beware my power . . . Green Lantern's light." The plots of these comics were all reassuringly alike: Some evil genius, loathesome alien or monstrous creature with seemingly unstoppable power plans to take over the world. For a while it looks as though our hero is beaten, often because of his single weakness (kryptonite, the need for regular immersion in salt water), but in the final pages he escapes almost certain death to reappear for a final epic battle in which the haughty enemy is vanquished—at least until a future issue, when the cover might announce, say, "The Return of Dr. Destructo."

I was also partial to Blackhawk Comics, the exploits of a corps of multitalented airmen from different nations (the Frenchman was always spluttering, "*Sacre bleu*"), and would sometimes scan the battle reports of Sgt. Rock of Easy Company, steal a respectful glance at the cowboy with a whip, Lash LaRue, or hold my breath at the narrow escapes among the dinosaurs of Turok, Son of Stone. In a pinch I might even flip through a Classics Illustrated if, like *The Time Machine* or *A Connecticut Yankee in King Arthur's Court*, it looked sufficiently evocative, fast-paced or humorous. But I never really cottoned to the earnest and didactic "classic comics." Washed-out inking and lackluster titles didn't help, either. Who would pick up something called *The Cloister and the Hearth* or *Tom Brown's Schooldays*? The covers were usually the best part.

Although I gradually accumulated a library of perhaps two hundred of what my parents called "your funny books," I was mainly, then as now, a reader and would unhesitatingly trade away all but my very favorite issues. Only my long pristine run of Green Lanterns remained inviolate and sacrosanct, though it too would disappear sometime after I trundled off to college, probably given away by my mother to some ungrateful younger cousin. But I never stopped enjoying comics, never feeling that they might be alien to a so-called literary life. Years later, in graduate school, I would combat periodic *taedium vitae* by escaping to the laundromat with a styrofoam cup of coffee, a maple-glazed donut and the most recent issue of Conan the Barbarian. As the mighty-thewed swordsman battled some newly awakened serpent-god, while a drugged, white-limbed princess lay fetchingly in the background on a stone altar, my tidily washed clothes would slowly spin dry and my soul would be refreshed.

Back then, my classmate Stan Paysor was reputed to possess a fabulous cache of superhero comics. Because he and I weren't particularly close—Stan used to pal around with a couple of my occasional playground oppressors—I had never been inside his house at the corner of 23rd and Washington. But out on the school monkey bars we arranged to get together one weekend to swap items from our collections. On the appointed Saturday afternoon I loaded a satchel with thirty or forty books and raced over on my red Roadmaster bike. The leaves had just begun to turn and they crunched satisfyingly beneath my wheels, while the coolish air was smoky with the deciduous fragrance of backyard bonfires.

For a while, I remember, the two bibliophiles lounged on a front porch glider, sipping Cokes and debating the existence of Santa Claus. I endeavored to demonstrate, by sheer logic, that the jolly old elf must of necessity exist. Stan countered that I was naively fooling myself, an altogether ill-advised skepticism, since Christmas was only a couple of months away.

Stan kept his comics on the bottom shelf of a bookcase in the hallway near the front door. There we hunkered down on the faded carpet with our treasures and thoughtfuly weighed the trade values of Uncle Scrooge's misadventures with the criminous Beagle Boys against the undeniable merits of Batman's never-ending crusade against the Joker and Penguin. Yet even after I had off-loaded everything I had brought, there nonetheless remained a good thirty of my classmate's titles that I still coveted. Oh well, another time. As I was packing up my new batch of Supermans and Captain Americas, Stan suddenly shrugged and said, "Here, you may as well take these too. I don't really want 'em anymore." And he simply—even now the mind boggles, the heart stops, the eyes widen in disbelief—handed me just those comics I yearned for.

Utterly light-headed, I pedaled home around six P.M. and en route noticed guys playing late-fall baseball in the field next to our elementary school, could even hear the *thwack* of bats and the *thunk* of balls against leather. At that moment, as when the dove descended upon the apostles, I felt the unmistakable presence of grace: The world was truly good and life a blessing. After supper I scattered my trove onto the floor, in a corner of the living room, next to a floor lamp, then flung myself into it like Uncle Scrooge diving into his accumulated riches. A plate of cookies and a mug of hot cocoa appeared, and, leaning against the heat register, I perused page after page of breathtaking exploits until way past my usual bedtime. Have I yet spoken the words "bliss" and "rapture"?

Of course, every ten-year-old then knew that the best place for reading new comics, at least if one remained sharply vigilant, was the corner drugstore. In the summer I'd frequently tramp the couple of blocks to Whalen's—REDEEM YOUR OWL STAMPS HERE—and enjoy a seven-cent cherry Coke at the soda fountain or politely ask if they had any empty cigar boxes (R. G. Dun, King Edward—ideal hold-alls for baseball cards, foreign coins and pieces of flint and granite). My refreshment and other business concluded, I would casually meander over to the revolving six-foot-tall wire rack of comic books. By careful positioning, one could stand or stoop, unseen by the cashier, for anywhere from fifteen minutes to an hour. Inevitably old man Whalen would eventually notice a pair of shuffling sneakers and rasp, "Hey, kid, this ain't no library. You going to buy anything?" At which point, I would dig in my pocket for a quarter and select mint copies of the two particularly action-packed adventures mentally put aside for more private delectation. But with any luck I would have already skimmed through a half dozen or more of the other "All-New" titles published that month—Superman vs. either the hairless and arrogant Lex Luthor or the pathetic Bizzarro, or even—holy cow, say it ain't so—a suddenly evil Batman.

Being sometimes denied by my prickly father the opportunity to watch all the television I wanted—especially such cartoony Saturday morning shows as *Sky King* and *Captain Midnight*, not to mention *Mighty Mouse* ("Here he comes to save the day") or *The Lone Ranger* and *The Cisco Kid* ("Hey, Cisco! Hey, Pancho!")—I gradually began to look forward, more and more, to visiting the library. Every two or three weeks now, Dad, in a dressy short-sleeved shirt and pressed khakis, would pile his offspring into the red and white '58 Ford. We would drive along the darkened streets, up Washington Avenue and just past Lorain High School, to the main library on 6th Street, each of the little Dirdas with a lapful of books to return.

In those days, being restricted to a diet of children's titles, I devoured juvenile adventure stories, science fiction and mysteries. How strange, it seemed to me, that the high-minded librarians refused to stock the Hardy Boys or Tom Corbett, the Space Cadet. But with its blond-grained card catalogue, cheery fluorescent lighting and sturdy wooden tables, the main library was clearly another great mother, warm and inviting. Among the first chapter books that I can remember checking out were the Danny Dunn thrillers (especially *Danny Dunn and the Anti-Gravity Paint*), and the Miss Pickerell misadventures (e.g., *Miss Pickerell Goes to Mars*). For a long period I also sought out the work of Howard Pease, old-fashioned nautical adventures teeming with frequent and arcane allusions to bilge, Lascars and fo'csles. For unknown reasons, I never read, nor cared to read, the standard children's classics. *Charlotte's Web* and *The Wind in the Willows* I would open only as a lucky grown-up.

My dad always enjoyed a rather seignorial tour around the library, glancing like a refined connoisseur at the "New Arrivals," then idly twirling the stand-up globe. But before long he would retreat to the Quiet Room, where he could doze through the *Cleveland Plain Dealer*. After half an hour, he would gather up all his chicks, and we would present our cards to the dour circulation librarian, watching with fascination as she inserted date-due slips into the envelopes glued to the pastedowns of our various treasures. Generally, we were each permitted to take home four or five books.

Like certain adult pleasures, a visit to the library offered both excitement and its satisfaction. I would start off by eagerly scanning the packed shelves, in search of a new title by Jim Kjelgaard or Beverly Cleary, but then snatch up anything that sounded good—

Richard Halliburton's illustrated travel exploits, Robert Heinlein's *Citizen of the Galaxy* (" 'Lot 97,' the auctioneer announced. 'A boy.' "), simplified introductions to geology or secret codes. Before long I had my cradled arms full and would wander over toward the children's periodicals. There one could riffle through a stack of tattered and worn *Boy's Life* magazines, each issue chockablock with reprints of classic mysteries ("The Problem of Cell 13," starring Prof. S. F. X. Van Dusen, the "Thinking Machine"), John R. Tunis's baseball stories, true-life wilderness tales, sanitized cartoons and jokes. At first it didn't register on me that the magazine was published by the Boy Scouts of America—which I snootily disdained as a goody-goody organization for losers. But for a year or two *Boy's Life* clearly provided just about the best casual reading in the world. Its pages left me craving a life of danger and excitement. Maybe someday . . .

I would usually start on one of my five library selections almost as soon as we pulled up our driveway. (If I tried to read in the moving car, I'd soon grow headachy, then nauseated.) Unbothered by the television's blare or my sisters' chatter, I might appropriate the recliner in the middle of the living room. I've always found it seductively easy to lose myself in print, and back then could read for hours and hours, repeatedly promising my solicitous mother that her son would definitely stop at the end of this chapter or possibly the next, and yes, all right already, I'll come to dinner. "You want cold meat loaf? See if I care." The phrase "Just let me finish this page" remains the universal mantra of every true book lover.

Though I might be happy alone with Green Lantern or Danny Dunn, school inflicted its usual angst and unhappiness. I had left Garfield for the newly built, one-story, yellow-brick Washington Elementary School, just around the corner from my house. Each morning my mother would wake me near eight, steer me to an unchanging breakfast—a small glass of orange juice, a bowl of Rice Krispies with half a banana sliced into it, a piece of buttered toast and a cup of coffee liberally sweetened with sugar and evaporated milk. Then she would bundle me up in a heavy wool coat, press a cap down on my head and send her big boy out the front door. Crossing guards called patrols—hulking sixth-graders—would help younger kids to navigate two quiet street corners. Sometimes my classmates and I would kick our gym bags at trees—"Three points!"—as we dragged our sleepy selves to school, ever wary of the yapping mutt attached to a sliding lead on a clothesline or the red-nosed, lawn-proud neighbor: "You kids stay off my grass, hear me!"

One afternoon, at 28th Street and Washington Avenue, a patrol unexpectedly glowered at me and demanded, for no apparent reason, "What's your name? I'm going to report you." Instead of informing this officer of the law that I was Mike Dirda in Mrs. Nuhn's fourth-grade class, the oral formula prescribed for such encounters, I panicked, bolted across the street and ran home. When I banged open the back door, breathing hard and queasy with fear, my mother asked, "What's wrong with you?" But I answered, "Nothing," and scurried upstairs. Rather than confess my transgression, I hid my anxiety. That night, my troubled soul generated Technicolor nightmares about the paddling machine in the principal's inner office, an ingenious torture device said to be reserved wholly for the punishment of particularly wicked and reprobate students. Those who had undergone a session with the machine—which in appearance was said to resemble an old-fashioned telephone booth—were rumored never to be quite the same again. Any spirit in them was agonizingly broken and afterward the victims dragged themselves like soulless wraiths through their remaining empty, pointless days.

The next morning I somehow needed to reach my classes without being observed by my silver-badged nemesis, almost certainly on the alert for a miscreant fourth-grader. So I explored alternate, roundabout routes to school that would circumvent the fateful corner. In the days that followed my encounter with the totalitarian jackboot, I successfully hid myself behind umbrellas and in a crowd of noisy sixth-graders. But at night, in my narrow bed, I found myself tormented by increasingly horrible visions of the principal's office and the paddling machine into which I would be pushed, pleading for mercy. "Please, please. I didn't do anything. I'm sorry I ran. Please, don't close that door. . . ." Years later, when Don Giovanni is finally dragged down to Hell at the end of Mozart's opera, I recognized his final, soul-wrenching scream as my own.

Haggard and worn, I confessed the entire shameful story to my father. The next morning he promptly drove his distraught child to school, then accompanied my trembling self into the thronged hallway. Near the main door we immediately spotted the patrol who had threatened to "report" me. "Just what has my son done?" demanded my Dad. The patrol looked up, confused, puzzled. Then he stared down at me and laughed, "Oh, him. I remember now. I was just joking around," and he started to laugh nervously. His friends joined in and even my father began to smile. Everything was all right. Just a little mistake.

Or was it? Later, I realized, with a sinking stomach, that the smirking bully had had to proffer such a casual and seemingly dismissive explanation: He was addressing a parent, an alien from the Planet Grown-Up. Nobody was ever really let off. Hardly. Someday I'd be sitting glassy-eyed in class, sipping milk through a chocolate Flav-R-Straw during the afternoon snack break or watching my teacher diagram sentences on the chalkboard, and there'd be a tap on my shoulder and I'd be hauled off by a pair of burly student aides to the principal's office, where the inexorable paddling machine hummed and patiently awaited me, its promised sacrifice.

From that day on I never completely shook off the conviction that swift and merciless doom might come crashing down on me at any moment. Without my knowing the term, my entire mindset grew mildly Kafkaesque: In college I later recognized the school paddling machine in the torture apparatus of "In the Penal Colony," while the first sentence of *The Trial* perfectly captured my childhood paranoia: "Somebody must have been spreading lies about him for one day without having done anything wrong Joseph K. was arrested." Who can say when—or from where—the blow will suddenly fall? "Never drop your guard," I murmured to myself, "and always cover your tracks."

Washington was, I suspect, in most ways much like any other 1950s elementary school. Boys traded or flipped baseball cards in the restrooms, avoided one cootie-infested water fountain no matter how long the line at its identical twin, played a game called Hunt with cat's-eye marbles and gunmetal steelies in the tall weedy grass off the playground and administered painful Indian burns to each other's wrists as the penalty for losing at Paper, Rock, Scissors. This last was the pastime of choice as we sat, cross-legged, on the waxed wooden floor of the darkened gymnasium, while the janitor fumbled with the projector for the grainy eight-millimeter film about bicycle safety or the wonders of Ceylon.

Once a week each teacher's classroom would troop down to the school library for an hour's instruction in the intricacies of the card catalogue, the ineffable mysteries of the Dewey Decimal System and the approved methods for effective research (which at our age might be summed up as "copy from more than one source"). For the most part, our school library was a paltry, halfhearted operation, dull and official, with strong holdings in uplifting educational nonfiction and outmoded reference works; it echoed with the grating whir of kids endlessly sharpening pencils.

Most of my reading soon concentrated on a set of the Landmark titles—"You are there at Valley Forge"—and two and a half shelves of blue-bound biographies: *Davy Crockett—Boy Pioneer*; *Clara Barton—Girl Nurse*; *Zeb Pike—Boy Mountaineer*. I can still picture the opening to the Davy Crockett opus: the ten-year-old free-spirited woodsman, sporting a bowl on his shaggy head, struggles to run off rather than wait for his homespun mother to finish trimming his hair. There must have been sixty of these romanticized lives and I sucked up nearly all of them—except, naturally, those devoted to Betsy Ross, Florence Nightingale and other "girls."

Occasionally, I used to speculate about girls and books. Could tales about student teachers and Candy Stripers like Cherry Ames possibly equal whodunits with boy detectives? How would it feel to be a girl and have to read about dumb old Nancy Drew, Judy Bolton or Trixie Belden instead of Tom Swift and Ken Holt? More confusedly, I wondered whether gentle Phyllis Armelie or intellectual Kathy Petro could even *read* a Tarzan adventure. How did that work? Did she imagine herself as a female queen of the jungle? Or as Jane? Surely not as Tarzan. Of course, all such perplexities remained purely abstract and never once did I think to question my sisters or female classmates about their tastes in books. Still, I vaguely began to suspect there might be other ways of reading than simply identifying with the dauntless hero.

Having been judged a moon-faced dolt for most of my elementary school years, in fifth grade I unexpectedly awoke from my academic stupor. At the opening of the school year the principal showily ushered a new pupil into our hushed classroom. Solicitous attentions showered down on Tom Mikus from every side: Not only the son of the county prosecutor, he was also reportedly a genius at math and reputed to possess an astonishing IQ. After one quick glance at this blond cherub, I instantly despised his pampered guts. Naturally, he was to become my best friend (to the delight of my father, who came to relish the occasional chance to chat about democratic politics with "old man Mikus"). But at first Tom elicited nothing but envy, touched with repugnance: "I'm as good as he is," I whispered to myself, adding, with fierce resolve, "I'll show them. I'll show them all." In the course of the school year I moved up from class dunce to academic whiz kid. When, that spring, the school organized its annual "book fair," Michael Dirda was even elected its king, honored to reign from a chair—my throne—up on the gymnasium stage while holding a stiff banner whose emblazoned words I proceeded to proclaim aloud to the assembled parents and pupils: "Who hath a book hath but to read/ And he will be a king indeed."

Still, my rise to scholastic powerhouse was hardly without its cost. Back in the halcyon days of the 1950s, social clubs—more accurately gangs—dominated much of a school's extramural life. Two rival organizations—better not to mention any names, lest they seek vengeance even now—actually took shape back at Washington Elementary. Their then-sixth-grade leadership, ever on the lookout for new ways to scrap, rumble or otherwise divert themselves, soon started betting on whether Dirda or Mikus would garner higher marks on the weekly math or spelling test. This meant that I'd be busily calculating how many tomatoes a farmer would have left after he'd sold $\frac{13}{22}$ of his crop when a pencil would prick my neck and I'd hear a throaty Don Corleone-like growl: "Me and the guys bet the Bachelors fifty cents that you'd get a better grade than Mikus. You know we don't like to lose our money." If Tom outperformed me, I'd quite likely get pushed around or beaten up out on the blacktop by the losing bettor and his helpful associates. Similar "accidents" might befall Tom should I outscore him. Naturally, we two milquetoasts—one elfin and silly, the other four-eyed and dreamy—decided that our safest course lay in earning exactly the same marks, which would cause all bets to be canceled. In other words, I started doing well in school not because of any innate gifts, but first out of envy and later out of fear.

Despite my newfound academic success—in some ways as bewildering to my teachers and parents as to me—I remained essentially an isolato, a loner without close friends apart from my chums Rick Brant, Joe and Frank Hardy, Lord Greystoke and Superman. My happiest school days still focused on books generally—and on the TAB Book Club in particular. Ah, the TAB Book Club! Once a month our teacher—in fifth grade, Mr. Jackson; in sixth, Mrs. Pierce—would distribute a four-page *Weekly Reader*–like tabloid, listing titles available from this mail-order clearinghouse. This flyer reproduced in miniature the cover of each paperback for sale, with a brief description that highlighted its thrilling contents:

"From the pool near an old mine emerged the Piper's Ghost, moaning dreadfully! Michael Cunningham, an orphaned boy, stared at the glowing creature with the horns on its head, a bagpipe under its arm, and webbed feet. Who or what was this weird creature?" (Back cover of *The Mystery of the Piper's Ghost.*)

In fourth grade I bought *Snow Treasure*, a true account of how Norwegian kids cleverly smuggled out something—gold for the Allied cause? the plans for heavy water?—from under the very gun barrels of the Nazis. No storm-coated soldier ever thought to look under the children's sleds (shades of Ulysses' escape from the Cyclops!). Then too I succumbed to the obvious blandishments of *Treasure at First Base* and *The Spanish Cave Mystery*. I can remember declaiming passages aloud from the latter—about the sudden apparition of a Nessie-like sea monster—to my terrified younger cousins. Years later I figured out that this spooky adventure had been written by none other than Geoffrey Household, whose classic survivalist thriller of the 1930s, *Rogue Male*, I was to find unputdownable as a teenager.

Each month my mother allowed me to buy four TAB books, at twenty-five or thirty-five cents apiece. Carefully, methodically I deliberated on exactly which titles to choose. Should it be *Big Red*? Or a novel about drag car racing by William Campbell Gault? How about *Mystery at Thunderbolt House* (set at the time of the San Francisco earthquake and fire)? Or that collection of Mr. Wizard science experiments? "Come on, Ma, how about five, just five? Please." But no matter how much I beseeched the parsimonious Mrs. Dirda, she would never shell out for any more than four books. "What do you think we are, made of money? You want more books, what's wrong with the library?"

After our teacher posted the class's order, several weeks would pass and I would almost, but not quite, forget which masterworks I had selected. Then, in the middle of some particularly dull afternoon, when spitballs were beginning to fly, a teacher's aide would cautiously open the classroom door and silently drop off a big, heavily taped parcel. A murmur of anticipation would ripple along the rows of the slant-surfaced school desks—the kind where the hinged top opens up to reveal an enclosed storage tray for crayons and pencils—and we would squirm restively, hoping that Mr. Jackson or Mrs. Pierce would distribute the goodies that very day. Sometimes, groaning with disappointment, we'd be made to wait, especially if the package had been delivered close to three o'clock when school let out.

Romantic poets complain that in later life they can intellectually appreciate the wonders of nature but no longer truly feel them as they did when young. So too I can recall, but never wholly re-create, the breathtaking joy of holding in my hands four bright new paperbacks, so tight and sleek and shiny. At my desk I would patiently study each title's artwork, review the brief descriptions on the back covers, even check out the faint edge of glue at the top of the perfect-bound spines. I would then lean over to envy the treasures on my classmates' desks. No rare first editions have ever been so lovingly cherished as those ordinary TAB Book Club paperbacks.

Of these purchases the most memorable was doubtless *The Hound of the Baskervilles*. Both its title and the accompanying blurb electrified me: "What was it that came out of the moors at night to spread terror and violent death?" What else, of course, but a hound from the bowels of Hell, pictured loping across the moonlit horizon? Eager as I was to plunge into obviously suspense-filled pages, I resolutely put off starting the book until conditions were just right.

One propitiously gray Saturday in early November my parents announced that they would be visiting relatives that evening with my sisters. Yes, I might stay home alone to read. The afternoon soon grew dark, the wind off the lake picked up, rain threatened. With a dollar clutched in my fist I pedaled my bike to Whalen's, where I bought two or three candy bars, a box of Cracker Jacks, a twelve-ounce bottle of Orange Crush. After my family had driven off into the lowering evening, I dragged down a blanket from my bed, spread it on the reclining chair, carefully arranged a floor lamp and my assorted snacks. I then turned off all the other house lights, and crawled expectantly under the covers with an emergency flashlight and my new TAB paperback of *The Hound*—just as the heavens began to boom with thunder and the rain to slap against the curtained windows.

Under these near-to-ideal conditions I turned page after page, more than a little scared, gradually learning the origin of the terrible curse of the Baskervilles. At the end of chapter two, the tension escalates unbearably. Sherlock Holmes and Dr. Watson have just been told how the latest Baskerville has been found dead, apparently running *away* from the safety of his own house. Their informant, Dr. Mortimer, pauses, then adds, hesitantly, that near the body he had spotted footprints on the damp ground. What kind? eagerly inquires the great detective; to which question he receives the immortal answer: "Mr. Holmes, they were the footprints of a gigantic hound." I shivered with fearful pleasure, scrunched farther down under my blanket, and took another bite of my Baby Ruth. This was living.

Chapter Three

*All the things I write of I have first known, and they
are real to me.*

—Katherine Anne Porter

Sandy, Pam, Linda. After I'd read *Macbeth* I sometimes referred
to them as my three weird sisters. In my childhood they generated a continual background noise—a staticky buzz of voices
arguing about dolls, clothes, food, friends, their stupid brother—and
for weeks at a time I would contrive to ignore them. They were
forced by straitened circumstances to dwell in close proximity—three
single beds in a small room with just one closet—and I have sometimes idly mused how they managed. Basically each was allocated
two drawers in a bureau and a dozen hangers. Little wonder that they
now reside in airy modern homes with vast closets and giant family
rooms.

The eldest, Sandra—round-faced, chubby and empathetic—
would alternate between maternal solicitude and hysterical outbursts
of tears and frustration, usually brought on by her insane family.
"Why can't we all just get along? Why do we always have to yell about
everything?"

Pamela, my middle sister, was skinny throughout our childhoods, hyperactive, sulky, contrary and determined. We fought constantly. Once she grabbed my hand and pulled my index finger back

as hard as she could, thwarted only by mischance from breaking it. Another time she slammed the car door on her younger sister's hand—an act of coldly nursed vengeance for some previous slight.

Pamela could be a fussy eater and when confronted by an unwanted piece of fried perch she might lodge the breaded fillet in among the wooden brackets beneath the dining room table. The decaying fishy remnants would be nosed out a week later. She repeatedly defied our mother, who more than once had to fetch "the spoon" after her. This was a wooden cooking spoon with which Mom liked to crack our bottoms when we misbehaved. Rather than submit to this corporal punishment, Pammy would sometimes pull away from from her righteous mother's grasp and race off. Mom would then call, "Sandy, Michael," and we would block various passageways so that the miscreant might not continue to flee the now-greater wrath to come.

Once or twice, the wayward child actually pronounced curse words—"damn" or "hell"—inside our house. Such blasphemy could never be permitted to happen twice. While her older siblings held Pam down on the kitchen floor, kicking and thrashing, Mom slowly forced open her clenched teeth and made our evil sister eat a quarter of a new bar of Ivory soap. "How does it taste, little girl? You going to say those words again? Are you?" Pam sputtered and tried to wriggle free. "I hate you. I hate you all." Mom again shoved the bar of soap into the blasphemer's mouth. "Eat it," she commanded. Pam made a terrific effort to escape. "Hold her down, Michael. Sandy, stop her from kicking me." Slowly, Pam's will broke, but it took twenty minutes before she said she was sorry.

As the baby of the family, "Little Linda" annoyed her big sisters. She was Dad's princess. "Linda gets everything," Pam would seethe. "I never get anything. That's because I'm the neglected middle child."

Then she would go on about how she was always shortchanged and overlooked.

In fact, Linda did learn how to soothe our savage dad and to maneuver deftly around his moods, often to her own benefit. Yet she wasn't inherently conniving or even particularly ambitious. For a Dirda, my youngest sister possessed a rare sunniness and equanimity.

As mothers tend to, ours liked to dress her three daughters in matching or similar outfits, so that they might parade into church like a trio of Shirley Temples. "Sit pretty," Mom would order. But, of course, they would jab each other with their elbows, and she would have to angrily shush them. As they grew older, they were sometimes ordered to run the sweeper or pick up their clothes from the floor— "this isn't a barn"—and they would loudly complain about these monstrous burdens. Even Sandy once burst out, "Sometimes I think the only reason you had us is so that we could do the housework for you." In fact, the division of labor in our house was exacting but lenient: Mom would shop, cook and wash clothes and dishes. Dad would maintain the house and the property. The children were all-purpose roustabouts and any or all of us might be ordered to shovel snow, weed the grass, water the vegetable garden, clean the garage. If you wanted a favor, you might take on a chore without asking.

Now and then, my parents would vanish for the evening and leave their four offspring at home, sometimes with an older cousin for a babysitter. At such times, we'd rearrange the furniture in the living room and then make death-defying leaps from couch to chair to stair railings, all to avoid the ravenous gape-mouthed crocodiles just waiting for one of our stocking feet to touch the floor. Occasionally we'd douse all the house lights and play hide and seek in the dark. And, now and again, we'd even surprise the poor shoemaker and his wife by washing the dishes, Windexing the windows, vacuuming and generally making every room tidy and spotless. Mom would always feign astonishment at what the "elves" had accomplished during her two-hour visit with Auntie Stella.

The girls and I always ate our meals together. Breakfast, lunch, dinner, the last usually around five o'clock. Then Mom would wipe down the table with a dishrag and we would open our three-ring binders and copy spelling words or practice cursive handwriting or figure out story problems in math: a vision of harmonious child labor—every parent's dream.

Back in those slow-paced, small-town days, it was common practice for entire families to pick up and go "visiting" on Sunday afternoons. So every few weeks Dad would announce, "Let's take a drive," and my mother would rush through the noontime dishes, rouge her cheeks and lips and then round up her three princesses and moody son. The Ford would be already idling, its antsy driver growing increasingly impatient to be off.

We would usually stop first at Uncle Joe and Aunt Mary's— my godparents. There we would sit primly in the dark, *tschotchke*-cluttered parlor and munch on tasteless homemade cookies, while Aunt Mary retailed her family's ongoing travails of the spirit and the flesh. My uncle had somehow injured his hand—falling from a ladder—such that it was now oddly flattened, misshapen and hardly usable: For years its condition, along with hesitantly advanced medical opinions, supplied the burden of all conversation at the Burtz household. My Uncle Joe would sadly wave his grotesque digits, and Aunt Mary would shake her head in tender sympathy. Following an obligatory peck on my aunt's cheek, we kids were usually permitted to scale the backyard plum trees or fiddle dangerously with my swaggering cousin David's animal traps; one Christmas we stared, mesmerized, as he demonstrated, with a twitch of a bony wrist, his gleaming new flick knife.

Sometimes Dad would swing out toward genteel Amherst or run-down South Lorain, to say hi to Frank or Eddie or John. Were all uncles, I used to wonder, florid of face, loud and stubble-cheeked? And what did the men actually do all day? Surely, one couldn't spend every weekend hour slumped in a softly padded creaking rocker, popping cans of beer and watching *Perry Mason* and *Cheyenne*. My aunts, either thin and cranky or plump and solicitous, generally twittered about, setting out lechvar turnovers or plates of fatty sliced ham. Nearly all my relatives, no matter how kind or welcoming, struck me as deeply unhappy souls, caught up in stunted jobs, marriages and lives. Their houses, some just a cut above those in a trailer park, might look tidy and welcoming, but often felt lonesome inside, claustrophobic with heavy oak furniture. But perhaps everyone sang like birds when I wasn't around, and it was only my young self who felt dissatisfied and restless.

Both my parents had grown up in Lorain, and neither they nor most of their siblings ever really left it. For me this resulted in a dozen aunts and as many uncles and scores of cousins, all local. Some bore odd-sounding names like Fritzi, Schpun and Frankie Boy. Nearly all of them guarded secrets and unspoken sorrows, for my family seldom shared emotional traumas or personal adversities. Did my father's mysterious half-brother, John, who knocked late one night at our back door with a mess of lake perch, suffer from depression? Could a proclivity for the illness run in the family? No one discussed it. Had one of my uncles actually been a foundling, adopted by my Grand-mother Burcl? No one would say.

Then there were the tragedies. During World War II one of Mom's favorite high school dancing partners flung himself onto a grenade to protect his comrades and was awarded a posthumous Medal of Honor. My Aunt Stella's fiancé perished when a Kamikaze dive-bombed his ship. At some point my own mother suffered a miscarriage and lost the child who would have been my brother. When I was ten or so, one Sunday morning my Uncle Eddie appeared at the front door, tears flowing down his cheeks, to announce that his son had been shot in the eye with an arrow. "See," my mother said later, "I've told you kids over and over not to throw stones or shoot those bow-and-arrows and slingshots at each other. Do you ever listen? No, you don't. Well, this is what happens." In years to come, cousin Eddie—when provoked—would threaten to take out his glass eye and my sisters and I would turn away, shrieking.

Only occasionally did my father reminisce about his years in the South Pacific aboard the heavy cruiser *Pensacola*. He had manned both the eight-inch cannons and the forty-millimeter machine guns, either shelling islands or shooting down enemy planes. One day I unearthed an album in the dining room bookcase devoted to the "Gray Ghost" and her missions. Dad had annotated the volume, penciling an arrow to one sailor in a group picture—the beloved friend Peterson, who was killed a few days after he transferred to a new gun mount. The *Pensacola* herself was torpedoed twice; nearly a third of the men died the second time. After this debacle at sea, my father fashioned a huge Bowie knife—for sharks, he explained with a faraway look—and a leather sheath to keep it in. The dagger lay, carefully locked up, in the cedar hope chest with other family treasures and yellowing wedding mementos.

My father was brought up Russian Orthodox but after the war converted to a lukewarm Roman Catholicism for my observant mother. Every Sunday at ten A.M. we attended Mass at St. Vitus for an eternal hour and ten minutes. We children were instructed to sit erect, to kneel without allowing our bottoms to touch the pew behind us, to follow the drama of the miraculous transubstantiation of bread and wine into the body and blood of Christ. After a while I found this tedious beyond belief and took to reciting the rosary instead, racing through the beads, mouthing Our Fathers, Hail Marys and Glory Bes as fast as possible, just to see how many cycles I could finish in seventy minutes. Half drunk on incense, I would also drowsily listen to the Latin phrases: Did the priest really chant, "Leave Her on a Sunny Day" and "Dominic Go Frisk 'Em"? Later, when English clarified, yet further dulled the ancient rituals, I couldn't wait to hear the words "Go, the Mass is ended," to which we kids responded with a fervent, "Thanks be to God."

Sometimes, though, the more gruesome readings from the two Testaments would thrill me in spite of ennui: Herod slaying every infant around in a vain attempt to destroy the baby Jesus; Doubting Thomas being compelled to place his hand in the bleeding wound. I shuddered at the plagues of Egypt and the destruction of Sodom and Gomorrah, loved the unexpected twists and reversals in the story of Joseph, marveled that the armies of Israel could triumph only when Moses held his arms extended. The economical richness of Jesus' parables impressed me too—all those kaleidoscopic permutations on cloaks and Pharisees and vineyards, on mustard seeds and brambles and wedding banquets, on the birds of the air and "a certain rich man." At Eastertime I waited expectantly for Peter to break down in tears, having fulfilled Christ's prophecy at the Last Supper that he would deny his Master three times "before the cock crew." And I reflected often about the weeping and gnashing of teeth and the outer darkness.

To designate our well-meaning priest's sermons as boilerplate is to be kind: Father regarded himself as the mouthpiece of received dogma and his homilies risked neither rhetorical flights nor Holy-Roller frenzies. Before he began his weekly platitudes, he would always announce that last Sunday the parishioners had given $173.50 or $187.50. For special collections he would add, "And special thanks for fifty dollars from the Altar Society and fifty from St. Theresa's Guild." Bored, I eventually asked my mother if I might study the Bible during Mass. She hesitated but yielded to my entreaties—after all, it contained the word of God. And so, as a youngster, I lost—or found—myself in the cynicism of Ecclesiastes and the ecstasy of the Song of Songs, which is Solomon's "Stay me with flagons, comfort me with apples; for I am sick with love."

After Mass my mother would "give us eat," that is Sunday dinner, plunking everything down on the table before grumpily saying, "Nuh. That's all there is. You don't like it, don't eat it." During the week my sisters and I might hurry home at lunchtime from school for a tomato sandwich—just a slice or two of ripe tomato lightly salted between two pieces of soft Wonder Bread. Nothing better on a hot day with a glass of cold milk. On more wintry afternoons she would sometimes fry up potato pancakes—certainly one of the supreme delicacies of Eastern European cuisine. But Sundays were always true feast days. Ham, stuffed cabbage, pierogi, kielbasa with sauerkraut, sweet potatoes, city chicken (kebabs of breaded veal and pork), kolachy walnut rolls. Even when leaving the table I'd secretly swipe one last roll or even a slice of bread that could be kneaded into a hard ball of dough and nibbled on later. At Thanksgiving, Easter or Christmas there would be vastly more of the same bounty, plus a kind of dirty rice, made with turkey juices, and stuffing and apple pie. To underscore the sacerdotal nature of such holiday meals, we'd all solemnly receive a torn piece of bread dipped in honey and a shot glass full of Concord grape wine. The body and blood of Christ. My mother would take a tiny sip of the Mogen David, smack her lips together and girlishly announce, every time, "Ooh, I can really feel that wine."

In my extended family, marriages, graduations and even funerals were all opportunities for lavish bumper suppers worthy of some Dutch painter of peasant life. The women, having cooked all day, would set out huge earthenware bowls of potato salad, Pyrex pans of baked beans and white-flecked navy-blue roasters brimming with juicy stuffed cabbage or crispy fried chicken. Hands would grow cold rooting in steel washtubs of sloshing, icy water, fishing around for an Orange Crush or grape soda. Teenage boys would try to inveigle Rolling Rock or highballs from the youthful bartender, usually just an older cousin armed with a bottle opener. At the boisterous annual church picnic one could even buy hot pork sandwiches and watch the steaming meat sliced off a snouted carcass slowly turning on a spit over dying embers.

However, no occasion could aspire to the truly festive without a dance band. These would almost always include an accordion, so that my aunts—more often partnered with their sisters than with their overstuffed husbands—might swirl around the floor at the Slovenian Hall to the driving rhythms of a polka or czardas. As she spun by, my mother would ululate periodically, "Yah, ha, ha!" and grab a child's arm and try to teach clumsy feet the basic steps. Not for bashful me. Instead my cousins and I would slip and slide on the sawdust-covered floor, dodging the manic, sometimes barefoot dancers. Outside the young men would congregate to smoke an illicit Lucky Strike, brag how much weight they'd bench-pressed down at the Y or whisper about some curvy female cousin. "Did you get a look at that dress she's got on? Man, you can practically see right down the front."

At every such party mothers or fathers would eventually introduce their hesitant children to some shrewd-eyed crone who rattled away in broken English or fluent Slovak. Or was it Russian? Cousin Helen, we'd be told, was a DP, a Displaced Person come over after the war, your father's mother's sister. Or possibly your mother's cousin's aunt. Who could remember? After all, my grandmothers were both dead by the time I was seven and my grandfathers had died long before them. The Dirda offspring were wholly American, though we loved the food and the babble of foreign languages and the oompah music of the accordion.

Ah, the accordion! That would be just the thing for "little Mikhailo." Before long I was signed up for lessons at the Music Center, on my way to stepping into the black patent leather shoes of Myron Floren, the curly-haired virtuoso accordionist and chief lieutenant of Lawrence Welk, whose Saturday television program my mother revered. The bubbly champagne music, Norma Zimmer or the four Lennon Sisters—"aren't they just beautiful?"—the groomed, clean-cut look of the orchestra: "Wunnerful, wunnerful!" This was music, not that rock and roll, not that screeching Elvis Presley on *The Ed Sullivan Show*. So I ran through my scales from a book by Pietro Deiro, memorized "Lady of Spain" and Frankie Yankovic polkas ("Roll out the barrel, we'll have a barrel of fun") and dutifully practiced the bellow-shakes. Finally my red Lira and I were ready to join—what else?—a thirty-six-member all-accordion band.

No doubt a public relations venture for the Music Center—and a soft-sell encouragement for more parents to give their children the gift of keyboard music—the band soon won blue ribbons at county fairs around Ohio and appeared in Fourth of July and Memorial Day parades. We bowtied *artistes* would sway on wooden folding chairs on the back of a long flatbed truck decorated with patriotic bunting. From there we'd launch into our renditions of John Philip Sousa's "Washington Post March" or "Under the Double Eagle" while our parents beamed. Twice we competed in an international accordion-band competition at the Cedar Point Amusement Park in Sandusky—and took home trophies.

But it was hard for a ten- or eleven-year-old to lug a heavy instrument around and I hated missing *Zorro*, my favorite Thursday night TV show, because of practice: "Out of the night, when the full moon is bright, Comes a horseman known as Zorro." "Time to go to band," my dad would announce, just as the black-caped figure would slash a Z with his rapier—*Hwit, hwit, hwit*—into a frightened soldier's tunic: altogether much more satisfying than the somber *Have Gun, Will Travel* or the self-important *Gunsmoke* (with gimpy Chester always hurrying behind the sheriff and murmuring, "I'm a-coming, Mr. Dillon, I'm a-coming"). Ah, smiling, pencil-mustached Don Diego! Still, I stuck with the accordion for five years of weekly lessons and eventually joined another more Welk-like orchestra with saxophones, trumpets and drums. I even perfected a special solo piece: "Boogie Woogie on the Squeeze Box."

My mother had never heard this razzle-dazzle number in public and so stayed behind one evening at the church hall where I was to perform. "That's my son," she enlightened all those near her, as the youthful virtuoso swung into his signature tune. But I noticed her from the stage and instantly my mind went blank, my fingers gradually ceasing to fly up and down the keyboard. I fumbled, stopped, smiled wanly and started once more at the beginning, got only a little further and stalled again. Finally I had to skip the entire first section and limp from the middle to the end. Tepid applause couldn't disguise snickers and compassionate murmurs. To this day, when nervous before some public event, I remind myself that no adult gaffe or embarrassment can ever be as sheerly awful as the night I played for my once-proud mother.

As I grew older, I tried to spend more time with my omnicompetent cousin Henry Kucirek, a year or two my senior. My Uncle Henry's son, he was nicknamed Cookie and lived outside the municipal limits, in what my family always called the country. To me his yard and neighborhood rivaled Peter Pan's Neverland. Cookie's house, for one thing, was actually heated by a wood-burning furnace, which my uncle would frequently feed and stoke. I loved to watch him open the cast-iron grate and poke at the fire before tossing in a block or two of wood, then closing the heavy metal door with a dull clank. Dad always complained, of course, that Henry kept his house too hot and that wood heat gave people headaches. "I don't know why he can't get a gas furnace like everyone else."

During the summer, after I had received my obligatory June buzz cut, what we called a "butch," I would sometimes pass a week with the Kucireks. After breakfast, my cousin and I would push off to the railroad tracks a quarter mile away to load up old wheelbarrows with scrap lumber—firewood for the furnace in winter. My uncle would pay us a nickel-pack of BBs a trip; so by working for two or three hours each morning an eleven-year-old could earn enough ammo for the afternoon. Usually Cookie and I would take aim at birds or frogs, though I never really wanted to hit any, even when the county government was paying a two-cent or nickel bounty on crows. (Once I did shoot a big crow with a bow and then stared as the tough old bird actually flew off with my arrow stuck in its bottom.) With my trusty Daisy air rifle I liked best to plink away at bottles and watch them shatter with a direct hit.

One June this passion for tinkling glass led me to knock out the corner streetlight—quite a brilliant shot—and all BBs were cut off for a few days. By virtue of necessity, then, Cookie and I started to experiment with other projectiles and discovered that our rifles could be satisfactorily loaded with half-ripe elderberries. Whenever we "wounded" each other, a realistic splotch of red appeared on our white T-shirts. As a result, when we staggered home for supper, drenched in "blood," my aunt nearly fainted. Being foolish, we kept up these war games even after we returned to real shot, such that I carry to this day a BB buried in the fat of my lower left forearm. It was Cookie too who "branded" me on my left hand—we were street-fighting with two cigarette lighters from an old car. I flaunted a very cool circular burn mark, like a Yakuza tattoo, for at least a dozen years.

Those summer visits encouraged great childhood adventures— climbing into and under coal cars (while keeping an eye out for the railroad bull and his guard dog), smoking cattails or trapping snapping turtles at the Turtle Pond (where I learned to hockey-skate one winter on rough, wind-rippled ice), constructing elaborate tree forts, shooting the "slinkies" that we manufactured from "crutches" and strips of inner tube and then carried in our back pockets like Tom Sawyer.

At the end of those timeless days, the lightning bugs would glint and flicker, bats swoop in the dusk and the overgrown woods chatter with insects. But in the last hour or so before night, seemingly the entire neighborhood would play softball on an unbuilt corner lot. Games might easily start off with a dozen or fifteen people on a side, including preschoolers and retirees. One year we actually painted the ball an iridescent orange so that it would shine in the darkness. That didn't work very well. Another time my dad stopped by, found himself enlisted as a pinch hitter and casually batted the ball across the road. He grinned sheepishly like the Babe himself. There was a sense of family picnic to those sportive evenings, a time when even a young misfit might feel part of a community. My mother had played just such baseball games in her own childhood—and in this very same neighborhood; she would sigh with longing when she recalled those distant innings and how she and her siblings would scurry home in groups of two or three as the older kids frightened the younger ones with tales about The Hook or ghostly revenants. Never such innocence again.

Uncle Henry owned guns, shotgun shell reloaders, all kinds of knives, a tool for every job and vast quantities of wire. His basement looked like an Aladdin's cave in which everything had rusted and mildewed. Bottles of screws hung from the joists. Coffee cans spilled over with old parts. Washtubs were fitted out with butcher boards for gutting bass and cleaning pheasants. There were a dozen rods and reels, five or six tackle boxes, a fruit cellar stocked with inedibles, a treadle sewing machine, a half dozen thin chains dangling from bare bulbs, galoshes and waders under the steps and a persistent odor of mold, since the basement periodically flooded. It goes without saying that Uncle Henry's side yard boasted several abandoned cars (one summer Cookie and I took propane torches, cut off a sedan's roof and created our own homemade convertible), a flourishing chicken coop squawking with hens (some of which started life as pink and blue "peeps" acquired by my mother at Eastertime and kept until they were too big for our household), a couple of steel barrels in which you'd sometimes find big snappers waiting to be turned into turtle soup and a behemoth, park-sized swing set. Occasionally Dad and I would sit on the porch with slingshots and take aim at bottles on a fence; now and again Cookie and I would target chickens to watch them squawk and run. Anything, absolutely anything in the world might be found on my Uncle Henry's property and when, half a lifetime later, I read the description of a wonder-filled Parisian junk shop in Balzac's gothicky novel *The Fatal Skin*, I recognized the place immediately. I'd been there.

On my family's periodic weekend visits to the Kucireks we would start by sitting around the dining room table, with my mother-hennish Auntie Alice pushing ham sandwiches or big marshmallowy "circus peanuts," or the black gummy candy called—by some kids— "nigger babies." Usually my uncle would have something boiling on the stove, frequently, it seemed, a haunch of venison or a homemade stew. I recall one summer when Henry was out on strike—from Thew Shovel, which bolted together diesel cranes and power shovels—and nobody had any money. For three or four days in a row supper consisted of just slumgullion, a repulsive vegetable chowder which I could barely force myself to taste, let alone swallow (though it sounds good and healthy to me now). In subsequent years, Auntie Alice would always remind me of my grimaces at dinnertime, especially when my mother would tease me on the phone by mentioning that she was just that moment setting out breaded pork chops or city chicken.

On those Sundays, after we'd all sampled Alice's nut roll ("too dry," my Mom would say later, "needs raisins"), the grown-ups would sit around the kitchen table and gossip while my sisters and I explored the house or joked with our cousins. Parents might teach the little kids how to play 500 Rummy, a card game at which my mother "Chris" and her sister "Alice" excelled. During Christmas or New Year's get-togethers my uncle Henry sometimes brought out a harmonica or dilapidated concertina; he would stumble through Old Country tunes while people danced or sang mournfully in Slovak.

Week after week, as we drove to church and called upon relatives, I gradually began to fathom the basic layout of Lorain. My own house naturally occupied the city's geographical center. Across from nearby Washington Elementary School were "the projects"—multiplex wooden housing for the poor, mostly "colored," as people typically said back then, or hillbilly. For a while, my sisters and I would visit a community rec center there for lessons in "tumbling"—forward and backward rolls, splits and the like. But whenever I'd wander alone into these blocks, dirty and weedy and ugly, I'd feel out of place, on edge. Kids, especially white kids, would get beat up there for pocket change. Or so it was rumored. Lorain's African-American population would, however, eventually find its laureate (in several senses) in favorite daughter Toni Morrison, and especially in her first novel, *The Bluest Eye*.

If one traveled south, down Oberlin Avenue, one would pass Whalen's, Willow Hardware, Yala's Pizza, Lorain Plaza Shopping Center, the Tick-Tock Lounge, Rebman's Bowling Alley. Eventually Oberlin intersected with North Ridge Road, site of Elmwood and Calvary Cemeteries, the first vaguely Protestant, the other mainly

Catholic. There, from my grandfather's tombstone, I learned that he had originally spelled our family name Dyrda. Some of my mother's family also adopted the name Burtz as sounding more American than Burcl. We would visit graves three or four times a year, recite a prayer or two and then leave bunches of violets or pansies in the chained metallic cups. On some gravestones one found old black and white pictures, encased in yellowing plastic and embedded in the granite. I would stare at the phographs of young brides and little babies and smiling soldiers from long ago. *Memento mori.*

Down the road from the cemeteries lay Clearview, the regional high school that my mother had attended, and a little farther on, over at Route 254, the O'Neil-Sheffield Shopping Center. From there a movie fan could peer up at the radio tower that gave Tower Drive-in its name. In the *Journal* the entertainment section listed its Dusk to Dawn films: I remember an ad picturing a sexy young slattern, in what looked like a giant crib, sucking her thumb: *Baby Doll.* Beyond that cinematic landmark, somewhere in the distance, spread the neighboring city of Elyria, the county seat (and former home to Sherwood Anderson, when he managed a paint store). Elyria was only eight miles away from the much bigger Lorain—and yet I seldom visited there and always got lost when I did.

All these places and locales were loosely south of my house on 29th Street. To the north, toward Lake Erie, Oberlin Avenue first passed George Daniel Field—the stadium where the high schools played football and ran track meets—then continued a mile or so through largely residential areas, and finally debouched into Hot Waters.

This was a favorite fishing spot, a Lake Erie inlet kept warm by the adjacent electric power plant. When the white bass were running, they schooled so thickly in the "hot waters" that all you needed was a hook to snag them, and once my dad and I caught fifty in an hour or two. Only much later in my adolescence were the Erie perch, pike and bass deemed too toxic for human consumption.

To swim, my father would drive us to Lake View Park, a quarter mile west of Hot Waters and famous—well, sort of famous—for its Giant Easter Basket, spectacular rose garden and manicured bowling lawns for Italian *boccie*. Laden with blankets and coolers, we would clumsily descend the grassy lakeside slope to the beach so that Dad could teach his son, then daughters, how to stay afloat in polluted water. On a hot sunny day the wide expanse of sand would be stippled with colorful blankets and white, brown and black bodies glazed with Coppertone. It didn't seem ludicrous then that Lorain's motto could proclaim "Industrial Empire in Ohio's Vacationland."

My family seldom ventured farther west than Lake View except to the Roller Rink, where the girls and I used to skate in musical circles and make fun of the hand-holding or smooching teenage couples. Some of my classmates' fathers, though, worked out that way on the line at the new Ford Assembly Plant (Econoline vans). And every other summer or so we might drive another fifteen or twenty miles toward Toledo for the carnivalesque pleasures of Cedar Point, the latter a mecca for roller-coaster aficionados—and the source of innumerable July traffic jams that would leave our hot-tempered chauffeur fuming.

Lorain's downtown—Broadway—started at the lake and then ran parallel to Oberlin Avenue. Here all the local merchants congregated and thrived: Clothing stores like Louis Cohn's and Ted Jacobs, the Ohio, Palace and Tivoli Movie Theaters, a tiny hole-in-the-wall that sold peanuts, Klein's Department Store, Driscoll's Music, Rusine's Cigar Store, Cane's Surplus. When Mom wanted to take her children with her "to the sales" or out "bumming," we would usually end up downtown, listlessly traipsing behind her whining for penny candy, while she tirelessly checked out bargains on pillowcases, wash-and-wear shirts and flannel nightgowns.

To reach the East Side, where Lorain's big shots resided in lake-front splendor and ease, one needed to cross one of two bridges spanning the Black River. Both started from Broadway, and each offered distinctive pleasures. The Bascule, or jackknife bridge, could be raised to admit slow-moving freighters and ore carriers on their way up the river to National Tube. We kids always hoped to see its two halves slowly reaching for the sky. Off to one side one could also glimpse American Shipbuilding, with gigantic half-built vessels up in dry dock. The 21st Street bridge, by contrast, rose high and long in a graceful arc, and through its guard rails one could look out at the deteriorating back of Broadway on one side or admire the great red-dish slag heaps of the steel plant on the other.

Once on the East Side, Dad might announce, "Let's stop at Stella's, just for an hour," though sometimes he'd simply drive along for a while admiring the pillared manses of doctors, lawyers and plant managers. "How about that one, kids? Want to live in that one?" Dad both envied and hated the rich. He was convinced that politics was simply a means for the upper classes to protect their wealth and to get more of it. What could be more obvious? "The only other reason these guys run for president is to get their names in the history books." He would sigh, look daydreamy and then suddenly exhort his son, "Kid, just go out and make a lot of money. Get that house on the hill, drive a big old Cadillac. And vote Republican."

More than any of these "better" neighborhoods, however, South Lorain could lay claim to being the true capital of this "North Coast" industrial empire. Following busy 28th Street on the other side of Central Park, you passed St. Stanislaus Church and the Czech Grill, the Polish-American Fisherman's Club and Porkolab Insurance.

When your car emerged on the other side of the railroad underpass, Lorain suddenly grew serious. Thew Shovel loomed to the right, National Tube to the left. Picture a gargantuan junkyard, slowly rusting and corroding—huge steel-clad buildings, a mile or more of smokestacks, blacktopped parking lots, cords of blackened pipe, the iron tracks of the Lake Terminal Railroad. Near the smelly dilapidated YMCA or across from the Open Hearth Club, abandoned cars might be coated with wind-borne grit and the air fragant with sulfur.

In my day the neighborhoods around the steel mill were largely Puerto Rican and, to a lesser extent, black. Some older Poles, Hungarians and Italians still lived there, but most of their children had moved away from streets where people commonly referred to one another as Polacks, Hunkies and Dagos. Nearly all the wooden houses, each with a big porch sagging across its front, looked tired, gray, worn-out. Like their generations of owners, they'd been through a lot. On the edge of this ghetto stood our graceless red brick church, St. Vitus—the eight A.M. Mass always given in Croation—and a little farther down the road Oakwood Shopping Center. Across from that gimcrack merchandising venture, in the "woods," resided my Kucirek cousins in their wild splendor.

So here was my run-down, trash-spattered world, a Babel of languages—Spanish, Sicilian, Polish—and swarming with ethnic neighborhoods. Sweet Lorain!, as Bruce Weigl titled a collection of poems abour our hometown. I was soon to become the classmate of Sotirios Antonopoulos (Greek), Al Leyva (Mexican), Karen Staskiews (Serbian), Sal Scrofano (Italian), Ervin Mrosek (Czech), Rosario Pagan (Puerto Rican)—nearly all of whom could speak or understand at least a little, and often quite a bit, of their Old Country language. Little wonder that these days Lorain has been designated Ohio's "International City" and hosts an annual fair with an International Princess.

But back at the end of the 1950s, as I grew toward adolescence, Lorain seemed just about the most boring place on earth. Yet, in retrospect wasn't I obviously happier and far luckier than I realized? One snowy Christmas afternoon, when I was about eleven, the Dirdas went calling and ended up at my Aunt Stella's. Soon the various uncles started up a poker game and I wandered upstairs to check the shelves of my cousins' rooms. There, among the juvenile fiction that I was beginning to outgrow, I discovered a copy of *Bomba, the Jungle Boy*, which came downstairs with me to the seasonal festivities. I remember nothing much now about the book, and have been told that the series itself is fairly racist in its descriptions of native Africans, but back then I sank into the story with my usual obliviousness to all else.

About halfway through the evening, Mom, having noticed me squirreled away in a corner, brought me a Coke and a ham sandwich with sweet pickles on soft rye bread. . . . I've never forgotten that Christmas. To be warm and safe on a cold night, enjoying delicious home-cooked food, while reading an enthralling book, with the noise of nickels and dimes plinking on a kitchen table and the soft susurration of mothers talking about their children in a gift-strewn, brightly decorated living room was to inhabit, for an hour or two, what Wordsworth called a "spot of time," a rare moment of complete and unalloyed happiness.

Chapter Four

One's real life is often the life one does not lead.
—Oscar Wilde

In my later childhood I hungered after adventures in time and space. More and more I gobbled up the Hardy Boys, Rick Brant ("an electronic adventure"), and Tom Swift, Jr. (Why, I used to wonder, is the hero Tom Swift, Jr., and the author Victor Appleton II?) Once I borrowed three Hardy Boys novels from Drew Edelman, who lived down the block from me on 29th. A bit nervous, since the books belonged to an older brother or cousin, he would only let me take away *The Missing Chums* and two forgotten others for a weekend. So I rushed home that Saturday night and spent all of Sunday sprawled on my sister Sandy's bed, where the sunlight shone down through the open blinds and no one would disturb me. I finished all three by nightfall, my record for speed-reading.

Few now remember Ken Holt, but I grew especially fond of his exploits, particularly the first one, *The Secret of Skeleton Island*: Ken is a New England preppie on the run from sneaky foreign villains (who have already kidnapped his journalist father). Following some hairsbreadth escapes, our teenage hero makes his way to the seashore, where he is befriended by a working-class kid who will become his partner in all future adventures. Soon after meeting Sandy, Ken takes a shower and emerges from the bathroom to find his prep school uni-

form gone—the jacket and tie readily identify him to his enemies—
and in its place a pair of "dark-blue dungarees and a turtleneck
sweater." After Ken dons his new duds, he glances in the mirror and
smiles at the tough young sailor he sees there.

I read this scene over and over and it never failed to raise in me
a warm, tingly sensation. Naturally, I acquired a dark blue turtleneck
like Ken's, though the scratchy wool chafed my neck and with my
glasses on I could never be mistaken for anything but a round-faced
nerd. However, I suspect that this "transformation" passage touches
on the archetypal appeal of all boys' books: As kids, we yearn to cast
off our ordinary unshaped self and exchange it for a more heroic per-
sona, along with the matching adventures. No one, I finally knew,
could ever realistically hope to fly like Superman or zoom along like
the Flash, except in daydreams—for a few months I had once
assumed a secret identity as the Green Flame—but anybody, with
luck or training, might become Ken Holt.

As I wrote in a school essay at the time, "The main reason I enjoy
the Hardy Boys and Ken Holt is because I actually envy these ficti-
tious characters. . . . In these books I escape my dull world of school,
accordion, etc., in this dull unexciting town (nothing ever happens)
and I take the place of the hero and share his adventures in every corner of the world. I really like to have adventures, though to look at
me you would never guess it. But I actually do. I love to go camping,
take bike rides all over Lorain, mix chemicals in my chemistry set,
peer into the microscopic world with my microscope and dream up
weird inventions."

Weird inventions proliferated in the science fictional adventures
of Rick Brant and Tom Swift. Breathes there a boy with soul so dead
that he could resist the allure of *Tom Swift and His Jetmarine*? Or
Rick Brant in *The Caves of Fear*? From these it proved only a small

step to young Robert Silverberg's *Revolt on Alpha C* and Robert Heinlein's *The Rolling Stones*. The TAB Book Club even delivered my favorite Jules Verne adventure: *Journey to the Center of the Earth*. (Decades later I was to write an afterword to a Signet edition of the book—a belated homage to my younger self.)

Childhood reading possesses an almost holy power, and I still vividly recollect the plots of these and many comparably "worthless" books. *Tarzan and the City of Gold*, for example, concludes with Lord Greystoke facing certain death. Nemone, the sexy queen of some lost, vaguely Egyptian civilization has fallen in love with the ape-man, but he refuses to respond to her amorous entreaties, in part because she is a half-mad, sadistic nymphomaniac (or so the text hints). Eventually Tarzan so angers the queen that she declares that he will serve as the quarry for her powerful and vicious pet lion Belthar, a great tawny animal with whom she spiritually identifies. Given a less than sporting head start, the King of the Jungle quickly surmises that he can never outrace the beast or reach the safety of some distant trees. So he resolutely turns to face this monster with his bare hands. But just as the evil lion is about to leap at our hero's throat, a streak of golden fury races onto the veldt and an even more immense animal seizes the royal pet by the neck and kills it as a cat does a mouse. Then this "mighty engine of rage and destruction, a giant of a lion in the prime of its strength and velocity"—according to another contemporary book report—meekly trots over to Tarzan and the ape-man places his hand on the massive head of Jad-Bal-Ja, the Golden Lion, the two quietly facing the murderous queen. Who, bereft over the death of her pet and knowing that the good times are over, obligingly plunges a dagger into her own breast.

This jungle tale of Tarzan, *mirabile dictu*, led me to start thinking about a novel's form. All through the main narrative Burroughs periodically interjects short chapters following the halting progress of a great cat as it searches for someone or something. These interludes, related from the lion's point of view, suggest mildly "poetic" attempts to wax lyrical about the smells and sounds of Africa. For a long while the reader doesn't even know the identity of the beast. The two story lines intersect only in the final chapter, as Jad-Bal-Ja rescues his master from certain death. This was my first conscious experience of double plot, of creating rhythm and tension by alternating two strands of action that eventually become one.

Similarly, I experienced moral complexity in Beverly Cleary, of all unlikely authors.

Even though I was sometimes picking up more "advanced" books, I retained a longstanding fondness for Cleary's numerous juveniles. But I only remember one with vividness: *Henry Huggins*. In this novel the series hero finds the stray dog he dubs Ribsy. Henry nurses the starving creature back to health, gives him a name, a home and his heart. Unexpectedly, Ribsy's original owner reappears. But Henry doesn't want to give him up. Who, then, should take the dog? The two boys place their pet between them, move off a dozen paces or so, and then call to him:

"Slowly Ribsy stood up, and after a backward glance at the stranger, trotted eight squares down the sidewalk toward Henry. He paused, scratched again, and trotted the remaining squares to Henry. Then he sat down with his head on Henry's foot and closed his eyes again. Ribsy had chosen Henry!"

Happy ending. Right? Not precisely. Even then this scene—illustrated in the book—touched me with its inhererently sorrowful nature. All three characters are "good" and none of the possible denouements could ever be completely satisfying: The former owner loses his dog, the dog has to choose between two affectionate masters and Henry feels vaguely guilty about taking away another person's pet. *Henry Huggins* made me think about ambiguity and accommodation to circumstances, and played to a temperament that was growing ever more introspective. Maybe life was more complicated than it appeared in the Hardy Boys series.

To be an indiscriminate reader—as the luckiest young often are—means that the right books are all around you. Most Saturdays my mother would interrupt our backyard games to ferry her fractious children to catechism. At one P.M. my reluctant younger sisters would march into the kiddie class for those preparing to receive first Holy Communion; I would attend the later two o'clock class for older kids. This meant that Mom and I could spend the hour from one to two at nearby Oakwood Shopping Center. Most of the time she would shop for clothing-store bargains, while I scooted directly off to Gray Drug, where the policy about standees at the magazine counter proved extremely lax. There I could riffle through all the comics I wanted, while simultaneously nibbling from a box of Milk Duds secreted in my front pants pocket. My reading taste growing ever more refined, I was soon drawn to the sophisticated pleasures of *Cracked, Sick* and *Mad.* That last magazine's Don Martin authored and drew a series of absurd cartoon/novelettes about Captain Klutz, which made me laugh out loud. And who can forget his Fester and Karbunkle in "The Hardest Head in the World," wherein andirons, a blacksmith's forge and even a pyramid are unable to crack a doltish character's noggin? At Gray Drug, I also gratified my humiliating attachment to a celebrity rag called *Sixteen,* first bought when I was in fifth grade, mainly for a special spread on the heartthrob of my Mouseketeer youth, Annette Funicello. As often as I could, I used to tune in to *The Mickey Mouse Club* variety show on TV, hoping for a glimpse of this dark-haired beauty. For a few years around 1960 I suspect she was more popular than Shirley Temple in the 1930s. How I treasured that early issue of *Sixteen*, repairing to it regularly to sigh over a photo of teenage Annette sitting behind the steering wheel of her Thunderbird convertible.

In catechism itself we would suffer through consummately dull lessons from our parish priest, who repeated the same lugubrious phrases week after week like a tocsin: "Who made me? God made me . . . the one holy, catholic and apostolic church . . . the body and blood of Christ." I suppose such litanies of Q & A define catechism, but there's no gainsaying their monotony. Yet even before I was confirmed—with my Cossack grandfather's name Damian—I had begun to upstartishly argue about church dogma, often posing theological conundrums of near-Aquinian complexity, many of which involved the international date line, ships at sea and the prohibition against meat on Friday. As a teenager I eventually asserted that Marxism had more to offer the world than Christianity, and was banned from religious instruction for a week. It struck me as self-evidently more important to improve the conditions of life in this world than to worry about a dubious eternal holiday in the next.

Outbursts of rational humanism notwithstanding, I was nonetheless secretly attracted to the religious life, glad to have my throat blessed by a relic of St. Blaise and eager for angelic clarity over whether to become a monk—cowled, gravely meditating on graveled walks—or an urbane and sophisticated Jesuit, master of the world. But I lacked docility. At the end of my weekly confessions, Father would solemnly intone: "Do you promise to go and sin no more?" Normally, I would just whisper yes, but eventually could no longer stand my implicit hypocrisy and complained, "Father, forgive me, but you know I'll be back here next Thursday. I don't think it right for a person to make promises he can't keep. I'm bound to fight with my sisters." (More complex transgressions came later: Once I was even tempted, on a whim, to confess to the sin of simony—the selling of ecclesiastical offices.) Despite my pleadings, he dogmatically refused to absolve me or determine my penance—six Our Fathers, and six Hail Marys—until I agreed to go and sin no more. So finally I did promise, in part because my long sojourn in the confessional was exciting curiosity among other penitents waiting outside and in part so that I could please my pious mother by receiving Communion with her. Still, in the wake of such pastoral inflexibility, the would-be Benedictine or Jesuit began to question the unimpeachable wisdom of the church.

One Saturday afternoon, while waiting in a pew for Father to start catechism and tired of being elbowed by altar boy Mike Revta, I picked up our weekly *Catholic Messenger*—an instructional bulletin of some four or six pages—and noticed that that issue featured a short story called "The Blue Cross." An intriguing title, I thought, even if the main character, according to a drop-head, was a mousy priest called Father Brown. I began reading. "Flambeau was in England!" G. K. Chesterton's narrative gusto swept aside any resistance to clerical detectives, while the French criminal mastermind Flambeau—half Professor Moriarty, half Fantomas—appealed to my weakness for melodrama, special effects, flamboyant gesture. "There was one thing which Flambeau, with all his dexterity of disguise, could not cover, and that was his singular height." (Years later, John Dickson Carr took up the challenge implicit in that sentence to construct his ingenious "howdunit," *The Crooked Hinge*.) The very next day I hied my way to our branch library at the Plaza and checked out *The Father Brown Omnibus*. Unable to stop, I gobbled down thirty or forty of these short mysteries over the next couple of weeks. Even the titles delivered cozy shivers: "The Hammer of God," "The Sins of Prince Saradine," "The Oracle of the Dog." Each story chronicled a crime utterly beyond human ken and smelling of black magic. Yet Father Brown revealed, again and again, that mind alone, supported by a deep understanding of fallen human nature, could resolve any mystery.

At about the time I was reveling in the paradoxes of Chesterton (and the gas-lit hansom-cab atmosphere of Sherlock Holmes), I was also laying siege to the great nineteenth-century swashbucklers: Alexandre Dumas' *The Count of Monte Cristo* and *The Three Musketeers*; H. Rider Haggard's *King Solomon's Mines*; Jules Verne's *Twenty Thousand Leagues Under the Sea* and *The Mysterious Island*. The Dumas novels I encountered in abridged versions, but in the case of *The Count of Monte Cristo* this condensing only sharpened the object lesson and mythic appeal of the story. Is there a better treatise on the power of education than the chapters in which the imprisoned Edmond Dantès, under the patient guidance of the scholarly Abbé Faria, manages to transform himself from an ignorant young sailor into a self-assured, multilingual *homme du monde*? And wasn't this a lesson that any twelve-year-old longs to hear? Here was Ken Holt again, albeit in reverse. But the moral remained exactly the same: Through effort one could, even against great odds, radically remake oneself.

Before long, I was teaching myself chess, practicing fancy shuffles with cards, working my way through Fletcher Pratt's history of code-breaking, *Secret and Urgent*, and studying the shortwave radios in the Allied Electronics catalogue—as well as learning how to identify animal tracks, edible berries and the sure signs of mental illness. At Lent during my last year in elementary school I gave up sweets and lost fifteen pounds. I began to jog around the block, or even Central Park. "Atta way. Get yourself toughened up," said my father.

This Faustian craving for wisdom and sophistication soon fired a concomitant desire to check books out of the adult section of the library. My cousin Marlene had once mentioned that I might enjoy Agatha Christie's mysteries—but all of these were still technically off-limits to me. Adult material. Strictly *verboten*. Well, I wasn't a six-year-old anymore, to be told what I could and couldn't read. Besides, *Murder on the Orient Express* sounded almost as good as the soul-stirring *Tom Swift in the Caves of Nuclear Fire*; so did *And Then There Were None*, and several others about a detective called, improbably, Hercule Poirot. Still, if dumpy little Father Brown could solve mysteries, why not a vain and portly Belgian with "little gray cells"? I just had to get my grubby paws on these books. But how?

Through chicanery, of course. One afternoon I "borrowed" my mother's little-used library card, inscribed "Mrs. Michael Dirda." Having scoped out the precise location of the Christies, I swiftly selected a three-novel omnibus of Poirot whodunits, *Murder On Board*, and nonchalantly ambled to the checkout desk. There I hastily scribbled my name and presented my adult library card for inspection, carefully holding my thumb over the giveaway word "Mrs." I was certainly . . . Michael Dirda. The woman behind the desk stared down at me; my hand gently quivered as I clutched the card in a death grip lest my subterfuge be revealed. Her eyes narrowed with suspicion. She hesitated. Then she stamped the due date and handed the volume to me with a coy, knowing smile. "Enjoy your book, Michael Dirda."

I read the three mysteries with pleasure, but not with ecstasy: Hercule Poirot, for all his intelligence, hardly invited self-identification, and some of the denouements might be judged too clever by half. Still, Christie opened a door. For the next year I illicitly explored the library's adult shelves, moving on to Ellery Queen puzzlers and black-bound anthologies of stories about blind detectives, psychic detectives and scientific detectives. I also passed a brief but intense period with do-it-yourself manuals: Once upon a time I could explain how to construct a crossbow from parts easily found around the home.

As I was fast approaching puberty, my parents quite properly felt that their only son required a bedroom of his own. The building of "the addition" proved to be a major project, one which took months, required the help of my anorectic Uncle Danny and my hefty Uncle Roy (who delivered milk and owned a one-acre farm), and caused my ever-suffering father—as well as his hapless dependents—even more suffering than usual. Dad always thoroughly disdained the stoic virtues, and when he agonized, his world agonized with him.

My new quarters proved hardly spacious, but had room for a double bed, an easy chair and, most important of all, the heavy wooden desk that Dad and I constructed in the basement and at which I dutifully scribbled my homework and term papers. On one wall we also installed a set of shelves on steel brackets with room for perhaps two hundred books. I can remember arranging my TAB paperbacks and my adventure novels—with lots of space left over. When I graduated from high school, the shelves were still only half filled. My collecting addiction took hold in earnest only much later in life.

At about the time I moved into the addition—in sixth grade—I accompanied my mother one day to Hill's Discount Department Store in quest of new khakis. After the usual sartorial try-ons and errors, I grouchily made my way at last to the paperback racks and surveyed the wares on offer. Scanning the horizontal shelves, my piercing gaze—common to all romantic heroes, even those with myopia—zeroed in on a Pyramid paperback appealingly titled *The Insidious Dr. Fu Manchu*. As was my wont, I opened to page one then and there, and was immediately caught up in the maneuvers of Denis Nayland Smith as he tries to thwart the evil doctor's plans for world domination. I have never quite forgotten the description of Fu, with his brow like Shakespeare's and a smile (or sneer?) like Satan's, nor the novel's title: my first conscious awareness of the lovely word "insidious." Of course, no praise is too great for the doctor's ingenious if dastardly methods for inflicting sudden death, the Call of Siva being the most memorable. I shuddered at the prospect of a voice that could kill, and for months afterward used to peer up into our Ohio oak trees in the, alas, vain hope of discerning a lurking thuggee.

Pyramid reissued the first three or four installments of Sax Rohmer's pulpy saga, but my reading soon shot ahead of the company's production schedule. I desperately yearned to acquire the complete series, which promised such toothsome tantalizers as *President Fu Manchu*. Perhaps a year went by, however, when, quite by chance, a classmate told me that her mother (her mother!) possessed a dozen of the Fu Manchu classics in hardback. After considerable cajolery, Michelle lent me the books, all bound in black, their titles in faded gold lettering. I raced through *President Fu Manchu* and *Emperor Fu Manchu* and all the others with a zealot's enthusiasm, yet my nascent critical skills soon detected how repetitive the plots were: Invariably, the evil "Chinaman" would slip through Nayland Smith's hands in the tumultuous last chapter. Moreover, I didn't much care for Karamzeh, Fu's exotically seductive daughter—sheath dress, sinuous curves, raven hair, dangly earrings. I now wonder: What wasn't to like? Despite such blemishes, the novels' atmosphere of ancient evil, their blend of antiquarianism and exoticism, deeply appealed to my sense of the wondrous. As I noted in a contemporary book report: "I like stories about . . . ancient sorcerer type persons trying to take over the world using Dark Age secrets." For that matter, I still do.

As part of my ambitious program to transform myself into a combination of Lord John Roxton (the big-game hunter of Conan Doyle's *The Lost World*), Kenneth Robeson's Doc Savage ("The Man of Bronze") and Sherlock Holmes, I paid three dollars for a "balanced throwing knife" from Cane's Surplus, that home to camouflage gear, exotic cutlery and Pendleton shirt-jacs. In my backyard I took to throwing my knife at a tree, like Jim Bowie, but with virtually no perceivable improvement in getting the trusty blade to stick in the bark. I would also fling homemade spears at a cardboard box set up on the wooden picnic table.

One evening my evil sister Pamela mocked me while I was practicing with my weapons and I lost my temper, as she no doubt intended. She pranced off for the safety of the house, but I seized one of my spears—fortunately blunted by ardent practice—and, just as Pam was about to reach the sanctuary of our back door, some forty feet away, nailed her in the small of the back. I remember the Riefenstahlian beauty of those few seconds: the desperate throw, the high graceful arc of the spear, the way the hunted eland, uh, Pamela, simply collapsed onto the ground. Though it induced a bad bruise, the worn point of the peeled sapling never broke her skin—and yet my father, furious and appalled, administered the second-worst beating of my life. (The worst occurred a few years later, following an unfortunate afternoon in which I scratched the car with a wheelbarrow. That time he throttled me so hard and long that I peed my pants.)

The Dirda siblings spent a lot of time in our small backyard, swinging like Tarzan from the oak tree branches, romping with our (usually chained-up) dog Rinny (short for Rin-Tin-Tin), climbing the red brick fireplace and jumping from its smokestack into the leaves and clippings of the compost heap. When I was very young a runoff ditch flowed at the back of our property and the little kids of the neighborhood splashed in it after thunderstorms, sailing stick boats, stepping intrepidly across log bridges, leaping from bank to bank, eventually tumbling into the mud. But this "eyesore" was all too soon filled in, so that after the age of ten I started going out farther from home for wilderness adventures, into what we called "the field"—a miles-long tract of then-undeveloped land that started a few hundred yards from my backyard.

For most of my childhood one could slam my back door, dash across 30th St., and within five minutes be clambering on front-end loaders and downed trees near construction sites. Water-filled ruts and ditches buzzed with dragonflies. Overgrown paths wound their way through tall grass, marshland and blackberry brambles. A half-hearted creek meandered all the way up to North Ridge Road. In this unkempt realm, fluttering with monarchs and swallowtails, my dad and I would occasionally tramp with Rinny, or we'd scout for the mushrooms my mother would simmer into gravy, even though she hated their smell of decay. (Invariably Dad would announce at the dinner table, "Let Mike try that gravy first. There were a few of those mushrooms I wasn't quite sure about.") Sometimes our whole family would go out berrying while the dog romped. We'd come back scratched and stained from the purple juice, but with the prospect of soon tasting the finest dessert in the known world: my mother's blackberry pie.

Mostly, though, I'd just hike along the indistinct trails—could they have been blazed by Delaware Indians?—that led through copses of trees into tall meadows, which in turn gave way to more stands of trees and other meadows. Having learned to identify sassafras, I'd sometimes build a fire, boil the roots and brew a bittersweet tea. At other times the neighborhood guys—Jimmy Hamilton, Drew Edelman, Kenny Mize, Tommy Faroh—and I would roast potatoes in the ashes of the fire and squat back on a rock or log and aimlessly talk away the afternoon. "Do you think flying saucers have landed down in South America? I heard this radio program . . ." "What if that Michael Anthony guy on TV gave you a check for a million dollars? What would you do with the money?" "Right, we all agree that Green Lantern is the greatest superhero. So who's the next best? Superman? Flash?"

One winter I remember taking my secondhand hockey skates out to the creek and following the frozen logjammed stream through the woods—the skating equivalent of off-trail mountain biking. One summer I disturbed a swarm of bees and thrashed my way through a field of flowers and miraculously escaped being stung to an early death. I was probably looking for long dry stalks to pull up and fling like spears—the clump of mud around the roots gave them ballast and heft. Always the guys and I would keep an eye out for a sapling that could be shaved into a good hiking staff or homemade bow, and then we'd spend half an hour hacking through its trunk with our pocketknives. Sometimes one of us would sneak a hatchet from home. And though we worried about typhoid and even malaria, when thirsty we would kneel down and sip from the cleanest part of the creek or from what we hoped was a spring and not a trickle from a drainage sewer.

Those endless summers were also the great time of all-day Monopoly games on rainy Saturdays or for going to the movies downtown. The Palace Theater offered a special summer film series for kids, and the girls and I were dropped off nearly every Saturday. Mom would stuff fresh popcorn into brown paper lunch bags that we would smuggle into the theater. "Ridiculous to pay that kind of money for snacks. And my popcorn's good enough; you kids don't need Raisinets or Good & Plenty." The shows themselves tended to be D-grade "family entertainment" from the 1940s and even earlier: *Ma and Pa Kettle on the Farm*, Huntz Hall and the Bowery Boys, Francis the Talking Mule, Abbot and Costello, the Three Stooges, Johnny Weismuller as Tarzan, *The Wackiest Ship in the Navy*.

Occasionally, we'd see slightly better, current films—Kirk Douglas in *Ulysses*, Steve Reeves as *Hercules* and various Disney flicks such as *The Absent-Minded Professor* (about the invention of the super-bouncy flubber), *The Shaggy Dog* (a boy's brain inside a canine body) and *Third Man on the Mountain*. In this last a young Swiss mountaineer ends up rescuing a climber high up on some Alpine peak, possibly the

Matterhorn. At one point, he ascends a narrow fissure by placing his feet firmly against one rock face and his back against the other, then jerkily inching himself upward. It seemed really cool and easy.

Next to the Palace there was a narrow passageway, probably less than four feet wide. Instead of patiently waiting for my mother, I decided to replicate the mountaineer's stunt. I slammed my Keds against one brick wall and my back against the other, then half walked, half dragged myself up. And up. And up. Eventually I was able to clamber out onto the roof, perhaps forty feet above the ground. And then, with considerably more trepidation, I repeated the moves to descend. When my mother arrived, she saw that the back of my shirt was filthy. "What happened to you?" "Oh, I just leaned against the wall over there." "Be more careful. Those marks will be hard to get out. After all, you're not a child anymore." No, indeed, for that September I started junior high school.

Part Two

TURNING THE
PAGES

Chapter Five

*The function of education is to make one maladjusted
to ordinary society.*

—*Northrop Frye*

For seventh grade I trudged off to Hawthorne, one of Lorain's
four junior high schools, the others being Lowell, Irving and
Longfellow. Located a half hour's leisurely walk from my
house, it was three stories of crumbling red brick—penal in character, somber of hallway and rowdy with overcrowded classes. During
the summer I had received a letter inviting me to join what was then
denominated, with no nonsense or disguise, an Advanced Class:
Room 211, of blessed memory.

Our homeroom teacher, Richard Latsko, turned out to be a muscular, introspective young man with rounded shoulders who shuffled
sadly from the door to his desk and then sank into his wooden swivel
chair with a heavy sigh. Latsko hailed from Pennsylvania coal-mining
country, but appeared far more exotic, with his dark, handsome looks
and football player's body. He was in some respects the most important teacher of my life.

From the beginning Mr. Latsko treated his class as serious students, both able and eager to learn anything. Because we came to love
him so, most of us tried hard to live up to his expectations: We competed with ourselves and each other to earn his praise and intellectual

regard. For three hours every afternoon this brooding, philosophical soul, paid to instruct us in the niceties of English and social studies, actually opened up our minds to the excitement of ideas and the pleasures of the imagination. We were taking Latsko.

Surveying the desks in Room 211, he would whisper in his soft, lugubrious voice, "What is history?" Some of us would look quizzical. A hand would go up. "History is the study of the past." Latsko would then push for further clarification. "Can history be cyclical?" Yes. No. Maybe. We'd discuss, argue. For some thinkers, Latsko would continue, history is progress toward a certain goal—the Second Coming of Christ, the establishment of an egalitarian communist society. The so-called Whiggish interpretation, we learned, meant that things were supposedly always getting better and better. But Hegel felt that history worked through a dialectic: "Thesis, antithesis, synthesis." Others, including, I suspected, our world-weary teacher, believed that history was simply change and nothing more.

So for a week or two we all reflected on the nature of the past. And then Latsko inaugurated a series of lectures on the American presidency, stressing political ideas and personal scandal. My own understanding of national politics was then both minimal and romantic. Back in elementary school our *Weekly Reader* children's magazine had carried photographs of Dwight Eisenhower and Adlai Stevenson during their 1956 campaign. Since these were supposedly the two best leaders in the country, I convinced myself that the winner of the election would become president while the loser had to settle for vice president. Naturally, my father loathed Eisenhower—"All that guy does is play golf," he would complain in disgust. But in that fall of 1960 Dad took me out of Hawthorne one day—despite the protests of the principal, Dr. Shook—to accompany him to a rally at the stadium for the new Democratic candidate for president. The motorcade from Cleveland was late and the day was bitter cold, but that afternoon I glimpsed the face and heard the voice of John F. Kennedy.

"Government should never be regarded as sacrosanct. It was made by people and could be changed by people," Latsko told us. We ought to question everything, speculate fearlessly, peer always beneath the surface. Thought should then be followed by action. In that dark-paneled classroom on quiet afternoons I felt the first breeze of the gale-storms of the sixties.

Latsko was constantly dreaming up unusual projects. Was there even the pretense of a regular curriculum? Once we staged a mock trial for murder. A group of guys is trapped in a cave. Starving, they draw lots and dine on the loser, the short straw. More time goes by and again they draw lots. Finally only two men are left and one is eaten. A day later the sole survivor is rescued, and subsequently accused of murder.

The moral and legal issues, as I recall, boiled down to a matter of contracts. We agreed that the first guys dispatched had legitimately agreed to participate in a lottery and then borne the misfortune of losing. But what about the very last two? Would the short straw meekly submit to the winner? How can we know that the contract was actually fulfilled? Without the force of numbers, wouldn't the pair simply battle it out and the stronger ingloriously feast? Beyond this lay questions of morality, degrees of guilt, social Darwinism ("survival of the fittest") and the fun of turning the classroom into a courtroom. We divided up into public prosecutors and defense teams, expert witnesses, a judge and jury. Lance Teaman acted the role of the hapless survivor, and broke down piteously on the stand when he recounted his horrible ordeal, dwelling quite lipsmackingly on the gruesome cannibalism. An exceptionally exhilarating week.

I felt somewhat less enthusiastic about the class's experiments with oral declamation. To improve our speaking skills Latsko assigned a short talk, five minutes, no big deal. I laboriously set down every word of my presentation—its subject happily lost to memory—on several sheets of cheap notebook paper. On the way to school I doggedly recited my remarks over to myself, except for a few minutes spent chatting with some kid about why Catholic schools always seemed to be a year ahead of the public schools. (How typical of memory that something so insignificant should be recalled so clearly.) When, late in the afternoon, I finally stood up intending to deliver an oration of such silver-tongued eloquence that even William Jennings Bryan would envy it, my hands begain to shake so uncontrollably that my crumpled notebook paper snapped and crackled, and I actually had trouble making myself heard. It was both terrifying and profoundly embarrassing. Coupled with my recent debacle with "Boogie Woogie on the Squeeze Box," I was confirmed in my fears of appearing before an audience.

Unfortunately, Latsko didn't give up on oral declamation. "You kids need practice. Lots of it." He decided that we should take up impromptu speaking. Each member of the class scrawled the subject for a possible talk on a slip of paper, which was deposited in a big screwtop Mason jar. Other slips in another jar carried our various names. On rainy afternoons when we all grew bored with class, Latsko would lean back and, without looking, pluck out a name at random. Nancy Cadwallader. Jeanette Darvas. Bob Brent. The elected victim would then plunge his or her hand into the topic jar. After five minutes, in which one was gathering one's supposed thoughts, the student speaker would discourse on some improbable, silly topic for as long as possible. When the lot finally fell to me, I had to elaborate on "Why I am a playboy." Needless to say, the resulting apologia lacked both conviction and any in-depth, practical advice on the swinging lifestyle.

Latsko's particular interests, which for a long while became mine, were history, government and social studies. I can't remember reading any literature for his class, though we must have carried around an English textbook of some kind. In fact, the only book I do recall from that school year is a physics paperback that we resorted to in science. One day Tom Mikus—now best friend as well as rival—scribbled all over my copy's title page, changing "Physics" to "Physic" and making jokes about laxatives.

More and more, as our parents and teachers complained to one another, we kids were "filled with too much sass and vinegar." One lunch period Nancy Cadwallader—a tall beautiful girl with light brown hair who walked, according to Lance Teaman, as though she had a limp in each leg—brazenly ordered pizza from Yala's, which she somehow got delivered. When this infraction of school policy was revealed to the principal (by Mr. Brocklehurst, our shop, or "manual arts," teacher), Dr. Shook was livid. "It is strictly against regulations for nonschool personnel to enter this building without first checking with the main office." Nancy, disingenuously, replied, "But he didn't enter the building." "Then how, child," responded Shook with overdone sarcasm, "did you manage to acquire the pizza?" Nancy looked up with doe-eyed innocence: "Why, the man just passed it right through the window. He never came in at all."

In those days we were all quick, bristling with the intellectual equivalent of glad animal spirits. After years of feeling alone, I was grateful, and happy, to be among my own slightly weird kind. Not that we weren't genuinely silly, and even sophomoric. Once Mikus and I got into an argument after Mr. Latsko vanished from class for a few minutes. Tom suddenly threw my pencil out the window, so I threw out his; then he tossed my books out, so I tossed his; we were just lifting up our chairs when we regained our senses and rushed outside to retrieve our stuff from the bushes. Both of us were clearly going to keep competing, in nearly everything, for the next six years.

At lunch, boys would sometimes play a variant of the old English pub game Shove Ha'Penny. While the coin or a flat wad of folded paper was sliding across the slick tabletop, the contestants chanted, "Yatta, hey, Yatta, hey. Hey, Yatta." Why, I don't know—probably something that Tom started and Lance took up and then we all did. Another lunch period we discovered that our new slide rules could be manipulated into dandy miniature guillotines, ideal for slicing off the tips of carrots. Ideal, of course, until they broke.

We were always joking around with language. Mark Weber scripted a parody of the TV show *The Untouchables*, its highlight the stage description of a loud series of bangs and crashes. Elliot Ness: "What happened?" Rico: "My toothpick fell down the stairs." For some reason, we laughed and laughed. Not even Max Shulman, creator of *Dobie Gillis* (our favorite TV show) and author of the immortal classic of "campus" humor, *Barefoot Boy with Cheek*, could match that. Bob Brent composed a thrill-packed adventure story—waterfalls, cliffs, whirlpools—and in the last line revealed that the hero was . . . wait for it . . . an ant. Ingenuity could rise no higher. Or could it? One afternoon Tom and I were trekking down Broadway and he noticed a green post office box and, in a Eureka moment, blurted out, "U Smail." Get it? You smell. U.S. Mail. A classic.

A bit later, when television commercials during *77 Sunset Strip* or *The Jackie Gleason Show* revealed that the sleeping aid Serutan spelled backward yielded "Nature's," this created our knee-slapping predilection for pronouncing words back to front. Remember, we'd intone solemnly, Geritol—for "iron-poor blood"—spelled backward is Lotireg. Tom was Mot Sukim; I was Ekim Adrid (when I wasn't my nom de plume Raoul Schpitzenberg, international man of mystery).

Once a group of what were fast becoming my circle of friends—Tom, Ed Partyka, Lance, Ray Schwarz—composed a nonsense poem, some of which I still recall: "Zark Boople/ As tar the frosh/ Yet can it stand/ Nay the ret has not/ But soon the boople will zark/ And all shall fit rod." Was it for this touching lyric that one of us thought up the line "That nay for nither"? More typical of my preteen melancholia was "The Algae Poem for Small Children," a delicate meditation on life's brevity that builds to this dolorous finale:

> *So what if the algae are green, purple or red*
> *It won't matter at all, when I am cold dead*
> *For the algae, no matter, lives on, on and on*
> *But I soon enough am so utterly gone.*

Though Hawthone encouraged the members of the Advanced Class to bond primarily with one another, we still interacted with the rest of the school during the day—in shop or home economics, in phys ed, where we were embarrassed by our adolescent bodies, at lunch, when we doctored each other's sandwiches with dead maggots, and at assembly, as we listened to soporific choral concerts ("Oh, my father was the keeper of the Eddystone Light/ And he married a mermaid one fine night") or watched, bedazzled, a demonstration by the Harlem Globe Trotters. In fact, much of the school—perhaps a third—was African-American, for Hawthorne stood on the edge of a predominantly "colored" neighborhood. But I don't remember any black kids in Latsko's class.

Racial prejudice was pervasive in that era, and I grew up hearing all the stereotypes about African-Americans. These could range from outright contempt for "lazy good-for-nothings producing bastards to suck up more 'relief' money" to paternalist affection for "coloreds" who rose above their ethnic burden and worked as hard as any white guy at the mill or shipyard. In 1960 the town's blacks lived largely among themselves—but then so did the Hispanics. People of a common ethnicity and nationality still often huddled together—hence the Abruzzi Club, the Slovenian Hall, the Polish fishermen's club, the 8 A.M. Mass in Croation at St. Vitus, the cemetery for the town's small Jewish population. There were doubtless economic differences in the community, but excepting the well-to-do on the East Side or someone like Judge Mikus, basically every father worked in a job where he got sweaty and his hands dirty. This made for a kind of *de facto* equality. Nobody, regardless of the color of his skin or the language he spoke, had much money.

Kids, though, pass along clichés as folk wisdom. At Hawthorne I was told never to get into a fistfight with a black kid or a knife fight with a Puerto Rican. One afternoon, on my way home from school, I ignored this wise counsel.

A group of us were joshing each other, lollygagging on the broken, humpbacked sidewalks, kicking bits of glass or chunks of old blacktop onto the scraggly, weedy tree lawns. Once or twice a week I used to swing into a corner store near Central Park to buy an ice-cream sandwich or a Big Time candy bar (cheap chocolate but the biggest bar for the nickel). On this particular afternoon I hadn't quite reached my sweet-treat mecca when I noticed a black kid razzing a skinny white kid. Somehow I felt obliged to "do something." Doubtless picturing myself as a chivalric righter of wrongs, I butted in with the wildly original challenge customary upon such occasions: "Why don't you pick on somebody your own size, punk?" Well, Lucius Johnson immediately took up my thrown gauntlet. We exchanged a few more words and before I knew it we had dropped our notebooks and were circling and eyeing each other, moving stealthily, hands ready to grapple or pummel. "Hey, hey, they're going to fight" I heard someone yell, and maybe a dozen pubescent spectators gathered around us to watch or cheer.

Being heavier than my opponent, I figured that I had a good shot at wrestling him to the ground. Like most kids, I'd spent a lot of time roughhousing in the backyard. Unfortunately, Johnson knew how to deliver devastating punches, so I was soon desperately flailing about, trying to protect my face and stomach, and none too successfully. Fortunately for me, within minutes we heard the sound of an approaching siren, so everyone took off, scampering for home. Hobbling through Central Park, I felt incredibly sorry for myself: I was bloody, my clothes torn, one eye swollen, and I was worried that Lucius might want to continue my beating the next day.

When I reached my house, Mom clucked over her poor baby while Dad appeared strangely pleased. I certainly wasn't supposed to make a habit of this sort of thing, but occasional fisticuffs obviously meant that you were more than just a four-eyed, pasty-faced book-worm. (Dad would occasionally suggest that any nephew or neigh-bor kid who struck him as the least bit gentle or effeminate should be sent to Central Park, so that he could get beat up by the tough kids there and acquire "a new perspective on life.") The next morn-ing, studying my face in the bathroom mirror, I found out that an eye really could turn black. I looked a mess.

For several days while my face healed, and maybe a week or two after that, I slunk around school and tried to avoid Johnson. Eventually, however, we bumped into each other in the hall, nodded gravely like two *ancien combatants* who meet in Paris after the Armistice, and then proceeded on our separate ways. Later, in high school, I patched up any remaining differences with Lucius, coolly figuring that a friend who knew how to box just might be useful to have around. It goes without saying that sometime after we graduated I learned that Lucius Johnson had become a minister and pillar of the community.

If I had hoped to finish seventh grade with some illusions, my debacle on the field of honor brought home that I wasn't D'Artagnan or the Count of Monte Cristo quite yet. But there was worse to come.

Christmas had always been, and still is, my favorite time of the year. The girls and I penned long thoughtful letters to Santa, detailing our virtues as well-behaved children and carefully listing the presents to which we were consequently entitled (e.g., *Tarzan and the Lost Safari*, or *Roy Rogers and the River of Peril*). After school we regularly clapped along with TV's "Mr. Jingaling"—one of Santa's special helpers, the "keeper of the keys" at the toy section of Halle's Department Store in Cleveland. Some years, when the local AFL-CIO was flush, Santa would drop by the Union Hall and distribute pre-Christmas gifts to all the good little future workers.

Christmastime rituals never altered back then. A week or so before December 25, elves would tiptoe into our house at night—one never knew precisely when—and set up the tree in all its glittery, illuminated glory. The following morning I would stretch out on the couch, take off my glasses and stare at the now-blurry lights, especially the pointy narrow ones that bubbled inside. It was magical, like being inside a snow globe. One Yuletide evening Mom would pop popcorn and the family would gather in front of the black-and-white Magnavox for *The Wizard of Oz* or *White Christmas* or *Peter Pan*: Wickedness never looked so sheerly enjoyable as when Cyril Ritchard's Captain Hook rakishly sashayed about and, with infectious glee, sang about his poisoned "cake quite green." But the play's epilogue, in which Peter abandons Wendy because she's grown up, always made me cry. Time would steal our youth away, and soon, all too soon, we would be too old for the games of Neverland. Like the ending of *Henry Huggins*, the last scene of *Peter Pan* made real the premonition that life would, in some sense, grow sadder and grayer with each passing year.

Christmas Day itself was always sheer rapture. My sisters and I would wake up at six, assemble at the top of the steps, be ordered back to our beds. At eight, Dad would majestically descend to the living room to "check" that Santa had indeed slid down our chimney during the night. Hearing the all-clear, "Okay, come on," we'd rush down the stairs and then, in spite of ourselves, pause for a moment before the gaudy, circus brightness of four pyramids of presents, each aligned in front of a bulging stocking. But then, with shouts of barbaric, Ostrogothic joy, we'd start tearing and ripping away the wrapping paper, while our mother yawned sleepily and my father grew grumpy. "These kids don't need all this stuff. . . . Too much junk. . . . We've got to cut back." Following a Dickensian holiday dinner, I'd try on my new six-gun and holster or slip away to read *Spin and Marty* or *Secret Sea* or *Rapids Ahead*. Later in the afternoon or evening we'd bundle up, edge the car down the snowy driveway and putt-putt slowly through town, admiring the specially decorated houses. Crèche scenes. Santas on rooftops. Frosty snowmen. How could anyone not adore Christmas? When, at the age of seven or eight, I had been asked who or what I wanted to be when I grew up, the answer seemed self-evident: "Santa Claus." After all, you live surrounded by toys, loved by everyone, and only work one day a year.

But in seventh grade everything changed. One early December afternoon Latsko strode into class, chuckling to himself. In the mornings, we knew, he taught the so-called "slow learners"—though I always maintained to Tom that *we* were actually the slow learners and that the school system pretended we were "advanced" to spare our feelings. "Do you know," said Latsko that morning incredulously, "there's a kid in the morning class who still believes in Santa Claus?" Everyone around me—Tom, Nancy, Bob, Jeanette—burst out hooting and guffawing. I sank down into my seat. Hadn't I once proven to Stan Paysor, with faultless syllogisms, that St. Nicholas must exist? I had struggled with my suspicions, suppressing them as long as possible. But no longer. Childhood was truly over. Or so I thought.

In that first year of junior high, come Saturday, I'd often ride down West 29th Street to Central Park. Pedaling hard up its black-top pathway, I'd zoom past the four big boulders (ideal for tag), the baseball field, the swings, teeter-totters and monkey bars, the kid selling popsicles and frozen treats from a three-wheeled bicycle cart, the empty ice-skating rink and finally the tin-roofed shanty. This last held park equipment and board games. In the winter, kids were allowed inside to change into their skates or warm up on the wooden benches that ran along its dark walls. (It was here that I dragged myself when I broke my ankle on the ice.) During the summer one could buy penny candy (wax lips filled with Kool-Aid, bracelets made of sugar candy, powdered Lick-M-Aid in thin envelopes), or sign out a worn basektball or checkers set, or even pay a nickel for a potholder kit: Under the trees, high-school-age "counselors" would demonstrate how to attach the loops of colored cotton to the posts on the edge of a square metal frame and then to weave another loop over and under. Tying off was the tricky part. Cool guys, disdaining such feminine devices, preferred to buy lengths of thick plastic twine and weave elaborate lanyards with a whistle on the end.

Sometimes I'd meet up with Lance, Tom or Ed and we'd set forth on marathon bike rides, one of these, all around Lorain, earning the honored sobriquet "Ed's Tour." Nothing much ever happened on these lazy cycling forays. We'd race each other, then stop at a gas station for a can of root beer, or swing by the law offices of Mikus and

Bransztet—Tom's suit-wearing parents—and goof off in the empty labyrinthine cubicles downstairs. During election years that space blossomed with posters as the local Democratic headquarters, and I remember a couple of late nights there, watching sweaty men in short-sleeved dress shirts chalk up each precinct's balloting on a portable blackboard.

One Saturday, I persuaded my friend Ray Schwarz—inventive, thoughtful, hypercritical—to join me on a bike ride all the way into South Lorain. The previous Sunday my Mom had followed a new route home from St. Vitus and I had noticed a big shop window on Pearl Avenue crammed with picture frames, lamps, a bureau or two, some old tools and a few books. Above the door loomed the fateful words "Clarice's Values."

As I gradually discovered on subsequent bike journeys, Lorain supported perhaps five good places for a lad of bookish bent to acquire affordable reading matter: Amvets Value Village, the Salvation Army, Goodwill, the St. Vincent de Paul Thrift Shop and Clarice's. Between the ages of twelve and sixteen I cycled from one of these secondhand emporiums to the next. Paperbacks generally went for a nickel or dime, hardbacks ran a quarter and sometimes you could bargain for a special price when buying in bulk, which I, more and more often, was. Except for those occasions when rabid booking made me late for supper, thus risking a smack or two from the spoon, I have seldom passed better afternoons in all my life. Borges felt that his Heaven would be a library; mine will be a really well-stocked thrift store.

Of them all Clarice's most truly entranced me. You would enter through double doors, and Clarice herself would glance up from her counter, where she'd be fiddling with a broken appliance or ringing up a sale to a handsome Puerto Rican and immediately give out a cheery, slightly hillbillyish, "Howdy. Take a look around the showroom, honey." Her "showroom" displayed the de rigueur jumble of chairs, bedsteads, cast-off clothes, unwanted neckties, scratched records, broken kitchen appliances, barbells, radios, socket sets and alarm clocks. Department store paintings and amateur watercolors drooped from pegs on the walls; trays overflowed with mechanical pencils, tie clips and costume jewelry. Much of the stock, though, could be downright mysterious, so that a reasonably courteous thirteen-year-old could acquire a decent education just by asking, "Clarice, what is this? How does it work?" She always knew. "Why, hon, that's a Ridgewell pneumatic battery pull, with a built-in turn-buckle. Needs work, though." Rumor had it that Clarice actually commuted into Lorain from hoity-toity Shaker Heights, where she reigned as the chatelaine of a grand manor house on the earnings of her ghetto thrift store.

Such shops provide ideal hunting grounds for young biblio-philes. You can buy a good hardback book, or even a terribly trashy one, for the price of a candy bar. And don't discount the pleasure quotient attached to serendipitous discovery. At Clarice's you some-times needed to scramble across dressers and bureaus just to reach the book alcove, where everything was precariously double-shelved and cartons stood piled high in the corners. You might readily pass a cou-ple of hours climbing or crawling around, pulling out volumes, skim-ming dust jackets, setting aside likely purchases. A half-demolished paperback of Alfred Bester's *The Demolished Man*. An old school edi-tion of Burke's speeches. Innumerable volumes of *Reader's Digest Condensed Books*. Foreign language textbooks. Bulwer Lytton, War-wick Deeping, Frank Yerby. Dilapidated correspondence-school manuals covering basic electronics, the fundamentals of plumbing and the elements of gardening. There was always more too over in the backroom or out on the truck—old Clearview or Lorain High year-books in abundance, and quite possibly the *Neconomicon* of the mad

Arab Abdul Al-Hazred, the *Oath of a Freeman*, a mottled first edition of Poe's *Tamerlane*. In short, an entire world of words, layered with dust, smelling of mildew and history.

To this day I can still remember much of what I acquired at these consumer-goods graveyards. At Amvets I picked up the second American printing of the Homeric-sounding *Ulysses*, by James Joyce, the price of forty-five cents boldly scrawled in blue crayon on the front endpaper. "Stately, plump Buck Mulligan . . ." There too I bought H. G. Wells's *Outline of History* and dozens of Perry Mason mysteries and science fiction novels. At Clarice's, in a sudden transport of Highland enthusiasm, I carted home sixteen volumes, with steel engravings, of the complete works of Sir Walter Scott for five dollars. I must sheepishly confess that I still own many of these books, even the Scott. *Waverley* was moderately exciting, but not enough for me to go on to *The Heart of Midlothian* or *Ivanhoe*.

More than ever, then, books and I were drawn together, as though I emanated an invisible tractor beam for printed matter. For the most part, my parents had grudgingly come to accept that I was always going to have my nose in a book. One sunny afternoon, for example, in the summer between seventh and eighth grade, I was lazing in my room, idling turning the pages of *My Favorite Science Fiction Story*, a collection that I'd checked out of the branch library at the Plaza. Suddenly my father, just home from work, appeared in the doorway with a brown-paper grocery bag in his hands. "Here, you like to read. A guy was cleaning out his locker and gave me these."

Inside were perhaps two dozen Bantam paperbacks: *Prisoner's Base, Fer-de-Lance, The League of Frightened Men, The Final Deduction, The Second Confession, And Be a Villain, The Black Mountain*. All the books featured a private detective named Nero Wolfe and his lieutenant Archie Goodwin. They sounded terrific: The sixth-of-a-ton Wolfe never left his brownstone in New York, cultivated rare orchids, dined on gourmet foods and tended to pontificate impressively. Archie was a wisecracker, ladies' man and counterbalance to Wolfe's enormous bulk, intellect and stubbornness.

By comparing the copyright pages I figured out the order in which the novels had been published and for the next two months read them chronologically. *The League of Frightened Men*, a little overlong and even padded, didn't quite live up to its sinister title. But I was thrilled when Wolfe finally encountered his own Moriarty in the archvillain Arnold Zeck. Best of all, I treasured the portrait of New York City in the 1930s and 1940s, a swirl of dizzy dames, eccentric millionaires, dogged Irish cops, the Brooklyn Dodgers, love nests, sloe-eyed femmes fatales and debonair killers. Soon I wanted to down cocktails and took to muttering, "Pfui," and using words like "cogent" and "poppycock." Admittedly the later novels lost some fizz, but I relished the celebrated opening scene of *Gambit*: Wolfe tearing out the pages from Webster's Third International Unabridged Dictionary and feeding them to the fire. Why? Because its editors had allowed use rather than prescription to guide their definitions, thus opening the gateway for such solecisms as "irregardless," the misuse of "hopefully" and the acceptance of vulgarisms in polite speech. "Pfui" to that. Wolfe, after all, may have been born in Montenegro, but he spoke an accentless and perfect English.

Though my daydreams might be growing more sophisticated and I was boldly exploring my hometown on my own, come nightfall I often turned back into a slightly fearful child. In my bureau I still kept two stuffed toy bunnies, the comforts of my early years when I would send them romping through caves in my covers and up a mountain of pillow. If I read a story like Ray Bradbury's "Zero Hour" in *My Favorite Science Fiction Story*—aliens conquer the earth by turning children against their parents—I wouldn't be able to stop thinking about it. How could we know that aliens weren't already out there? Maybe those nuts on the radio were right. Hadn't I forced my indignant father to leave the theater just as the Martians emerged from the steaming meteorites in *The War of the Worlds*? It was obvious that we puny earthlings could never stand up to their laserlike death ray.

Kids nowadays watch Godzilla movies for laughs, yet back then I turned away, shuddering, from the posters advertising these very same films. Nothing could induce me to buy a ticket to *Godzilla vs. Mothra*. *This Island Earth* appeared one Saturday morning on television, and I suffered nightmares about exploding planets and dying civilizations. I would feel so sorry for the poor victims—trampled, eaten, hypnotized, turned into zombies. In particular, I found myself troubled by movies in which Good People, especially pretty girls, were transformed, via drugs or diabolical machinery, into soulless predators and sirens, desiring only to serve their new masters, often while wearing skimpy, revealing outfits. How dreadful—and yet, somehow, vaguely exciting too. I signed out some books on hypnotism from the library. Maybe I could transform Angela Ortenzi or Lois Gradisek into my willing and obedient slave? "Yes, I will do exactly as you say, master. . . ."

Bedtime could be especially terrifying. Just the sprightly yet ominous sequence of notes alerting the viewer to *Alfred Hitchcock Presents* would send my heart racing. Before I moved into the addition, I had had the company of Sandy, Pam and Linda. Back then, at night, my mother, settled on the floor like a big Raggedy Ann doll, would read aloud to us from a fat, tattered collection of stories, the edges of its newsprint pages already torn or chipped. These cutesy tales, geared toward my younger sisters, would soothe even their big brother. Afterward, Mom would usually take her nightly bath and I would further calm myself with the sound of the hot water running into the tub, then scrunch my head against the soft, fresh pillow, stretch and twist my body under the covers and gradually fall asleep to the tranquilizing splash and gurgle.

But sometimes this soporific routine didn't work and my father would need to climb the stairs to assure his overly imaginative child that vampires, aliens and ravenous ghouls absolutely, positively didn't exist. Not a one. Deep in my heart, I knew this had to be true. Yet my fear arose less from any reality than from mere possibility: What if, just for the sake of argument, such creatures actually, somehow, did roam the earth? Well, it logically followed that one midnight, and probably quite soon, we'd all be horribly torn to pieces and fed to its young. With equal rationality, I knew that by keeping my body wrapped tightly in blankets, with only my head exposed, I would escape this gruesome fate. (For some reason, I never seemed to care if my sisters were devoured alive or not.) And so I would lie under my covers, safe from harm, but dripping with perspiration from the summertime heat and humidity. Yet far better to suffer and sweat than to be snatched away by some monster of the id.

One restless night I recall waking up at two A.M. and glancing at the shade covering a nearby window. As I sleepily observed the shifting shadows playing across its surface, the splotches of darkness gradually solidifed into a single, vaguely humanoid shape, which—no, this can't be happening!—suddenly reached out and commanded me to take its gnarled hand. I could hardly breathe, for I knew, absolutely knew that if this evil demon but touched me I would be dragged into its shadowland forever.

Given my suggestibility, it is odd that I seldom remembered dreams or nightmares. I used to believe my conscious mind suppressed their unbearable horror, lest madness ensue. For that too was a recurrent fear: Didn't *Reader's Digest* calculate that one out of every ten people would spend time in an insane asylum? Could there be any doubt that I was destined to reside in the "loony bin" or at the "happy farm"? Better for my fragile mental stability that, come morning, daylight immediately blotted out my unendurable nocturnal visions.

But not the series of entrancing ones that thrilled me during the summer after seventh grade. I had been rushing through Robert A. Heinlein's *The Door into Summer*, which impressed me mightily, not only for its evocative title and time-travel theme, but also for the description of the young women of the future. The heroine and her friends, you may recall, basically parade about in Saran Wrap, leaving very little to the imagination yet much for a boy's subconscious. For three successive nights I traveled to this enticing future and beheld these wondrous girls in the flesh or at least in their plastic wrap, then fought, cutlass in hand, for love and glory: None but the brave deserve the fair. What impressed me, above all, was my strange ability, on successive evenings, to pick up my adventures where they had left off. For once, I could hardly wait to go to bed.

Chapter Six

An American is insubmissive, lonely, self-educated, and polite.

—Thornton Wilder

If Agatha Christie provided my introduction to "grown-up" fiction, then Fyodor Dostoyevsky deepened the casual relationship into a serious love affair. Somehow, perhaps from Latsko, I had learned that *Crime and Punishment* was a kind of murder mystery. So I bought a Bantam paperback, translated by Constance Garnett, and plunged into the troubled soul of the student murderer Raskolnikov. Never in my life did a long book move so quickly. Children's stories might allow the occasional speculation about the young hero's pluck or his playground fears, but in this novel thinking—brooding, really—turned out to be as important as talk or action. This was a journey to the center of the self. After *Crime and Punishment* I never willingly read any obvious kid's book again.

In eighth grade, Mr. Latsko carried on as our homeroom and social studies teacher, but the Advanced Class now took English with Delmar Wright. Where Latsko slouched and moodily ruminated, Mr. Wright proved jaunty, dapper and almost boyishly enthusiastic. He sported brown horn-rimmed glasses, dressed in casual but elegant checked sport jackets and drove an open two-seater MG. He may even have worn a tweed driving cap. Imagine a young Fred Astaire—

with children named Thomas Carlyle Wright, Sean O'Casey Wright and Emily Dickinson Wright.

Unlike most English teachers, Mr. Wright never spent much time on grammar, a subject for which I then had nothing but contempt, largely because of my failure to fully comprehend the proper diagramming of compound-complex sentences. Instead he would start reading poems or stories aloud in a clear, pleasing voice, somewhat precise and even sissified (in the view of some). After a while he would kindly ask one of us to continue. During the year we declaimed most of *A Tale of Two Cities* aloud in class, with Bob Brent—who had begged to be the final reader—stumbling slightly over Sidney Carton's famous last words. "It is a far, far better thing I do than I have ever done. It is a far, far bitter, uh, better rest I go to than I have ever known." A Freudian slip, we teased.

Lots of short stories suffered our nascent forensic skills too, among them Shirley Jackson's "The Lottery," E. B. White's "The Door" and E. M. Forster's "The Other Side of the Hedge." All three of these are startlingly allegorical tales—an ancient ritual in a picturesque New England town, a man trapped in life like a rat in a maze, a world where everyone must keep walking until passing through the thick hedge that lines the roadway. They were perfect for prolonged discussion, which doubtless accounts for why Wright chose them. How we argued about "The Lottery"! And with what wistfulness E. B. White invested his plain prose:

I remember the door with the picture of the girl on it (only it was spring), her arms outstretched in loveliness, her dress (it was the one with the circle on it) uncaught, beginning the slow, clear, blinding cascade— and I guess we would all like to try that door again, for it seemed like the way and for a while it was the way . . . for the world was young.

In class we probed, debated and sometimes simply wondered: Why should the people in Forster's story need to keep walking incessantly? Did their pedometers measure miles or years? Is the hedge death? And why does the narrator meet his brother when he finally crosses through to the other side? And so we would talk and talk away the sunshiny afternoon. But not always about literature: Once we spent several days debating a red-hot topic of the moment: World War III morality. If your backyard bomb shelter holds only enough food and space for your family, what do you do if your neighbor tries to break in? Would it be morally permissible to shoot him? Our ruthless, if pragmatic view was: Blast away.

To enhance his teaching, Wright employed all sorts of "aids," especially phonograph records and audiotapes. We listened, for instance, to I. M. Synge's *Riders to the Sea*, Bernard Shaw's *Don Juan in Hell* (from *Man and Superman* with Charles Laughton) and the complete *Waiting for Godot*—and naturally argued about the identity of Godot, the character of Pozzo, the plight of Lucky, the differing personalities of Gogo and Didi. Mostly I remember being entranced by Samuel Beckett's wit and astonished by the cartoonlike *prestissimo* of Lucky's nonstop soliloquy. *Waiting for Godot* showed me that words might be funny yet their meanings still complex and confounding.

One afternoon Mr. Wright announced that he was going to play for us a recorded version of *Macbeth*. What? A play by Shakespeare. Groans of dismay. As the needle touched the vinyl, the bright day immediately vanished, replaced by the noise of storm and battle, the dull clang of iron weapons, thunder booming and lightning crackling, the wind rising, falling. And then, emerging above the din, hideous voices that chilled the blood and heart: "When shall we three meet again?" "When the hurly-burly's done/ When the battle's lost and won." And later, "Double, double, toil and trouble/ Fire burn and cauldron bubble." The weird sisters were clearly the scariest witches this side of Oz. Yet what dreamy kid could resist the sheer coolness of their double-edged, O. Henry-like prophecies, especially that "none of woman born" will ever harm Macbeth? Even when Macduff finally stands before the usurper, like some Highland Terminator, declaring that he was from his dead mother's womb untimely ripped, Macbeth still goes down swinging: "I will not yield,/ To kiss the ground before young Malcolm's feet/ and be baited with the rabble's curse." Everybody in our class agreed that Macbeth, though villainous, showed style.

Oddly enough, even after excluding the Little Rascals production of *Romeo and Juliet* (starring Darla and Alfalfa), this was not my first taste of Shakespeare. Earlier that year I had been lounging in the family Ford one Saturday awaiting my mother, who was busy picking up Krazy Day bargains at Klein's or Penney's. In the parking lot out back squatted one of those massive industrial dumpsters, from which I soon detected unexpected rustlings. Suddenly, what to my wondering eyes should appear but three kids my age scrambling from the rusting trash bin with their arms heavy-laden with long-playing records. It seemed that someone—probably a disgruntled, larcenous employee—had secreted the new LPs, which the three treasure hunters sullenly agreed to share with an interloper. "Where'd those records come from?" demanded my mother. "Some kids gave 'em to me." "Oh, Okay."

When I reached home, I learned that along with Vincent Price sighing the poems of Shelley ("I met a traveler from an antique land"), Renata Tebaldi singing her favorite arias (years passed before I listened to that LP a second time) and an album entitled *Dream Dancing*, which eventually provided background music to my early adolescence, there was also an abridged audio version of *Richard III*. As is universally acknowledged, John Gielgud possesses the most entrancing speaking voice in the world. From his very first syllables as Richard—"Now is the winter of our discontent"—I listened as mesmerized as poor Lady Anne. ("Was ever woman in this humour woo'd?/ Was ever woman in this humour won?") For the next week or so, I took to commandeering the bathroom, where I would demand of the surrounding tiles, in resonant tones aspiring to the mellifluous and orotund, "A horse, a horse, my kingdom for a horse."

Shortly thereafter, I happened upon a recording of Charles Laughton "reading" stories from the Bible—and sat spellbound to his tour-de-force one-man-show presentation of Shadrach, Meshach and Abednego and "the burning, fiery furnace." How I longed to speak with the radiant preciseness of Gielgud and shivery tonal range of Laughton! I even checked out the library's copy of the latter's anthology *Tell Me a Story* and practiced my own "oral interpretation," modulating from whispers to shouts, testing accents, performing for no ears but my own.

Back in seventh-grade social studies, Latsko had named me the only true nonconformist in his class. I was pleased but could never quite make out why he had arrived at this judgment of my character. Did it have anything to do with my attire? Liking the feel of soft cotton, I nearly always wore sweatshirts and khakis to school, and generally dressed geekishly, even compared to my geeky classmates. Or maybe he truly believed that I exhibited an odd and independent mind. Certainly on paper my rival Tom was technically smarter, and with a quicker wit. Nevertheless, I grew persuaded that I might seriously differ from my classmates only when Mr. Wright announced that, in addition to our class stories, plays and poems, we would be expected to read fourteen other assigned books over the course of the year. All but one person among the room's twenty-five immediately began to grouse about the huge amount of required work.

Even now I can remember nearly all the titles on Wright's required list: James Joyce's *The Dead*, Katherine Anne Porter's *Noon Wine*, Glenway Wescott's *The Pilgrim Hawk*. William Faulkner's *The Bear*, Nikolai Gogol's *The Overcoat*. (All these were included in a Dell paperback called *Six Great Modern Short Novels*.) There was Vance Packard's *The Status Seekers* (which mentioned Lorain as a town dominated by the steelworkers' union), Rudyard Kipling's *Captains Courageous*, James Hilton's *Goodbye, Mr. Chips* (about which Bob Brent and I had to present an oral report) and *Only in America*, Harry Golden's nostalgic vignettes of Jewish life in New York. Not least, by any means, we even read *Moby-Dick*, Faulkner's *The Unvanquished* and George Orwell's *1984*. This last proved the class favorite, in part because of the torrid sex scene between Julia and Winston Smith—was it on page 104 of the Signet paperback? I was hardly immune to the manifold charms of this passage, but found the entire book nearly as throat-constrictingly, breath-holdingly nightmarish as *Crime and Punishment*, to which—I only realize now—it is in some ways an evil twin, with comparable characters, plot and even denouement. Who could stop after that ominous opening sentence: "It was a bright cold day in April, and the clocks were striking thirteen"? Nor have I ever quite escaped the chill of its last simple, spirit-shattering words: "He had won the victory over himself. He loved Big Brother." Were we the masters of our fate, the captains of our soul? Could we ever be sure we hadn't been brainwashed? Was I really in the Advanced Class?

One day Mr. Wright made an announcement: "You all know that I drive up to Cleveland once a week for a course at Western Reserve. I usually stop at a paperback bookstore near the Terminal Tower afterwards, and I'd be happy to buy books for anyone here in the class. Just let me know what you want. Payment on delivery." During the school year that followed, Mr. Wright purchased a half dozen books for me, starting with two that altered my young life: Dale Carnegie's *How to Stop Worrying and Start Living* and Henry David Thoreau's *Walden.*

Some lucky people are happy by nature, hopeful and welcoming to the world around them. But I have always felt more or less discontented, either looking back to the past as a golden age or daydreaming about some future estate of perfect felicity. The introspection of the four-year-old who liked to dilly-dally in Central Park on his way to kindergarten and drop stones through a sewer grate to listen to their mournful splash remains quite near the surface of my adult self.

Such a hangdog personality, along with myopia, night fears and a temperamental father helped me to start adolescence as a worried, overconscious thirteen-year-old. (As the Underground Man taught me years later: "Too much consciousness is a disease, a positive disease.") Some author or magazine article must have alluded to Dale Carnegie, whose *How to Stop Worrying and Start Living* sounded as if it might provide solace to my soul's confusions.

Carnegie taught a number of techniques for dealing with worry—for instance, he endorsed William Osler's sound counsel that we should dwell in "day-tight compartments," refusing to allow the past or future to mar the present moment—but what I came to value most in the book were its anecdotes, quotations and pointers to further reading. In Carnegie I encountered Kipling's "If" and its corny but nonetheless admirable Boy Scout sentiments:

> *If you can dream and not make dreams your master*
> *If you can think and not make thoughts your aim,*
> *If you can meet with triumph and disaster,*
> *And treat those two imposters just the same.*
>
> *If you can force your heart and nerve and sinew*
> *To serve your turn long after they are gone,*

And so hold on when there is nothing in you
Except the will which says to them "hold on,"

If you can fill the unforgiving minute
With sixty seconds worth of distance run
Yours is the earth and everything that's in it,
And what is more, you'll be a man, my son.

Here—or in the companion volumes on public speaking and winning friends—I also learned the importance of proper pronunciation and how Cicero and Demosthenes practiced constantly to improve their speaking skills. Soon, the would-be rhetor Marcus Tullius Dirda had checked out a volume of classic speeches from the library and was reenacting noble perorations on the Athenian dead and the civic duty of Romans, sometimes with a mouth filled with pebbles. As Lincoln—himself no elocutionary slouch—once said, "I will prepare myself and my chance will come."

Carnegie commanded anyone wishing to acquire a truly extensive and precise diction to give over his days and nights to the Bible and Shakespeare. So I began to read these two sacred texts at bedtime. My father, perceiving that scriptural knowedge could only be a Good Thing, offered me a hundred dollars to go through our Douai version cover to cover, every chapter and verse. The challenge—only in Numbers and Leviticus an ordeal—took most of a year. Genesis, Proverbs, the Apocalypse, Job and Ecclesiastes appealed to me most, and I copied out gloomy passages like this one:

Light is sweet! And it is pleasant for the eyes to see the sun. However many years a man may live, let him as he enjoys them all, remember that the days of darkness will be many. All that is to come is vanity. Rejoice, O young man, while you are young and let your heart be glad in the days of your youth. Follow the ways of your heart, the vision of your eyes; yet understand that as regards all this God will bring you to judgment. Ward off grief from your heart and put away trouble from your presence, though the dawn of youth is fleeting.

Shakespeare I started in earnest somewhat later, in a little hard-backed volume from our dining room shelves called *Five Tragedies*. I opened to the first play, *Hamlet*. Lonely sentinels on a rampart. A ghost. Foul and unnatural murder. Revenge. Obviously, another mystery story, of sorts. Even more neatly, Hamlet resembled and reversed Raskolnikov, one university student agonizing before he kills and the other afterward. Most of all, though, I loved the play's rapier wit, the bitter repartee, the obsessive self-inquiry. "I could be bounded in a nutshell and count myself the king of infinite space, were it not that I have bad dreams." Oh, *mon semblable, mon frère*. Little wonder that I later plunked down some outrageous sum—perhaps $3.50—to see a filmed version of the Broadway production starring Richard Burton in a Ken Holtish turtleneck. For months I wanted to dress only in some modern equivalent to Hamlet's "customary suit of solemn black." "Goodnight, sweet prince, and flights of angels sing thee to thy rest."

Nowadays, most of our self-help books obsess about the state of one's soul or of one's self-esteem; Carnegie insisted on social interaction as the center of his message. "Always make the other person feel important." He also stressed, as had the Count of Monte Cristo, that through effort any boy or man can remake himself. Not least, despite his apparent emphasis on cocktail party glad-handing, he genuinely promulgated worthwhile civic virtues: empathy, courtesy, attractive diction, the necessity of hard work. Effort always paid off. Carnegie strikingly quoted William James that "compared to what we ought to be we are only half awake. We are making use of only a small part of our physical and mental resources. Stating the thing broadly, the human individual thus lives far within his limits. He possesses powers of various sorts which he habitually fails to use." Few people, I apprehended, ever employ more than a small percentage of their innate intelligence. I determined that by dauntless Kiplingesque will I would use at least three-quarters, and definitely no less than half, the mental capacity at my interior command. A grandiose ambition, yet hardly an unworthy one for an eighth-grader. I owe Dale Carnegie a lot.

At the very same time that I was attempting to "talk in terms of the other man's interests" and dreaming of emulating Bernard Baruch (the Wall Street millionaire, park bench wise man and Carnegie exemplum whose autobiography my dad had me check out from the library), I was also hearkening to the very different drumbeat of Thoreau. In its way, *Walden* is an equally All-American self-help book, one in which the sage of Concord exhorts people to adopt a simpler, better, more noble life. *Walden* undercut the foolish notion that wealth and position signaled success in this world, and dismissed entirely ambition's impulse toward self-serving obsequiousness and trimming. Instead, Thoreau spoke, in clean, aphoristic sentences, about living in harmony with nature, attending to the dictates of one's truest self and cultivating the soul. To this day I can cite by heart—never a better phrase than that—numerous sentences from his pages: "Beware of all enterprises requiring new clothes and not a new wearer of clothes. . . . If a man does not keep pace with his companions, perhaps it is because he hears a different drummer. Let him step to that music which he hears, no matter how measured or far away. . . . The light that puts out our eyes is darkness to us. Only that day dawns to which we are awake. The sun is but a morning star."

Walden bristles with insistence: "Simplify, simplify. Let your affairs be as two or three and keep your accounts on your thumbnail.

. . . If a man advances confidently in the direction of his dreams and endeavors to live the life he has imagined, he will meet with a success unexpected in common hours." Thoreau also tells you what to study and when, pointing out that we should always read the best books first lest we miss the chance to read them at all. In short, *Walden* compels the reader to think about how to engage the world—and does so in phrases as sturdy as oak, as lovely and supple as a willow branch. Thoreau's masterpiece provided the first model for my own prose and I still try to emulate its clarity and unassuming poetry when I'm at my most alert. Yet when Mr. Wright queried me whether Thoreau didn't have a lot more to say to people than Dale Carnegie, I answered, "Yes, Thoreau has a lot more to say to people," yet couldn't help adding, with my new taste for wordplay, "but Carnegie has a lot more people saying things."

The golden age of reading, if and when it comes, is early adolescence, and I was now devouring books like a banqueting teenage Falstaff. Some were established classics, like *Hamlet* and *Walden*, but most might be judged high- and medium-grade trash, not to overlook some plain rubbish. Which is as it should be. But even in midlist fiction a moody kid can discover occasions for lachrymose reflection. For instance, I bought a paperback of James Michener's *Tales of the South Pacific* and in a book report for Mr. Wright pointed out that the final chapter, "The Cemetery at Haga Point"—a meditation on the people buried there, many of whom we've glimpsed earlier in the novel——particularly touched me:

The last chapter seemed to make you realize a little more about time. How fast it flies, yet how vivid remains the picture of the good times that are no more. Before you know it, you're an old man with nothing left except a few cherished moments from your earlier life. It is then and only then that you fully realize all the things you should have

done, seen or heard but, of course, it's too late. Time passes so swiftly.
You look forward to something for a week and when it finally comes,
and then goes, all that remains is a dim and fleeting memory.

I concluded this somber *tempus fugit* reflection by appropriately advocating a philosophy of *carpe diem*: "Do all the things you want to do, right away, for if you wait you may never get the chance."

Though highly energized by such omnivorous and catholic reading, I nonetheless began to feel the need for some expert guidance in my biblio-explorations. And one unlikely Saturday I found it at a shopping center.

That afternoon I was lingering in the book section of O'Neill's Department Store, surreptitiously turning the pages of *Tarzan the Untamed.* The Grosset & Dunlap editions of Lord Greystoke's adventures ($1.50 each) cost too much to actually buy, except on the rarest and flushest of occasions, but no store officials seemed to care if an obviously devoted student of the ape-man simply stood there, in that quiet corner, and read through an entire novel in the course of a lazy afternoon.

I was to meet my mother, that tireless bargain shopper, out in the parking lot at five P.M. Rather to my surprise I finished that Burroughs masterwork with half an hour to spare, examined the other books on the racks—various Hardy Boys selections that I'd read years ago, pricey Scribner's illustrated classics (parent-approved kiddie lit) that didn't appeal to me, numerous leatherette editions of the Bible. Nothing I was in the mood for.

A bit antsy by now, I started to roam through the store when, near the cash registers, I spotted what appeared to be a virgin stand of paperbacks. But as I approached I discovered that the revolving rack was stocked entirely with plastic bags, each containing three coverless books and each bag priced at some ridiculously low figure like twenty-five cents. I now realize that the store had stripped the paperbacks and sent the covers back for credit. Instead of discarding the now-coverless novels and self-help books, clerks had bundled them together as a special bargain.

It took but a moment for me to realize that no single package contained three books I wanted. What to do?

At this point it is important to remember that even as a kid I always carried a pocketknife.

Quietly, nervously, I slit open two bags and rearranged their contents so that I would be sure of acquiring Edward S. Aaron's *Assignment: Ankara*, a Sam Durrell spy thriller, and a humorous memoir called *Which Way to Mecca, Jack?* by William Peter Blatty (later to earn fame for his modern horror classic, *The Exorcist*). I didn't much notice or care what the third book might be.

Sweating like Peter Lorre in *M*, I put on a cheerful, innocent smile as I displayed my purchase to the cashier and handed over a sticky quarter. I scurried out through the sliding doors to my mother, who little suspected that she was driving a getaway car. As we pulled away, I fully expected to hear the sound of sirens, the distant baying of hounds.

But my worry soon passed. After all, I had not really stolen anything; just made a few trifling substitutions. As I sat restlessly in another parking lot, waiting while my mother continued her shopping rounds, I began to study my new acquisitions. I have utterly forgotten the thriller, eventually enjoyed Blatty's memoir ("Life is like a camel's back, littered with one goddam straw after another"); but the third book, the serendipitous one, turned out to be Clifton Fadiman's *The Lifetime Reading Plan*.

It was long fashionable to deride Clifton Fadiman as the quintessential middle-brow. But for me, and I suspect for many other people past forty, *The Lifetime Reading Plan* opened up the world of great literature. For a hundred books Fadiman composed brief essays in appreciation and excitement. Sometimes he expatiated about a writer's life; more often about the rewards or difficulties of his work. Whatever the case, one nearly always wanted to rush out and immediately start on *The Poetics* or *Vanity Fair* or *The Interpretation of Dreams*. In essence, Fadiman made classics sound as exhilarating as Tarzan or Dr. Fu Manchu. During the next half dozen or so years I would use the *Plan* as a guide, noting the titles I had acquired, checking off the books I had finished.

Naturally, I sought out Fadiman's own literary journalism, some of it going back to the 1920s (when he notoriously misjudged Faulkner's fiction). *Any Number Can Play* and *Party of One* offered reflections on famous novels, but also familiar essays on "privacy, conversation, house-hunting, cheese, mathematics, eccentrics, children, wine, puns, letter-writing, television comics, education, Mother Goose, fireworks and Judy Garland." I read and reread this genial *littérateur*'s books, underlined favorite passages and envied what sounded an idyllic, cultivated life.

Around this same time I began to notice that *This Week*—the Sunday *Journal's* magazine supplement—featured occasional pieces on bookish matters. Joseph Wood Krutch, a biographer and literary generalist, promulgated a Fadiman-like list baldly titled "My 25 Favorite Books—You'll Like Them, You Must Read Them." Then the naturalist John Kieran gracefully endorsed his twelve favorite books: among them, Boswell's *Life of Johnson*, which I acquired in an abridged Dell paperback, and Henry George's *Progress and Poverty*. This last I'd never heard of. "Here," wrote Kieran, "I disassociate myself from the single tax program of the author but this book is a literary jewel as well as a work of immense research, deep thought and radical conclusions on the economics of democratic nations." Soon thereafter, in an issue of *Popular Science*, I noticed—next to ads for the Rosicrucians, the Charles Atlas fitness programs and the ICS correspondence school—an address for the Henry George Institute. I wrote to its president, received back a typed letter and a monograph about the Single Tax and other Georgian ideas. Young Bernard Shaw, whose plays I relished for what was then called his intellectual sparkle, had been a great admirer of *Progress and Poverty*. So I plowed through the book and now remember nothing of it whatsoever.

Crackling with autodidact zeal, I began to study the book lists at the back of Signet Classics and its sister line Mentor Books. Their low-keyed blurbs possessed an almost Edwardian stateliness. *The Brothers Karamazov*: "The complete and unabridged classic about a passionate and tragic Russian family"—hmm, could be good, could be dopey. *Leaves of Grass*: "Whitman's enduring testament to a land whose vitality was the touchstone of his genius. A complete edition." How awful the thought of being inadvertently saddled with an incomplete edition. But what were *Persuasion, Adolphe, Lord Jim, The Ambassadors* and so many other books really like? Over the years I would find out.

In the 1950s and 1960s, mail-order subscription book clubs flourished and multiplied. Besides the Literary Guild and the rival Book-of-the-Month Club, one could scrutinize ads for the Science Fiction Book Club and the Detective Book Club (which offered omnibus volumes collecting three or four titles: "$40.75 worth of Perry Mason mysteries for only $1"). From garage and yard sales our household accumulated a handful of these criminally economic threesomes, which allowed me to fantasize over Erle Stanley Gardner's *The Case of the Lucky Legs* and Fredric Brown's spooky blend of whimsy, supernaturalism and suspense, *Night of the Jabberwock*. For the most part, though, I disdained the all-too-ubiquitous *Reader's Digest Condensed Books*—to read such abridgements felt like cheating—and can only remember whipping through a couple of these shortened novels: Alan LeMay's western classic *The Searchers*, and John P. Marquand's late Mr. Moto thriller *Stopover: Tokyo*. I kept wondering what was being left out.

One Sunday *This Week* magazine's back page carried an ad for something called the Walter J. Black Classics Club. For a dollar one was invited to enjoy in one's own home three high points of philosophical antiquity and then cancel if not completely satisfied. I sent in my dollar and a few weeks later received the *Meditations* of Marcus Aurelius coupled with the *Discourses* of Epictetus; the *Dialogues* of Plato (principally those dealing with the life and death of Socrates); and *On the Nature of Man*, selections from Aristotle's various treatises. All these works had been covered by Fadiman, so I dipped into them—after, of course, canceling my order for further Walter J. Black Classics: I wasn't my mother's son for nothing. Aristotle's categorical mind defeated me, other than for a couple of splendidly punchy sentences: "All men by nature desire to know" and "All education is accompanied by pain." An interesting, if slightly paradoxical, pairing. I read Plato's *Apology* soon thereafter, and concluded that Socrates, despite his cogent arguments about the immortality of the soul, was a fool to die rather than go into exile. Oddly, Epictetus never attracted me, but like called to pessimistic like in Marcus Aurelius and I underscored a number of passages in the *Meditations*: "Soon you will have forgotten all things, and soon all things will have forgotten you. . . . Retire into yourself. . . . Attend to the matter which is before you, whether it is an opinion or an act or a word."

Though longing to join the Literary Guild, the Walter J. Black Classics Book Club or the BOMC, I could figure no way to afford any of them. I didn't have ten or fifteen dollars a month to spend on new hardbacks. Nor did my parents. Dad was sometimes working double shifts at National Tube; the second eight hours paid time and a half. Mom landed a part-time cashier's job at W. T. Grant's (but was always home to give my father and her children hot meals). We never went on vacations. My sisters and I were growing up and in a few years all of us would need money for college or for hope chests and weddings. No, I couldn't afford any of these book clubs. Still, it was pleasantly literary just to lie on the living room floor under a lamp and study the dozens of titles available to new members. Someday.

Infected by these magazine ads, I actually checked out the library's copies of various best-seller "classics" by the likes of Louis Bromfield, F. Van Wyck Mason and Taylor Caldwell. I enjoyed Thomas B. Costain's historical swashbuckler *The Black Rose*; James Michener's aforementioned *Tales of the South Pacific* (racy at times); James Hilton's 1930ish *Lost Horizon* (the story of Shangri-la, with its heartbreaking close: "Oh, no, she was most old—most old of anyone I have ever seen"); Allen Drury's *Advise and Consent*; somewhat later, Harold Robbins's soft-core romance *The Carpetbaggers* (admiring the lean Nevada Smith cowboy novella in its middle) and that thousand-page popular history, William L. Shirer's *The Rise and Fall of the Third Reich*. Unfortunately, my all-too-embarrassing favorites in eighth grade were Lloyd C. Douglas's *The Robe* and *The Big Fisherman*. These sanctimous and manipulative tear-jerkers about the early Christians I found—let this cup pass away—masterly, and expected to reread them at intervals all my life. In my defense I can only point to my penchant for melodrama and sententiousness.

Clearly, given my growing soulfulness, it was high time for me to swoon over lyric poetry, and this happened in the usual improbable fashion.

One Saturday afternoon in the summer after eighth grade, I was strolling down Broadway in the company of Tom, Ed and Ray. We'd been to the movies—it might have been Jules Verne's *The Mysterious Island* with its Ray Harryhausen giant crab and behemoth honey-bees—and the four of us were dawdling our way home, stopping at various dimestores, checking out our feet in a shoe shop's X-ray machine, sharing a bag of bridge-mix chocolate. On some bizarre impulse, we stormed into a rather fancy emporium that sold stationery, greeting cards and "writing implements." While the guys tried out various ballpoint pens, I beelined over to a small section of paperbacks. Nothing in the least sinister or swashbuckling could be found on the racks. But on an impulse I picked up *Immortal Poems of the English Language* edited by Oscar Williams and on a whim bought the paperback for sixty cents.

My buddies poked fun at my purchase, and I could hardly blame them. We'd read some verse in school, but everyone knew that nothing was more percy—a then current slang term of contempt—than poetry. But I sullenly ignored the gibes, being unable to explain why I had wanted to own this brown-and-tan volume, its cover framed with tiny inset pictures of Byron and Shelley and Keats (that trio of lyrical treats, as Dorothy Parker once called them), as well Emily Dickinson, Robert Frost and scores of others. Once home, I flopped down on my bed, late afternoon sun slanting through the window, and began to read.

I was astonished by what I discovered. Sir Walter Raleigh's delicious cynicism, for instance:

> *Tell zeal it wants devotion*
> *Tell love it is but lust;*
> *Tell time it is but motion;*
> *Tell flesh it is but dust;*
> *And wish them not reply,*
> *For thou must give the lie.*

The world, I guessed, hadn't altered that much since the sixteenth century.

Single lines entranced me: Wordsworth's "Our birth is but a sleep and a forgetting." George Meredith's "The army of unalterable law." Ernest Dowson's "I have been faithful to thee, Cynara! In my fashion." I laughed at Pope's couplet for a dog's collar: "I am his Highness's dog at Kew,/ Pray tell me, sir, whose dog are you?" And marveled that Marianne Moore could begin a poem, entitled "Poetry," with the words: "I, too, dislike it . . ." To my surprise, I found that I, at least, didn't dislike it at all.

At this point my giant brain conceived the Great Plan. With a daily twenty-minute trudge to high school awaiting me in the fall, what better way to pass the time than by memorizing some of the "immortal poems of the English language"? Over the next several years, off and on, I committed to memory hundreds of lines of verse: Shakespeare soliloquies, Dryden couplets, reams of Romantic effusions, high points of high modernism. Swallowing whole the A. E. Housman selections in Williams's survey, I even stopped at the Plaza's branch library and took home *A Shropshire Lad*, the first book of poetry I ever read all the way through. I didn't tell anyone. Some of the more epicene pages bored me, but not many. Has any English verse ever been so simple and perfect?

> *With rue my heart is laden*
> *For golden friends I had,*
> *For many a rose-lipt maiden,*
> *And many a light-foot lad.*

> *By brooks too broad for leaping*
> *The light-foot boys are laid;*
> *The rose-lipt maids are sleeping*
> *In fields where roses fade.*

In years to come verse frequently soothed a broken heart, though this is to look ahead, if only a little, to my hot youth. Spurned by one raven-haired beauty in tenth grade, I consoled myself with Tennyson's lines about kisses "sweet as those by hopeless fancy feigned/ On lips that are for others." Rejected by a blond temptress shortly thereafter, I copied out and sent her Yeats's lines: "Never shall a young man thrown into despair/ By those great honey-colored ramparts at your ear/ Love you for yourself alone and not your yellow hair." During my own radical sixties I would often repeat Sarah N. Cleghorn's devastating quatrain: "The golf links lie so near the mill/ That nearly every day/ The laboring children can look out/ And see the men at play."

Sad to say, over the decades I have gradually forgotten a fair amount of what I had once committed to memory. Still, "though much is taken, much abides," and I have been known to thunder out at parties, when it's long past midnight and time to go home, Prospero's valedictory: "Our revels now are ended. These our actors/ As I foretold you, were all spirits, and/ Are melted into air, into thin air . . . We are such stuff/ As dreams are made on, and our little life/ Is rounded with a sleep."

Newly sensitized to the existence of poetry, at about the time I acquired Oscar Williams's anthology I also ran across an article, again in *This Week*, by the actor Richard Burton. He'd been asked to choose five favorite poems (for recitation) and these were reprinted in the Sunday magazine. I only remember two now—Dylan Thomas's "Fern Hill" (an inevitablity for a Welshman, I suppose) and Gerard Manly Hopkins's "The Leaden Echo and the Golden Echo." The first I couldn't understand; the second's relentless wordplay left me dumbstruck:

"How to kéep—is there ány, is there none such, nowhere known some, bow or brooch or braid or brace, láce, latch or catch or key to keep/ Back beauty, keep it, beauty, beauty, beauty . . . from vanishing away?"

Much as I revered Housman's limpid diction and lyricism, Hopkins's words rose off the page like barely harnessed ecstatic ululations, and revealed that not merely wit or melancholy but also a more visceral power could be found in poetry. Soon I was mouthing the stirring alliteration of "The Windhover" ("I caught this morning morning's minion") and "God's Grandeur" and "Carrion Comfort."

At the end of eighth grade Mr. Wright asked his pupils to produce a short story in lieu of a final paper. Over one weekend I sat diligently at the picnic table in our backyard, laboriously scribbling "Faster and Faster." My tale focused on Mitch, a kid obsessed with speed—with running faster than anyone at track, with riding his bike like the wind, with drag racing cars. The story doesn't really go much of anywhere, though it obviously moves right along. We simply follow the kid as he travels faster and faster in life. Having become a test pilot, one clear, blue-skyed afternoon Mitch simply flies to Mach 1, 2, 3—faster and faster—until he quite literally disappears. The narrative ends with the reflection that maybe our hero is still moving ever more quickly through space, time and the universe.

It wasn't a very good short story and Mr. Wright only gave me a B, which seems about right. Since then I've now and again wondered why I plumped for that particular subject and plot. What drew me, I think, was less the idea of speed than the attractiveness of disappearance, coupled with the notion that one may need to transcend ordinary life to fulfill one's innate destiny. Never content with who or what I was, I dreamed of becoming an Other, of finding fulfillment in a radical change of being. Like so many of my fictional heroes, I was seeking transformation.

And so I ran away from home.

Chapter Seven

The specific virtue of the hero is self-control.
—E. R. Curtius

L ate one summer afternoon in 1962 I came home from the park to hear my parents quarreling about me. How could their son be such a misfit? Why wasn't he more like other kids? Who said what, I have no idea anymore. After all, hadn't I been listening to parental, especially paternal, criticism all my life? I walked like a drunken sailor, I didn't tinker with cars, I never built anything, couldn't play ball, ate too many snacks and certainly read too much. "All that kid wants to do is stick his nose in a book," said my father with disgust.

Crouching outside the front dining room window, hidden by the evergreen bushes from view, I resolved that it was finally time to hightail it out of this household, this insane asylum. I was tired of being afraid to open the back door because I never knew whether my father would be "on the warpath" or not. Who needs this? And if I was such a loser, let them lose me. What the hell, I'd just take off, maybe for a couple of days, maybe for longer.

Bear in mind that I was fourteen years old and, though I'd camped out in the woods and occasionally slept over at my cousin's, I'd never really been out of Lorain or on my own overnight. Still, I decided to hitchhike to . . . well, anywhere. But first I should see if anyone wanted to tag along.

Like most adolescents, my friend Lance was frequently mortified by his parents. How he envied the daring blasphemy of a slightly older kid who, instead of singing, "Hail Him! Hail Him!" during Baptist services, would chant, "Nail Him! Nail Him!" Lance wanted in. So we sat on his porch steps the next day and considered various options.

"Let's go to Cleveland. Remember when we walked there?" The year before, Lance and I had hoofed about two-thirds of the way to the Big City to visit his aunt; it was our attempt to emulate young President Kennedy's fifty-mile hikes for fitness.

"No, not far enough away. Plus they'd find us right off."

"How about southern Ohio, then—I know this cool guy who lives down there in Coshocton. Met him at trombone camp."

Southern Ohio sounded too vague to me, so I suggested Pittsburgh, and we settled on that smoky metropolis as our destination.

Naturally such a great escape required careful coordination and the utmost secrecy. We agreed that we should decamp in the middle of the night, after everyone was asleep. We'd rendezvous on the boulders in Central Park at three, then walk across town to Route 57 and start hitching as soon as the sun rose. With luck we'd be miles away before our families sat down to breakfast and figured out that we were gone.

Funds might be a problem. I had all of $2.75; Lance had nothing. "How about we break into my grandmother's house? I know where she keeps her cash." This struck me as a terrible idea. "You must be crazy. The police would be after us for robbery or breaking and entering." So we resigned ourselves to heading out with just my personal savings. "We'll probably be able to mow lawns or do odd jobs to earn some money."

So late the next afternoon I carefully packed a green canvas knapsack with a change of clothes, rooted around for my dad's old steel-toed workboots, which would make perfect hiking shoes, and pasted together some peanut butter and jelly sandwiches. That night I politely excused myself, explaining I felt strangely tired, and "hit the hay" by nine. At two I jolted awake to an alarm clock muffled by a pillow, dressed, retrieved my gear and supplies and with some trepidation silently opened the backdoor and stepped out into the dewy cool of night.

When I reached the big rocks I didn't see Lance, waited for a few minutes, then concluded the fink had chickened out. But all at once his gangly silhouette came traipsing up the blacktop path. "Had some trouble getting up." He yawned, then added, "I still think we should get some more money. My grandmother won't miss it." "Lance, forget that. Let's get out of here already." And so we finally set off.

As we tramped toward South Lorain, I quickly deduced what a big mistake I'd made. I'd never worn my father's size-nine workboots before, and they were already chafing the sides of my ankles; before long the blisters were hobbling me. By the time we reached the Czech Grill, I needed to stop. To my surprise, the grill was open, with men already drinking, or still drinking, at four A.M. As I hunched down on the doorstep, applying Band-Aids to my bleeding feet, a couple of early morning drunks yelled, "Hey, what you two boys doing?" I answered, "Running away from home. What else?" They laughed, disbelieving.

On we trekked, down 28th Street, then up Route 57, until finally we arrived at the outskirts of Elyria, several miles south of Lorain. It was around seven in the morning.

"Lance, I think it's time we started hitching."

"Okay, Mike. Go for it."

With my best imploring, waiflike smile, I stuck out my thumb as the next car approached, but Lance simply stood there on the grass, a few feet off the berm. "Why aren't you helping?" Only now did my fellow traveler disclose that he had been taught that hitchhiking was bad, wrong, improper and, well, he just couldn't do it. Ah, that old-time Baptist training. My smile and thumb would have to hook nearly all our rides.

The first turned out to be an old guy en route to work in Cleveland, who rattled on and on about his hobo life during the Depression. Then a suited-up businessman carried us a few miles farther, following which a black dude took us on a wild spin along winding roads at high speeds. Even a college girl, with short blond hair, stopped. I think she was a mite disappointed at how young we were.

About eleven we lounged under some maple trees and wolfed down our sandwiches. Lance had spread mayonnaise on his bread and was worried that it might have gone off in the hot sun. "What happens if I get sick?" "I'll leave you here to die." An hour or so later, we were dragging our feet along the graveled edge of a back road—to avoid the attention of troopers, we stayed off major highways—when I suddenly realized that I felt happier than I'd ever felt in my life.

There I stood, on my bedraggled own, a hundred miles from home, on an empty stretch of nowhere, not a lift in sight, without any resources but myself. I didn't even have a book with me. And, for once, I didn't want a book. This—what shall we call it? living?—was far more interesting, far more exciting than anything I had experienced on the printed page. Maybe Huck Finn's adventures were more action-packed, but mine were just beginning. I felt open and ready for anything. If a copy of Whitman had been in my knapsack—a "complete edition," of course—I would have recited the "Song of the Open Road":

Afoot and light-hearted I take to the open road,
Healthy, free, the world before me,
The long brown path before me leading wherever I choose.

Henceforth I ask not good-fortune, I myself am good-fortune,
Henceforth I whimper no more, postpone no more, need nothing,
Done with indoor complaints, libraries, querulous criticisms,
Strong and content I travel the open road.

We reached Pittsburgh at five P.M., and briskly surveyed the river-scape from one point of the downtown Golden Triangle. The Monongahela lay to one side, the Allegheny to the other, and the mighty Ohio—their confluence—flowed westward before us. Strong brown gods, all three. Urban Pittsburgh still bustled, and it was quickly apparent that we wouldn't find anywhere to flop there for the night. Worse, we were getting hungry.

So I squinted across one of the rivers toward what looked like a run-down residential area, high on a bluff. "Let's go there, Lance. It looks a little like South Lorain." But once we had crossed a rusty bridge, I noticed that the road wound its way, back and forth, lazily upward in loops and curlicues, while off to one side steel steps appeared to ladder their way directly up the riverbank. "I'm going to see if that's a shortcut. I'll meet you at the top."

Alas, the metal stairs led only halfway up to where railroad tracks had been cut into the bluff. I started to follow the rails, hoping that other steps or a path would take me the rest of the way to the top. About then I sensed my danger. On one side these tracks butted right up against a vertical cliff, leaving no more than a couple of feet clearance. On the other side a several-hundred-foot drop beckoned the unwary or suicidal. What, I mused, do I do if a train comes now?

I heard a whistle, put my ear to a rail as I'd been taught by my cousin Cookie and immediately began to hotfoot it down the tracks. The whistle grew closer, louder. I ran harder and kept looking desperately at the cliffside, hoping for some refuge there. After a minute or two, the bank started to flatten out, and then—thank God—a path. I leapt onto it and a guard dog leapt at me, barking, teeth bared, muzzle foaming. With this slavering hound of Pittsburgh at my heels, a terrified Sir Michael Baskerville tore through grass, rubbish, bushes and finally reached a four-foot wire fence. I threw myself against its mesh and scrambled over, tumbling hard onto some broken glass and gravel on the edge of the pavement. The monster-dog slammed into the steel grating, just as the locomotive, its whistle blowing, rumbled by below.

Later, with a dollar of our travel fund I bought a jar of Welch's grape jelly and a loaf of Wonder bread. Supper. I remembered my father's school lunches during the Depression. We didn't leave a slice.

Lance and I wandered like derelicts through this blasted neighborhood, yet couldn't find a quiet corner or, better yet, an unlocked car to sleep in. There seemed no choice but to head out of Pittsburgh toward some grassy knolls we had noticed on the way in. So the two of us wearily retraced our steps to the main road into the city, then began working our way through a tunnel using its service catwalk. Repairmen in a truck noticed the two tramps and motioned us back, back toward the city.

"You kids can't use that walkway."

I attempted to plead with them, but to no avail. So, at the end of our reserves, strength and tether, we straggled to a side road and sank down, exhausted, under a billboard, while the cars whizzed along nearby.

We woke up an hour later, wet with dew and pockmarked with insect bites. "Come on," I said to my now-haunted-looking, hollow-eyed friend, "let's go check out that twenty-four-hour gas station."

Before long Lance was asleep, while his companion spent the next several hours keeping the night attendant company. Enthusiastically, Jim described the correspondence school course he was taking in how to operate bulldozers. He proudly showed off his manual with a photograph of a front-end loader on the cover. "Don't get me wrong, Jim, but I want to get this clear: You're learning to operate construction equipment from a book?" Indeed he was, claimed it wasn't that different from driving a sixteen-wheeler. I tried to sound supportive, but even one who believed in books as much as I did had to wonder whether Jim wasn't being taken for a ride. At least it was warm inside the station.

The next morning we stumbled back into southern Ohio, eventually making our way to Coshocton, where we bunked in the garage of Lance's friend, sleeping on aluminum chaise longues, and earned a few dollars caddying on the local golf course. I'd never done this before, but had always heard it was easy money. Just carry around some clubs, spot balls in the tall grass, occasionally recommend, oh, a No. 5 iron. And that's just what we did.

After a couple of days, somewhat refreshed, Lance and I started off again, but couldn't persuade anyone to slow down for a pair of now exceptionally disreputable-looking kids. Something was going on. "Hey, Mike," said Lance, "have you noticed how all these drivers keep giving us funny looks?" "Yeah, I can't figure it out." All was made clear when the local sheriff rolled by, stopped and motioned us over to his cruiser. Beer-bellied, slow-talking, slower-moving, he might have been ordered up from Central Casting: "Now, why don't you two boys just climb into the back of this here vehicle?" Turned out a couple of young prisoners had escaped from jail and my work-boots added just the right touch—obviously what any fashionable inmate would wear. The sheriff, a jovial enough lawman, entertained us with tales of his derring-do all the way to the county line, then firmly told us never to come back to his jurisdiction again. "Yes, sir. Anything you say, sir."

By this point, Lance and I were pretty sick of each other's company and my eyes were growing tired of staring down empty highways for cars that never came. So, after five days away from home, we pointed ourselves north toward Lorain. When I finally dragged myself in through my back door, Mom broke down in tears. First she hugged me—"Oh, Mikey, you're home, you're safe"—and then she began to spank me as hard as she was able. "How could you do this to your father and me? Don't you know what we've been going through? You're supposed to be smart. Oh, Mikey, I was sure you were lying dead in a ditch on the side of some country road." My father, restraining his happiness at seeing me again, refused to believe that I hadn't simply camped out at some nearby farm. "Probably slept in a barn five miles away down 254."

In fact, the state police had been alerted about a couple of juvenile runaways and radio bulletins were broadcasting our description. But all was well again, now that the wayward prodigal sons were home—though to be scrupulously exact we were only wayward sons: After those five days on the road I still had a dollar in my pocket.

Part Three

ADULT MATERIAL

Chapter Eight

The only thing one can be proud of is of having worked in such a way that an official reward for your labor cannot be envisaged by anyone.

—Jean Cocteau

"Hail to our colors gold and blue/ Hail to our alma mater true. . . . Oh, Admiral King so strong and bold/ Our endless love can ne'er be told/ The light that you created here/ Will be a beacon through each year/ And bring us always home to sing/ The glory of our Admiral King."

When I entered ninth grade, Admiral King High School— named after Lorain's favorite son, Ernest J. King, commander of the fleet during World War II—was only a few years old. As a boy I had two or three times filled my wagon with Pepsi and Orange Crush and sold pop for extravagant sums to the bricklayers erecting its hallowed walls of tan block. I paid something like ten cents a bottle and charged fifty cents. But on a hot day it didn't take long to unload a couple of cases.

Going off to high school signaled the breakup of the Advanced Class's tight little Hawthorne group. We were all assigned different homerooms now, spread out among several teachers for each subject, crowded in with twenty-five hundred other students in a three-story building designed for two thousand. That population of supposedly eager scholars was roughly twenty percent Hispanic and twenty percent black, the remaining majority consisting largely of the children and grandchildren of Italian and Slavic immigrants.

A fair proportion of my fellow savants belonged to "social clubs," i.e., gangs: Bachelors, Barons, Dukes, Cavaliers, Southerners (from South Lorain), Islets, Bishops (black guys only) and half a dozen others, not to overlook their sister clubs with names like Junior Gems, Emeralds, Debs and Rainbows. During winter pledge week Bachelors reportedly beat up any prospective member, stripped off his clothes and dropped him naked into the cold, gray waters off Lake View Park. The pledge's job was to survive and make his way home. (Years later, reading around in J. G. Frazer and modern cultural anthropology, I would recognize this process of ritual death: To initiate a truly new identity the old self must first be wiped away.) Naturally, apocryphal, I hope, stories abounded about weaklings who succumbed to hypothermia, or were never seen again. One year Dukes (or was it Cavaliers?) adopted a plain white T-shirt as its unofficial uniform, since a boy couldn't wear gang "colors" in school. Members would strut for blocks without a coat in January as a sign of being tough. Which is what we all wanted, secretly or publicly, to be—even though I disdained the clubs as fraternities of the mean and the stupid.

In those years gangs might be threatening but hardly murderous: Nobody carried a gun and only Hispanics tended to flash knives or know how to use them. Rumbles were simply orgiastic fist fights, sometimes resorting to rocks, chains or car jacks. Kids might get drunk, and some might have sampled marijuana, but I never heard of any harder drugs being used. During school hours you might get shaken down for lunch money or punched out in the restroom for jostling the wrong guy. The best fight I ever saw, though, was between two girls in the second-floor hall one morning just before the homeroom bell rang: They clawed each other's faces and tore each other's clothes, to the delight of everyone standing around in absolute silence, so as not to attract any adult attention.

Of course, truly dangerous, even potentially deadly things did occasionally happen. Once a math teacher failed the vice president of the Barons: the next day the teacher was hustled into a janitor's closet by gang members, who then set fire to the door. He emerged shaken and otherwise unharmed, but never flunked anyone again. Another year, two friends, both stars of the basketball team, lost their cool in the cafeteria: one picked up a table knife and stabbed his teammate in the back; the wounded guy then grabbed a metal chair and clobbered his assailant to the ground. A week later both had healed and were again the best of friends.

Admiral King, with purportedly one of the highest juvenile delinquency rates in Ohio—one Puerto Rican guy acknowledged three illegitimate children by the time he graduated at twenty—was thus mildly perilous, the home to first-rate basketball and football teams and academically lackluster at best.

By ninth grade, I had developed into an impassioned, unstoppable power-reader, perpetually on the lookout for ever more challenging books, demanding classics, impossibly dense works of philosophy. Now legitimately entitled to an adult library card, I had read Will Durant's *Story of Philosophy* and had then started working my way through the library's set of *The Story of Civilization*—roughly a dozen fat black tomes containing, I presumed, all knowledge. The Pyrrhonist first, *Our Oriental Heritage*, caused me to question further my already shaky religious faith by chronicling numerous sects that had believed in hanged gods who returned from the dead. Christianity hadn't started anything special. In subsequent volumes Durant (eventually in partnership with his wife Ariel) introduced Greek philosophy, Roman civilization and Renaissance science. I confess to bogging down eventually somewhere in the Age of Reason. Mock on, Voltaire, Rousseau! Mock on!

Adults and classmates were sometimes astonished that I cared about such works, and I deduced that books might serve as a way of showing off. During that first year of high school I took to toting around a copy of Kant's *Preface and Introduction to the Metaphysical Elements of Ethics* and made a to-do of casually opening the monograph in study hall. Not that I understood much of it, though I thought Kant's description of the conscience strangely thrilling:

Every man has a conscience, and finds himself observed by an inward judge which threatens and keeps him in awe (reverence combined with fear); and this power which watches over the laws within him is not something which he himself (arbitrarily) makes, but it is incorporated in his being. It follows him like a shadow, when he thinks to escape. He may indeed stupefy himself with pleasures and distractions, but cannot avoid now and then coming to himself or awaking, and then he at once perceives its awful voice. In his utmost depravity, he may, indeed, pay no attention to it, but he cannot avoid hearing it.

To "stupefy" oneself with "pleasures and distractions" or to sink into "utmost depravity" sounded surprisingly appealing, even Byronically romantic. The corridors of Admiral King thronged with attractive girls, and I noticed every single one of them. But, so far as I could tell, none of them looked twice at the straitlaced, dreamy kid in thick glasses with a book under his arm.

Having benefited from the attentions of Latsko and Wright, I assumed that my ninth-grade English teacher would be at least their equal. Wasn't high school "better," more serious than junior high? Alas, I was assigned to a class taught by "The Purple Cow."

That was her students' cruel nickname for the elderly, portly, evangelically old-fashioned Miss Raymond. Miss Raymond fervently believed in grammar, discipline and baggy purple dresses, which she wore frequently and with a mistaken but apparently unswerving faith in their attractiveness. After reading such terrific books as *1984* and *Moby-Dick* in eighth grade, I was eager for more. Instead the Purple Cow launched the semester with a long discussion of the indirect object and the proper method of diagramming the same. Naturally, I raised my hand and spoke these ill-advised words: "Miss Raymond, I don't see the point of grammar. If you want to learn to write, all you have to do is read a lot of books and pay attention to the sentences." This, an eminently sensible observation, is in fact the way most of us do learn to write. But Miss Raymond took my animadversion, quite correctly, as a declaration of war.

Today I value grammar and the ordered study of prose far more highly—indeed, have been known to browse for pleasure in Curme's manual of syntax—and very nearly agree with Gertrude Stein's remark: "I don't think anything has ever been more exciting than diagramming sentences." So I probably learned more than I can even now admit from the much put-upon Miss Raymond. Yet back then I resolved that my true, unstated purpose in ninth-grade English would be to drive this blowsy spinster crazy.

My cardinal rule as a fledgling intellectual cut-up was simple: Never do the expected. For example, when assigned a composition on "the animal one would most like to be," I handed in an essay titled "I'm glad I'm me." ("I'm glad I'm I," Miss Raymond coldly corrected me—but I contended that that usage sounded too formal, almost like Yahweh in the Old Testament, and besides, "People just don't talk like that.") Only inadvertently would I write on any assigned topic, instead choosing a tangentially apposite one that would allow humor, provocation or grandstanding. I was awful, no question. Still, none of my belligerent surliness quite prepared Miss Raymond for my book reports.

Though written out in longhand and later collected ("Please pass your papers to the front of the row"), all our analyses were first read aloud by their nervous authors to their bored classmates. In late September, the Purple Cow asked us to choose a work of fiction for our first reports. When my turn could no longer be dodged, Miss Raymond hesitantly called me to the front of the room. "My book," I casually announced, with a glance toward the mass of purple at my left, "is"—and I paused, cleared my throat, waited for the moment— "*War and Peace* by Count Leo Tolstoy." Then added, with an obnoxious simper: "Complete and Unabridged." Miss Raymond stared incredulously at her class *provocateur* and began to splutter. "You ask us to believe that you, Mr. Dirda, have read *War and Peace*?" Then, as now, Tolstoy's epic of family and nation during the Napoleonic invasion of Russia was frequently accounted the "world's greatest novel," and its sheer length had long been proverbial. Looking pained at her suspicion, I spoke aloud my elaborate summary of the novel's multiple plot lines and persuaded her that, yes, I had indeed finished Constance Garnett's translation (which I had). I recall pointing out, for particular commendation, the epilogue chapters in which we view the heroes and heroines of the main narrative grown fat, dull and middle-aged. And here I glanced again at my poor teacher, who was by now all too clearly unnerved. Which was just what I wanted. To her vast regret, she had no choice but to give me an A.

Inevitably, come October Miss Raymond prissily informed the class that we should devote our subsequent book report to a work of nonfiction. Nearly every third girl, and a few guys as well, opted for the onetime best-seller *The Night They Burned the Mountain*, by Dr. Tom Dooley, the inspirational (and propagandistic) story of a missionary doctor in Southeast Asia. In one scene, I recall from the innumerable tedious reports on the memoir, the cinematically evil Chinese communists pound chopsticks into the ears of the good Asians. When my turn came around at last, I consequently proclaimed, with a dramatic Red Guard flourish, that my report would outline the manifest truth of . . . *The Communist Manifesto* by Karl Marx and Friedrich Engels. I then quoted the famous opening admonition about the specter haunting Europe, alluded with sham familiarity to *Das Kapital* and eventually concluded by intoning the ringing final sentences: "Let the ruling classes tremble at a Communist revolution." Here, a scornful smile at Miss Raymond. "The proletarians have nothing to lose but their chains. They have a world to win. Workingmen of all countries, unite!" Shortly after this I was asked in for a little talk with the school principal.

Jowly, graying Dr. Calta was obviously nonplussed. My test scores disclosed intelligence and my Hawthorne record apparently revealed a star student. Why, how, had I become such a troublemaker?

"I'm sorry, Dr. Calta, but I find Miss Raymond dull and her classes a waste of time."

I then added—just between the two of us—that Mike Dirda was a nonconformist and neither he nor anyone else at Admiral King could do anything about it. Dr. Calta rightly pointed out that nonconformity might bring its costs: Did I want to receive a D in English?

"Not really, but I don't much care one way or the other."

In fact, I did begin to receive D's on my report cards, in English and other subjects, even as late as the first grading period of my senior year (1965), when I was applying for college. To my eye, a well-chosen D or two softened the gaudy vulgarity of massed A's. Besides, I wished to cut a flamboyant figure, like the bacchanalian hero of J. P. Donleavy's "underground" novel *The Ginger Man.*

The weeks of grammar rolled on, and for a while I hesitated over the theme of my next outrage in English class. Religion? Education? No, let it be sex and reproduction. My third report, again fiction, took up Aldous Huxley's *Brave New World*, and I lingered on its test-tube babies, feel-good drugs and hedonistic freedoms. In fact, I expostulated so warmly about these matters, with relevant quotation, that Miss Raymond's countenance slowly turned as violet as her dress and she was obliged to quit the room in the middle of my close textual, sexual analysis. There was another talk with Dr. Calta, but what could he do against such recalcitrance? School was no longer exhilarating, and I mourned for the lost horizons, the daily intellectual excitement of Hawthorne.

Toward the end of the academic year I searched hard for my final provocation as an intellectual guerrilla. Where should I strike after my penultimate barrage, a synopsis of the somewhat leaden *Education of Henry Adams*? Where would the enemy least expect the blow to fall? First, I considered reviewing the twelfth-grade English grammar textbook. "Somewhat lacking in narrative drive, rather dry in tone, and with a plethora of incident, *Sound and Sense* is nonetheless . . ." Then I toyed with the idea of a report on the latest issue of Superman, treating the usual plot—what has red kryptonite done to the Man of Steel this time?—with scholarly solemnity. "Kryptonians such as the mature Kal-El, whose journalistic *nom de plume* Clark Kent masks his so-called 'true identity' as Superman, react to the surprisingly common *green* shards of their birth-planet in the following distinctive ways: (1) Severe abdominal cramping, leading to almost immediate collapse, (2) Quick gasps for breath, often accompanied by such locutions as 'Must get behind the lead wall before it's too late' . . ." Oh, well, either of these would have been fun, but in the end I settled on a book I'd actually been meaning to read for quite a while: *The Concise Cambridge History of English Literature*. "In," as I snidely emphasized, "two volumes." Miss Raymond simply gave up at that point. She was, I fear, a broken woman.

Still, I owe her more than I then realized, even if I've never regretted my antics: She should have been a better, more inspiring instructor. Nonetheless, our conflicts made me start thinking on my own, provoked me to read difficult books and encouraged me to stand up for what I believed and be willing to pay the price. Unfortunately, Miss Raymond also made me feel cockily, insufferably sure of myself—in English anyway—and, from ninth grade on, I always assumed I had read more than my teachers. That I was a fool goes without saying, but at least I seldom behaved with such blatant smart-alecky obnoxiousness again. At least I don't think I did.

By the time I enrolled at AKHS, the halcyon days of the TAB Book Club were long over. Missing that sodality's calming influence, I assuaged some of my bibliolatry at our high school bookstore. Located inside the concession stand across from the gymnasium, it opened only a short time each day, usually for a half hour or so just after the last period. At first I would lean across the laminate counter, tilt my glass lenses to a slant for maximum visual acuity and simply stare at the paperbacks displayed, face outward, in the wire racks. After I had insinuated myself with the upperclassmen who worked and flirted there, I was permitted to leaf through mint-fresh copies of Edith Hamilton's *Mythology* or *The Gold-Bug and Other Stories* by Edgar Allan Poe, thus refining my taste and gradually maturing into a connoisseur of softcover editions. Unfortunately, I never saw any Penguin Books, nor more than a few of the elegant Anchor Books, now highly esteemed for their Edward Gorey cover illustrations and typography.

Back then nothing surpassed Signet Classics, with their creamy stiff covers, bright paper, clear text, useful prefaces or afterwords and guides to "further reading." Yet sometimes, if opened too enthusiastically, Signets might crack down the center of the spine, leaving the ham-fisted reader with two chunks of text block, loosely attached by glue to the outside cover. Dell Books flexed with yogi-like suppleness, but the paper was too dark and their whole format struck me as less classy. On the other hand, when my Dell edition of Conrad's *Heart of Darkness* did fall apart, I complained to the publisher, who dispatched a new copy gratis. Pocket Books were okay for Agatha Christie mysteries, but wasn't there something cheap and bestsellerish about them, starting with that hokey logo, a kangaroo named Gertrude? Mentor Books "of special interest" focused on nonfiction, with volumes devoted to the teachings of the Compassionate Buddha or collections solemnly, if accurately, titled *Eight Great Tragedies* (Eugene O'Neill's *Desire Under the Elms* sounded a lot better than Yeats's *On Baile's Strand*). Image Books often bore the imprimatur Nihil Obstat and were visibly oriented toward Catholics, but then almost everyone I knew was Catholic. The house did publish G. K. Chesterton's biographies of Thomas Aquinas and St. Francis, as well as his essays ("If a thing is worth doing, it's worth doing badly"). Bantam tended to cut corners by using small type, though my soulful *Crime and Punishment* appeared under its rooster insignia. Some early Avon Discus books, refusing to cut corners, at least rounded them, literally, for no discernible purpose, and I remember a thick copy of Henry Roth's classic *Call It Sleep* in this format. At the lowest rung were Airmont Classics, with corny painted covers, using a paper stock that would embarrass self-respecting newsprint, altogether cheap and ugly publishing. I would never buy or read these if I could possibly help it.

To my surprise, the oak-tabled and airy Admiral King Library housed a better-than-expected collection of books, and not only the classics with which I gleefully annoyed teachers. From its shelves circulated the three key anthologies for any youthful admirer of genre fiction: Wise and Fraser's *Great Tales of Terror and the Supernatural,* Healey and McComas's *Adventures in Time and Space* and Dorothy Sayers's *Omnibus of Crime.*

In the first of these I read my all-time favorite short adventure story: Richard Connell's "The Most Dangerous Game": " 'Off there to the right—somewhere—is a large island,' said Whitney. 'It's rather a mystery . . .' " I've never run across anything else by Connell, nor has anybody I've ever met, but that one suspenseful tale of the hunter and the hunted, of suave Cossack General Zaroff and the increasingly desperate Rainsford, manages to achieve something almost mythic or archetypal, a stroke of genius as immortal in its way as the single remembered line by the Victorian poetaster John William Burgon: "A rose red city half as old as time."

That phrase from the poem "Petra" might have been penned by the writer I soon fell in love with: Lord Dunsany. For some reason the AK library owned a copy—hard to find these days—of the story collection *Jorkens Remembers Africa.* I can still visualize myself picking it out from the travel or geography bookcase where it had been mistakenly shelved as nonfiction. I opened to the title page, which revealed a woodcut of a big-game hunter, knocked to the ground, about to be skewered by an angry unicorn. After reading a few pages, I couldn't bear to stop when the bell rang for math class.

What kind of stories are better? The crackling fire of an English men's club. A dark and stormy night. Old colonials lingering over their whiskies. A chance remark. Then one of them, always Jorkens, murmurs something like, "That reminds me of a rather rum thing that once happened to me in Africa." Chairs are pushed closer to the fire, drinks refreshed, everyone settles back in comfort as the rain pelts the leaded windows. "We had come up to Zambeziland to hunt rhino and were having the most beastly luck. I had just acquired a new gun, a double-barreled Smith-Hawken—you know the one—

that could supposedly stop a steam locomotive in its tracks. Naturally, I longed to test it out on something really big. When the local natives began chattering about a huge creature in some kind of off-limits holy land beyond the hills, I decided to take a look. None of the pack-boys would come with me though, and the headman kept mumbling something like, 'Niripsa, Niripsa.' I was young then, so decided I'd just go it alone. Worst mistake of my life. . . ."

Ah, Jorkens! Start a tale in a gentleman's club—the above example I made up just this minute—and I become again as a little child and cannot choose but hear. Pure artifice, these tall tales can embrace anything from mermaids to Martians and yet never be so threatening as to provoke nightmares. Later, I turned up some of Dunsany's non-Jorkens stories—"How Nuth Would Have Practiced His Art Upon the Gnoles," "The Three Sailors Gambit"—and learned just how intensely imaginative he could be: Certainly "The Two Bottles of Relish," about the man who chops down trees to work up a macabre appetite, ranks high among the cleverest short mystery stories of all time. But most of all I treasured Dunsany's decorated, fin-de-siecle prose, from the drowsy word-music of "Idle Days on the Yann" to the pointed first sentence of "The Hoard of the Gibbelins"—"The Gibbelins eat, as is well known, nothing less good than man"—to his flair for proper names redolent of the *Arabian Nights*: "Toldees, Mondath, Arizim, these are the Inner Lands, the lands whose sentinels upon their borders do not behold the sea. . . ."

By my mid-teens the sound of sentences stirred me at least as much as their sense. Even though I agreed with Somerset Maugham's *The Summing Up* about the virtues of clarity, simplicity and directness, and even though I would always try to emulate the manly examples of Dryden, Swift and Addison in my own prose, my heart nonetheless lifted and soared in the presence of Latinate diction and lavish filigree. Only years later would I discover the stirring organ roll of Thomas Browne, Robert Burton and Jeremy Taylor, the tone poems of Pater and Ruskin, the arch pitter-patter of Firbank and the precise and silken lyricism of Nabokov. But these are all examples of my "fatal" type. Little wonder, then, that as an adolescent I succumbed to the spell of Dunsany, and, soon after, surrendered my soul to the charnel joys of H. P. Lovecraft.

A god, an elder god, of horror writing, Lovecraft composed prose so overblown, so heavily laden with menace, it cannot fail to appeal to a romantic naïf with a taste for gloomy mystery. Fungi from Yuggoth! Cthulhu! Yog-sothoth! At his best (worst?) his sentences approach a condition of incantation that to the mundane may sound like eldritch gobbledygook: "Ahonas's dholas ort . . . agus leat-sa . . . Ungl . . . ungl . . . rrlh . . . chchch." I first read those last words—the final chilling ejaculations of "The Rats in the Wall"—in a gruesomely illustrated anthology, edited by August Derleth and unearthed at Amvets, titled *Sleep No More* (its other highlights included such classics as M. R. James's "Count Magnus" and M. P. Shiel's "The House of Sounds"). From that day I combed through other collections for Lovecraft, gradually locating "The Call of Cthulhu" and "The Dunwich Horror" and "The Whisperer in Darkness." One day I actually paid fifty cents for a newly issued paperback of the deeply unsettling, novel-length *Case of Charles Dexter Ward*. How I relished the gnawing sense of the uncanny with which Lovecraft imbues the off-kilter opening paragraphs of his tales:

When a traveller in north central Massachusetts takes the wrong fork at the junction of the Aylesbury pike just beyond Dean's Corners he comes upon a lonely and curious country. The ground gets higher, and the briar-bordered stone walls press closer and closer against the ruts of the dusty, curving road. The trees of the frequent forest belts seem too large, and the wild weeds, brambles and grasses attain a luxuriance not often found in settled regions. . . .("The Dunwich Horror")

Be still my beating heart! I had clearly come to terms with at least some of my nocturnal fears.

What with all this varied reading, and I was now doing little else in my free time, my father began to worry about me more than ever. Sometimes he'd march into my bedroom, discover me lounging in the blue chair with a book and kick Plutarch's *Lives* out of my hands. "It's too nice to be inside," he'd mutter. "Get out. Go play ball or take a bike ride" or, if the weather was bad, "Go down the cellar and build something." Naturally, such parental assertiveness, directed at a rebellious teenager (who was also a nonconformist), merely resulted in my wanting to read all the more. Living in a room of my own, alone on the ground floor, I could usually stay up late with Dante's *Inferno* or Mickey Spillane's *I, the Jury* ("How could you? . . . It was easy, I said")—at least until my worn-out mother would notice the light, shuffle downstairs wrapped in an old housecoat, her hair in plastic curlers, and order me with maternal gruffness to stop reading: "Mikey, turn off that light and just go to bed. It's one o'clock in the morning." Usually, I would.

But not always. Early one evening I was being serenaded by a disc jockey named Jerry G with current hits and golden oldies ("Runaway," "Moon River," "Cathy's Clown") while simultaneously trying to finish my New Math homework with its rebarbative terminology (commutativity? distributivity?). Suddenly I heard the DJ mention that at ten the Cleveland station would be broadcasting "Words in the News" with Dr. Bergen Evans. I'd never heard of the pompous-sounding Dr. Evans—Bergen, what kind of a name was that? murmured the kid named Dirda—but I was interested in words. That

night at ten the acolyte of Cicero, Thoreau and Charles Laughton lay
in his bed, half asleep, with a little beige transistor radio pressed to
his ear.

Dr. Bergen Evans, a professor at Northwestern, spoke with a
slightly high-pitched, slightly fussbudgety pseudo-British accent, yet
something in his voice and manner soon bewitched me. During his
half-hour program he discoursed about words he had noticed in
Time, *Newsweek* and the *Wall Street Journal*. He would speculate
about neologisms and slang, trace etymologies, clarify usage errors,
and in general display an awe-inspiring breadth of linguistic expertise. Could this be Miss Raymond's subtle revenge? Suddenly I hungered for the kind of language lessons at which I had recently turned
up my nose. The next day I visited the library and checked out *Comfortable Words*—a volume in the spirit of Evans's radio show—and
The Dictionary of Contemporary American Usage, written with his sister Cornelia: "Bone of contention," they wryly explained, "as a figure
for a cause of discord, is obviously drawn from the dogs, and, by
overuse, has gone back to them." Only years later did I learn that Dr.
Evans had been the (blameless) researcher for the questions used on
the rigged quiz show *The $64,000 Question*.

I tried never to miss an installment of "Words in the News" and
would lie blissfully warm beneath my covers, as that tenor voice
enunciated careful sentences about Indo-European roots and the
vowel shift in Germanic languages. Absolute enchantment. For a
while one could also watch a television show called *English for Americans* featuring Dr. Evans, but it broadcast just as we normally left for
church on Sunday. Later, I did catch a four-part "course" on the radio
in which Evans surveyed the work of Shakespeare. One night he
expatiated with particular enthusiasm about the song "When That I
Was and a Little Tiny Boy," giving rather wistful assent to the
somberness of "A long time ago the world begun," especially when

contrasted with the stoic gusto of "Hey, ho, the wind and the rain." He also recommended Mark Van Doren's *Shakespeare*, which in its turn led me to a couple of other books by the Columbia prof, in particular *The Noble Voice*, a study of epic poetry.

About this time I first started to think, in a vague, unfocused way, about writing as a possible career. Suffering from teenage acne and still sporting my heavy black-framed Clark Kent glasses, I naturally yearned most for the life of Adam Troy—played on TV by Gardner McKay—who sailed around the South Pacific on his schooner-for-hire enjoying "adventures in paradise" with sexy young women in two-piece swimsuits. But being some kind of writer, or even a journalist, might do as a backup job until I could afford the boat.

My family subscribed to the daily *Lorain Journal*, but on Sunday the *Cleveland Plain Dealer* also landed on our front doorstep. The *PD* actually allocated a section to arts and culture and I took to glancing at this occasionally. There, unbeknownst to my innocent soul, I one day glimpsed my improbable future.

Picture the scene: Our lightsome lad, prone upon the faded blue-green living room carpet, has just perused, with his usual Talmudic rigor, the *Plain Dealer's* comics section. For some reason, he starts flipping through the arts and entertainment pages and remarks an article about an omnibus volume of Raymond Chandler mysteries. Soon the young teenager of letters is reading the first book review of his life. Alas, I have quite forgotten its author—the unhappy destiny of so many who have hitched their wagon to the shooting star of literary journalism—but have never forgotten the long, somewhat overblown passage quoted from *The Long Goodbye* about blondes, their various qualities and quiddities. Being fifteen, I'm not sure if it's art, but I possess more than a passing interest in blondes:

There are blondes and blondes and it is almost a joke word nowa-
days . . . There is the small cute blonde who cheeps and twitters, and
the big statuesque blonde who straight-arms you with an ice-blue glare.
There is the blonde who gives you the up-from-under look and smells
lovely and shimmers and hangs on your arm and is always very very
tired when you take her home . . . And lastly there is the gorgeous
showpiece who will outlast three kingpin racketeers and then marry a
couple of millionaires at a million a head and end up with a pale rose
villa at Cap Antibes, an Alfa Romeo town car complete with pilot and
co-pilot, and a stable of shopworn aristocrats, all of whom she will treat
with the affectionate absentmindedness of an elderly duke saying good-
night to his butler.

The dream across the way was none of these, not even of that kind
of world. She was unclassifiable, as remote and clear as mountain
water, as elusive as its color . . .

That review naturally steered me toward the premier literary
magazine of the era, the *Saturday Review*. I remember the cool night
I strolled up to Whalen's Drugstore, studied its wooden periodicals
shelves (next to my old haunt, the revolving rack of comics) and purchased my very first issue of *SR*. Sliding it into a brown paper bag to
keep the cover uncreased and pristine, I sauntered across Oberlin
Avenue to a hamburger joint that had recently opened in the Plaza.
There I ordered a plastic cup of coffee and a cellophane-wrapped
danish, then selected a clean Naugahyde booth by the streetside window. I stared out into the fast-arriving twilight and indulged myself
in doleful night thoughts. After finishing the pastry, I cleaned the
tabletop with a napkin, before carefully opening my new magazine
and reading about the literary life I aspired to join one day. I gingerly
turned those glossy pages, laughed with assumed sophistication over

the cartoons and comic poems, wondered if my own personal library might one day possess any of the books so enthusiastically reviewed. A new work by the young John Updike? A collection of humorous poems by Richard Armour? The darkness grew thicker. One day I would surely dwell high above Manhattan in a penthouse apartment, type at an IBM Selectric and nightly assuage the jealousies of an emotionally volatile French mistress.

But should I become a novelist? Or a poet? I'd written one bad short story and some nonsense verse about algae. Maybe it was more fun just to read? One afternoon, as I was doing just that, my father peered at his myopic namesake and solemnly pronounced: "A reader reads, a writer writes."

And so I began to keep a journal. Definitely a journal. The word "diary" sounded girlish, suggesting a little vinyl-covered album with a lock and key, decorated with hearts, flowers and either prancing ponies or apple-bottomed *putti*. I recorded my higher-order thoughts in a serious, muted green "record book" purchased at a real stationery store.

At first it was more a catch-all in which to preserve adages and favorite passages from Dale Carnegie's manuals, *Walden* and various borrowed library books. I had also recently paid seventy-five cents for a shortened paperback edition of *Bartlett's Familiar Quotations* and would scan its microprinted pages for exhortation and inspiration. I transcribed a lot of Churchill and Kipling. Where was it that I found "Two men looked out from the prison bars,/ One saw the mud, the other stars"? I copied out passages from Ecclesiastes and Lovecraft, Shakespeare and Dunsany, even from my apothegmatic dad: "Every fifteen-minute job takes an hour. . . . If you liked it all the time, they wouldn't call it work."

To improve my pathetic vocabulary I started to make lists, with definitions, of useful-sounding words: anomaly, mordant, cacophony, acumen, trenchant. When did I pick up *30 Days to a More Pow-erful Vocabulary* by Wilfred Funk and Norman Lewis, a self-help manual whose title ushered in a catchphrase? And one my father took to mocking: "Improve your vocabulary in ten hard lessons or twenty easy ones." In my journal I listed the four most "poetic" book titles, though I hadn't yet read any of the actual novels: *The Sun Also Rises, Tender Is the Night, Of Time and the River, The Call of the Wild.* In another entry I catalogued all the "classics" I had finished by the age of fourteen, then later took the list up to sixteen (see page 323).

Soon, in yet another gesture toward self-improvement, I took to taping three-by-five cards to my bathroom mirror, to my bed's head-board, even to the ceiling above my pillow: "Find a need and fill it." "There is no expedient to which a man will not resort to avoid the true labor of thinking." "I stand in the doorway with a dagger or a sabre and I say 'As long as I live, no one shall enter here.' That is what I call conviction." Such gung-ho sayings, and others, were drawn from a black tin box in which I copied onto index cards not only quotations but also my favorite chess gambits, the odds of drawing certain combinations at poker, and even my own high-minded analy-sis of what made a woman beautiful. The key notion, I recall, cen-tered on "sweet excess," a reasonable exaggeration from the norm (in length of legs, size of breasts, sway of hips) that made for pulchritude without going so far as to fall into the grotesque.

But as I grew older, I did more in my journals than copy quota-tions and set down uplifting homilies. Before long my notebooks drifted into sustained reflections, nearly all of them focused on either the passage of time or my burgeoning interest in girls, less often on day-to-day activities or my various part-time jobs. Yes, jobs. By the time I was fifteen, I could, at least in the summer, count myself a workingman of the world.

Chapter Nine

Work is best, and a certain numbness, a merciful numbness.

—*D. H. Lawrence*

Even before high school I had delivered the *Cleveland Press* for a brief period, but quit after a hideous two weeks because I couldn't rouse myself at four thirty in the morning, day after day (and because I was afraid of the pack of mongrel dogs that roamed Central Park just at dawn). While very young, I frequently sold Christmas cards and chocolates door-to-door or peddled soda pop from a red metal wagon at construction sites. During my first year at AK, I even joined the disdained "bleacher crew"—mainly Puerto Rican and black guys who swept up the gymnasium after basketball games (and then shot hoops themselves in the middle of the night). At the end of ninth grade I was primed and ready for some serious employment.

So along with lanky Ray Schwarz, now more querulous and crotchety than when we first explored Clarice's Values, I signed on to pick cucumbers for a farmer out toward Sheffield. I had had some vague notion that farming might be good for the soul—getting in touch with the land, with "the good earth," as Pearl Buck called it in the sorrowful novel I had recently read.

Instead, it was simply hot, dirty, mindless and dull routine. Stooping, pushing leaves aside, plucking only the proper-sized "pickles"—no "culls," as the stumpy ones were dubbed—Ray and I soon recognized that the very essence of farming is repetitive, constant bending. Hour after hour, week after week, we crouched on our haunches and picked cucmbers. "Dirda, how did you talk me into this? I don't even like pickles—except for those sun-dilled kind." "It's not so bad, Ray," I said, trying to sound mildly upbeat, as my hands grew scratched and stained. "A farmer," my dad told me, "has to have a swivel in his back."

To occupy my mind I eventually tore out some pages from a paperback poetry anthology and kept them in my back pocket, hoping to memorize a few lyrics during the cool mornings. But the farmer objected: "I ain't paying you to read no books." So while the sun shone down with what seemed preternatural intensity, I took to amusing myself out in the field by translating popular songs and lyrics into "sesquipedalianese." Thus, "I want to hold your hand" could be transformed into "I wish to perform sexual interdigitation with you." Lyrics from the Rolling Stone's "Satisfaction" would be transmuted into "While absorbing visual information from my kinescope a gentleman appears and informs me in the art of how much more completely reflective my body's upper wearing apparel could conceivably appear." That is, "While watching my TV, a man comes on and tells me how white my shirts could be."

We would start work in the fields early, at the latest by seven, and knock off for the day by two or three, having ravenously devoured bologna sandwiches and hunks of pie at eleven. At quitting time we'd take off our straw hats and remove the bandannas from around our necks, douse our dusty faces and matted hair with pumped well water, then lie prostrate on the ground under a chestnut tree and wait for my dad or Ray's mom to come drive us home. After seven or eight hours of picking cucumbers, it felt blissful to bask in the shade and talk about lasers and cryonics while trying to identify the various makes of the cars hurrying by on Route 254. "Ford Fairlane, Dodge pickup, Corvette, GTO—" "Oh come on, Dirda," Ray would interject with a superior air, "where's the challenge in that? What years are they?"

That job lasted only about three weeks. At its end, we were planting potatoes from a jib on the back of a tractor. Kind of fun, but there didn't seem to be much future in farming, at least not for dazzling urbanites such as ourselves. So later that summer Ray and I, joined by our friend, the serious, even occasionally solemnical Ed Partyka, landed slots at M&M Home Improvement in Elyria. Ed's dad was its chief sales rep and his uncle, John Muzick, owned the company and supervised the work crews. I was to spend five of the next seven summers working at M&M.

Since we were only fourteen or fifteen when we started, the three of us generally acted as gofers and helpers for various "skilled craftsmen," most memorably a pair of raffish carpenters who had taken up installing aluminum siding as easier than building additions and family rooms. Alfie was actually an English cockney, Sonny a West Virginia redneck: They got on famously. In fact, too famously, for the pair spent their lunch hours quaffing beer after beer in whatever honky-tonks were open near our work site. We used to joke about how the siding installed in the afternoon always looked crooked, wavy or out of plumb.

Mostly what I recall about those first summers was loading and unloading—ladders, tools and vast quantities of scrap aluminum. Though grunt labor, it paid reasonably well and we were supposed to be observing the work crews, studying the skilled craftsmen so that one day we could take on actual siding jobs ourselves. In fact, over the course of those summers I learned to install triple-track windows, storm doors, gutters, downspouts and aluminum siding. Though I've now forgotten virtually all those skills, in reveries I can still feel the weight of a full nail pouch of "whities" at my aproned waist or the comfortable heft of a sixteen-ounce hammer knocking, like a holstered six-gun, against my thigh.

Much of the time, at least on bigger siding jobs, I operated the brake. This last was a ten-foot long, viselike machine that allowed one to bend lengths of aluminum coil into elaborate shapes. Ed and Ray would call out measurements, while I laboriously figured out what combination of bends, and in precisely what order, would reproduce in metal the look of a bit of window trim or decorative fancy work.

Ed and Ray possessed a real flair for siding work (the former became a doctor, the latter an engineer), but I often felt unsure of myself, though in retrospect no job could have been more suitable for an all-too-bookish kid. Here was real life. Sort of. Once I electrified an entire wall of aluminium backer foil by nailing through a hot wire. Another time I tried to kill a wasp in the cab of our Dodge pickup with my boot and dramatically shattered the windshield. On yet another occasion Ed went zipping up a driveway, and before I could warn him, the ladder on the rack of the Dodge raked a low side awning and neatly ripped it off the house. Because of M&M I received my first traffic ticket: A trooper pulled me over for hauling downspout without a red flag. "But I'm just the driver, Officer. It's not my fault the warehouse didn't stick a flag on the back. My dad'll kill me for getting a ticket. Can't you let me off with a warning?" I had to pay the twenty-five dollars out of my own pocket.

Still, the most impressive mishap occurred late one afternoon when Alfie and I were working up on ladderjacks. Ladderjacks? Bear with me. Imagine two sixteen-foot-long railroad ties nailed to the side of a house; on each is a kind of mechanical bracket that can be cranked up and down, and into which one fits one or the other end of a fifteen-foot work scaffold. Typically, the siding man sits astride this bracket and in tandem with his partner cranks the whole scaffolding unit up or down to the level needed. Rather than work the crank all day, you lean a ladder against the raised scaffold and use it to scamper up or down after tools, water, what have you.

Well, on one particularly larky afternoon Alfie and I had been installing siding halfway up the side of a house and needed to crank to a higher level. It being after lunch, Alfie got it into his groggy head to race me. Not a good idea. The danger here is that the scaffolding plank can slide dangerously to one side or the other if it doesn't remain roughly horizontal. So naturally I had to crank like mad to keep up with my half-drunk coworker. Unfortunately, both of us, caught up in this stupid contest, forgot about the extension ladder, which grew more and more perpendicular to the ground as we moved the scaffold—Excelsior!—ever higher. By the time we both noticed what was happening, the ladder was swaying and standing virtually straight up and down. We tried to reach it in time, but our desperate movements provided just the push needed. For a moment, twenty-five feet of metal extension ladder trembled in the breeze and then slowly, with silent-movie perfection, fell backward into the huge picture window of the house next door.

Good times.

Still, half the kids in Lorain—the boys—hoped to "get into" the mill during the years when National Tube was hiring temporary summer help. So six months after I turned sixteen, following the usual paperwork and physical probings, I found myself being issued with prescription safety glasses, a green asbestos coat and pants, an orange hard hat and a locker. I was the lowest-grade laborer, class two, and the pay was slightly better than at M&M—but you could make time and a half or more if you worked double shifts. I labored in the mill's fuliginous world for two summers as a teenager.

Early that June, between my sophomore and junior years, my mother packed my work clothes into one paper sack and my lunch into another, and off I trudged to sweat for eight hours just like my dad. I would plod heavily, now in my very own steel-toed boots, across the blackened gravel of the small parking lot, flash my badge to the guard at the gate and make my way to the locker room.

On my first day I nearly got into another fight. Ten or fifteen men were plopped around the lunchroom table when I noticed that some louts were making fun of a round-faced, roly-poly guy with a crew cut. If not always, at least occasionally a righter of perceived wrongs, I told them to stop—even as the face of Lucius Johnson flashed through my mind. A showdown was avoided, however, for it soon grew obvious that as a newcomer I didn't understand about Georgie.

"Cool down, kid," said one grizzled millwright. "You're getting worked up over nothing. George don't care what we say. He's not loony, exactly, but he's not right in the head either."

Mentally retarded, nearing thirty, Georgie entirely lacked any reality check, inhabiting a world of his own, where daydreams swiftly modulated into detailed and vivid memories. One Monday he told me—the two of us had quickly become friends—that he'd just returned from a weekend cruise around the world. He constantly spoke about his girlfriend, a blond pinup whose picture he kept taped to his locker door. Once, out driving near the Oneil-Sheffield Shopping Center, I nearly ran the smiling dreamer down in the middle of the street, where he was recklessly—and fortunately wrecklessly—directing traffic.

Every so often I would glimpse this holy innocent in some dark corner of the plant, often quietly singing to himself like any Fool in Shakespeare. Sometimes he'd carry on conversations with the ether about his curvaceous hottie Miss Cindy. One afternoon, though,

Georgie arrived at work in tears, blubbering that his beloved had left him. "How could she?" he wailed. We all assured him that the foolish hussy would come crawling back. "Yeah, George, ain't many women could resist a handsome fellow like you." Georgie broke into a huge dopey smile. "Am I really handsome?" "Like Little Joe Cartwright on *Bonanza*," we said (though in fact he quite resembled the Paul Bunyanesque older brother Hoss). Happily, Miss Cindy returned home a day or two later, tearful with regret over leaving, even for a moment, a man so thoughtful and generous as George.

Which in truth he was. I have seldom enjoyed conversing with anyone so much. After all, we shared a passion for daydreaming and he possessed the enviable capacity to fully inhabit his wildest imaginings. At times I quite envied George. Who could not? Rumor had it that this grinning, simpleminded soul was able to keep his job mainly because his uncles were big men at U.S. Steel, one or two even in management. I don't really know. I hope Georgie lives and remains, now as then, untouched by time.

Old Martinez headed our little cleaning crew. As unoffical foreman, he would set us to work, clearing slag from some railroad tracks or sweeping up in the rolling mill, and then retire to a secluded bench or corner to nap for a few hours. Most of the time I sweated side by side with a handsome guy who hoped to be ordained a Baptist fundamentalist preacher. I've forgotten his name, but reveled in our disputations about religion and the moral life. We liked each other, even though he was exceedingly devout and I was then calling myself, with due pomposity, a rational humanist.

Much of the time our work unit spent its eight-hour shift deep underground. As the hot ingots, the size of minivans, scudded on railroad cars toward the rolling mill, they gradually cooled and a metallic skin would form on their surface. This scale would either fall off naturally or be knocked off, ending up on the floor of the underground refuse tunnels that ran beneath the railroad tracks. Our job was to shovel up this scrap, load it into wheelbarrows and roll these through the minelike passages to various open-air pits, where the accumulated waste metal would eventually be picked up by cranes and melted down again to form new ingots.

At its worst this work approached the life-threatening. We'd be sealed up in protective clothing, breathing through respirators, groping through smoky darkness and close to extremely high heat. If you wandered into one of the side chambers off the main tunnel, you had to be sure there wasn't an ingot sitting above your head, with a lump of scale waiting to drop off. In the mornings or afternoons I would step heavily down steel ladders into the dusty, subterranean half-light. With my partners, I'd start shoveling up the big chunks of metal, wheel my barrow for the equivalent of a city block, dump my load of scrap and then go back for more. I couldn't help but remember the summers I'd spent hauling firewood for my Uncle Henry. Once the larger shards were taken care of, we would push heavy industrial brooms to sweep clean the concrete flooring. In this netherworld Georgie liked to crawl away and dream about his sweetie. In this same Stygian darkness I would argue about the existence of God and the meaning of life. Perversely I came to like being a true Underground Man—the work felt real and I drove home bone-weary.

Best of all, I thrilled to a sense of masculine power when I directed the overhead crane operator in loading up the scrap. Most of this task was then managed purely by hand signals, though today factories usually employ walkie-talkies. With the proper flick of a wrist you could call over a huge-jawed bucket that would be slowly let down at your feet. It was like having Godzilla for a pet.

Now and again, we'd have to sweep up in the rolling mill, and here the work could be considerably more dangerous. "Son," my father warned, "you be real careful in there. And take those salt tablets. You don't want to get dizzy and pass out." All around us an assembly line of huge machines would be tirelessly pounding a hot ingot into a long thin pipe. The noise in a rolling mill is literally deafening: to talk you then needed to enter special rooms off the floor, since not even shouting could compete against the clangor and roar. There were frequent stories about people who'd lost fingers or limbs because of a moment's inattention, and after I'd spent a little time amid this Brobdingnagian machinery, I could see how easily it might happen. Even in the "safest steel mill in the world," as the sign outside the main gate proclaimed, there was no margin for error.

Occasionally we were detailed to the pickling vats, pools of sulfurous liquid that made you nauseated if you breathed the rotten-egg fumes too long. On my second summer, as a bricklayer's helper, we used to reline silolike vessels where the air was thick with graphite dust. Our respirators would clog or grow so hot and sticky that it was almost impossible to keep them on. Most of the full-time workers gave up on the damn things. But not me. On the first day at the start of my turn I had noticed that the ground was clean; eight hours later I was wading in three or four inches of graphite. I planned to live longer than my grandfather, who had died here at fifty-two from some nameless lung disease—at least in part because he didn't have the money to go to a hospital.

Let no one ever tell me that steelworkers—or auto workers or coal miners or truck farmers—don't deserve every dollar they earn "by the sweat of their brows." My father drained away his youth around the coke ovens, throwing shovelfuls of coal into hellish furnaces. The work was so hot and perilous that you could only do it for thirty minutes out of each hour, but you got a bonus in your paycheck. A job for a young man, a young man with a wife and new son. In subsequent years Dad worked as a skilled laborer, mainly in the

Four-Seamless Pipe Mill. Just before his retirement he became a steel checker, evaluating the quality of pipe turned out during each shift. It required the kind of expertise you pick up after three or four decades working shifts and time and a half.

One night at two in the morning I found myself high up on an exterior gantry, staring out at the expansive vista of National Tube through my grit-mottled prescription work glasses. White smoke poured from the stacks, orange fires burned off excess gas, dimly perceived workers far below me scurried by and in the distance wound the river, the Black River. A vision of Hell or of Mordor. And to finish that tableau, in the background I could hear the steady pounding of the rolling mill, like the beating heart of the damned.

I don't exaggerate. That summer I forgave my father everything: He could be overbearing and worse, but his soul-deadening labor gave me the time to read and to know that my life would be privileged compared to his. When writers talk about the "dark satanic mills," I know they're not just being poetical.

Chapter Ten

We have sought truth, and sometimes perhaps found it.
But have we had any fun?

—Benjamin Jowett

I remember almost nothing of my English classes after ninth grade. One male teacher preferred to keep pretty girls in the front-row seats on the off chance that they might languidly cross their legs and display a shapely thigh or a flash of pink underwear. He did make us write brief autobiographies—mine received a B, and the criticism that I'd devoted more than two-thirds of the paper to a hitchhiking trip to Pittsburgh. But I did reflect, in passing, on public education:

In first grade they teach you that Columbus discovered America, in second you learn that Columbus discovered America in 1492, and in third grade you discover that Christopher Columbus, an Italian, discovered America in 1492. This goes on getting more and more complicated until you reach seventh grade when you find out that Leif Ericsson discovered America.

In eleventh grade I regarded my literature teacher as another well-meaning disciplinarian, always questioning us about the color "symbolism" of *The Scarlet Letter* and *Moby-Dick*. Red, if I'm not mistaken, stood for passion, blood and sin, while the "unnatural" whiteness of the whale seemed rather ambiguous, but basically Not Good. I didn't much care for Hawthorne, though Melville has always appealed to my taste for the grandiose and orotund. I could once recite the entire opening paragraph of *Moby-Dick*, starting with "Call me Ishmael," and underscored and memorized several other long, metaphysical passages: "There are certain queer times and occasions in this strange mixed affair we call life when a man takes the whole universe to be but a vast practical joke, though the wit thereof he but dimly discerns, and more than suspects that the joke is at nobody's expense but his own." People would look at me queerly when I would pronounce such passages aloud. But I was used to such reactions by now.

During this same junior year I was appointed a class aide to Miss Delano, who taught twelfth-grade Honors English. Despite rather severe, black-framed eyeglasses, she was an attractive dark-haired young woman in her twenties, for whom I would grade papers and mimeograph exams. Normally, I would crouch at a table in a corner of her classroom and perform my clerical tasks while half listening to her discuss, say, Chaucer's "Miller's Tale." At the end of the year she somewhat bashfully presented me with a Cross pen and pencil set in silver chrome. To my regret, I found them too slender for my thick paw, so they have reposed these many years in one dresser drawer after another. Occasionally, I take them out and think about Miss Delano. Our relationship was perfectly normal and chaste, yet once or twice I detected a faint sexual buzz in myself. This must be common among teachers and favorite students. Of course, at this age I was erotically hypersensitive to begin with and Miss Delano *was* attractive.

My actual twelfth-grade English teacher, Mr. Japczynski, was a former paratrooper, lean and sinewy, with sunken cheeks and a quicksilver teaching style. In his class we memorized sections of Gray's "Elegy in a Country Churchyard," as well as lines from Pope and Milton. Here I first learned the rhetorical terms "oxymoron" ("cold fire") , "litotes" ("not unbeautiful") and "epizeuxis" (repetition for emphasis: "O dark, dark, dark amid the blaze of noon"). We also studied and analyzed *Oedipus the King* in Bernard Knox's translation (meeting the classicist in Washington, some fifteen years later, was like being introduced to Sophocles himself). J, as Japczynski signed his name, enjoyed spelling and vocabulary games, and sometimes offered books like that medical classic, Paul de Kruif's *Microbe Hunters*, as prizes. I nearly always won, for spelling then appeared to be my only natural talent: According to my file, in fourth grade I spelled at the level of a second-year college student—this, sniffed Tom, was just one more proof that I was an idiot savant.

On Fridays after school Tom, Ed and I would congregate in Ray's basement, which we called Lethargy Hall after a similar playroom in Robert Heinlein's *Stranger in a Strange Land*. Nothing useful or truly productive was permitted there. For hours we would play a lightning-fast card game called Sixty-Six, something like Euchre or simplified bridge, with bidding, marriages and tricks. While the cards were dealt for each hand, we would lounge at the round oak table, under a low-slung light, imagining ourselves as real-life gamblers. Usually we'd start our weekly game after watching modern spies Napoleon Solo and Ilya Kuryakin in *The Man from U.N.C.L.E* and nineteenth-century spy James West in *The Wild, Wild West*, then interrupt the action around ten P.M. for a quick run to Yala's for a half-mushroom, half-pepperoni pizza, which we'd bring back and wolf down with Orange Crush. At 11:30 we'd generally tune into the late-night horror movie hosted by the kitschy, tongue-in-cheek "Ghoulardi." At other times we'd just joke around, strum a guitar or fiddle with various "scientific" projects. A natural-born tinkerer and inventor, Ray constructed a primitive laser that could burst balloons; another time, he welded up a motorized minibike. Every so often, we would risk sampling Mr. Schwarz's homemade wine.

Sometimes, on a Saturday night, the Four Musketeers would go out cruising. Occasionally we'd even take two vehicles: Ed would drive the M&M pickup, with Ray's Honda 160 motorcycle lashed down in the back; Tom and I would rev up his '64 GTO, Li'l Blue Tiger (three two-barrel carburetors and a nonstandard 429-cubic-inch engine, the biggest then made by Detroit). Roaring down the dark streets, we felt that we were ready for any adventure, that together we could—let's be scrupulously honest here—conquer the world. Until the advent of our global regency, we were usually content to ride up to the McDonald's near Lakeview Park, then drift back along Lake Road, follow Broadway south to the 21st Street bridge and then turn around and do it again, the radio blasting out the Righteous Brothers, the Beatles or the Beach Boys. Once we swooped down on a young woman, stranded with a flat tire. Would-be ravishers? Hardly. We pretended to be an elite NASCAR pit crew as we changed her tire in under four minutes.

Now and again, Lance, my old hitchhiking buddy, would come along too. Being the most openly sex-maddened of our group, he formulated the three cardinal rules of girl-watching: Never judge a chick at night, from the back or at a distance. This seems obvious and sensible advice, but back then it struck me as the worldly, practical wisdom of an urbane boulevardier.

Though I now labored every summer at M&M or National Tube, during eleventh grade I also latched on to a Sunday afternoon gig at the Tick-Tock Lounge. From two to five I would be locked in, all alone, to mop and buff the floors, swab out the kitchen and scour the bar's noxious restrooms. For this scut work I earned five dollars a week—cold cash—and was permitted to eat Slim Jims, Barbecue

Chips and beer nuts to my stomach's content (or distress). Best of all, I could keep any money lying forgotten under the tables and metal stools.

It was, in fact, a pretty good job. Sometimes I'd switch on the jukebox—"It's now or never," the King would croon at full blast—or I'd sip RC Cola and munch away on bar snacks until I felt vaguely nauseated. Nearly every week I'd find money on the floor. At the very least this might amount to a dollar in change, but a couple of times I picked up five-spots; and once I actually swept up a crumpled twenty-dollar bill. Of course, some of Lorain's more sophisticated oenophiles would also come knocking now and again, pleading desperately for a drink or even—"for the love of God, buddy"—a shot of Thunderbird. "Come on, kid, help me out, just a swallow." Once a ravaged-looking doxy pounded at the door and screamed at me, while her two children stared white with fear from inside an old station wagon. "Open up this goddam door, you sonofabitch." But I was really locked in and couldn't open up even if I had wanted. (In retrospect, this all seems highly illegal and dangerous.) Still, I did contrive to jimmy a rear window a bit and through the crack would sometimes pass beef jerky and candy to Ray and Ed when they'd make a pit stop on their way out to Tom's place.

So much of high school now survives only in brief, strobe-lit flashes: Listening to "Pretty Woman" (Cleveland's No. 1 hit for thirteen straight weeks) while I struggle with quadratic equations; playing joke-tennis at the park while wearing roller skates; reading *The Magic Mountain* in the backyard after a Sunday spent installing aluminum siding; popping the clutch on our '58 Ford and practicing "Bat-turns" on deserted roads late at night; playing the basketball game Pig with my dad and realizing, with a shock, how much he loved me.

I do remember an early morning summer school course in world history. One day during the first week the teacher happened to murmur to himself, "No man is an island," and then, on a whim, wonder aloud if anyone in the class knew the origin of the quotation. He was just about to continue his review of Egyptian civilization when a hand went up. "Yes?" he asked. "John Donne, *Devotions Upon Emergent Occasions.*" I paused, savoring the stunned silence, then delivered the capper: "Number Seventeen." Groans all around. Dirda, again. The teacher, however, was properly flabbergasted and, in a fit of enthusiasm, announced that I must be the smartest kid ever to attend Admiral King (loud mutterings from Tom at this point). In fact, brains had nothing to do with this trick, just pure luck. A day or two previous I had picked up a ratty Scribner's paperback of Hemingway's novel *For Whom the Bell Tolls* and had copied out his epigraph from Donne's most celebrated chunk of prose, then checked up on its source. "No man is an island, entire of itself; every man is a piece of the continent, a part of the main. . . . Therefore never send to know for whom the bell tolls. It tolls for thee."

With such a highbrow reputation to maintain, I needed to turn in an extraordinary term paper at the end of the three-week class. I worked like mad on the life and ideas of Jean-Jacques Rousseau. First I read a Dell paperback of the *Confessions*, indulging myself in sensual Venetian reverie in my favorite section, where the young Jean-Jacques makes an assignation with a celebrated Italian courtesan. When she undresses, he notices a birthmark on her breast and is taken aback. Properly offended, she gathers up her clothes and spits out to her abashed would-be lover: "*Lascia le donne, e studia la matematica*"—"Give up women and study mathematics." Oh, to meet such a goddess!

Because the Lorain libraries didn't carry much Enlightenment philosophy—there wasn't, apparently, a lot of demand for it—I rode my bike to the Elyria Public Library (eight or so miles), where I spent an afternoon taking notes on, of all things, Rousseau's idiosyncratic

Profession of Faith of a Savoyard Vicar. I remember dust motes swirling in the five P.M. sunlight. The following Saturday I pedaled thirteen miles down Route 58 to Oberlin College and skimmed through a half dozen secondary works on this founder of romanticism. Now I can recollect nothing at all about the paper, beyond my adolescent conviction that it was the best thing I had ever written.

Maybe. Certainly I was honing my descriptive skills on another Rousseau. For some class I penned a one-paragraph description of Henri Rousseau's painting "Rain in the Jungle":

Wild foliage struggling, uselessly, against pounding wind and rain. Fronds, broken and swept away by the sudden storm. Upwards and half hidden by the huge arms and fingers of tropical trees, the sky rests an impassive gray, a drab broken only by an occasional and momentary blaze of light. Partially concealed by shadow and vegetation, a once-proud tiger crawls the jungle floor, fearfully searching for some shelter from Nature's unexpected onslaught. And everywhere there is the rain.

I think this reasonably good for a kid, but I received only a B. Teachers maintained standards in those days.

Though cocky enough in English and history classes, I still grew visibly nervous whenever required to deliver a real speech. Yes, I listened to great actors enunciate and I practiced declaiming aloud to my bathroom tiles and I studied Dale Carnegie's manual and I copied out inspirational remarks onto three-by-five cards: "The ability to speak well, will, by its nature, develop self-confidence, a logical mind, an ability to think quickly and accurately and a talent for expressing one's thoughts with clarity and efficacy." But none of this helped enough.

So I enrolled for a speech class with Mr. Bakalar, a.k.a. mellow-toned radio personality Ron Scott. We practiced oral interpretation

(I performed Edward Lear's "The Jumblies"—"their heads are blue and their hands are green"—to an uncomprehending audience) and debate (how we studied *U.S. News & World Report!*). We were taught to give impromptu speeches with only a single note card, and we weren't supposed to look at that very often. I would practice in front of my parents' bedroom mirror studying my delivery, willing myself to stop shuffling back and forth, to stand tall, smile and survey my audience. Gradually I improved, but for all my efforts in Mr. Bakalar's class, not to mention those hours of funeral orations and soliloquies to which my bathroom fixtures were histrionically subjected, it would be years before I really came to enjoy speaking in public.

Sometimes, as I recited poems or reviewed my speeches on my morning walks to Admiral King, I would find myself interrupted by an auditory hallucination. Strolling along, I'd abruptly hear a faint voice calling, "Mike, Mike." For a while I was convinced, and even hopeful, that a particular sidewalk square was actually some sort of time machine or space portal and that one sunshiny day I would simply disappear from this world, like Mitch in "Faster and Faster." Wasn't it a dulcet-toned girl's voice that whispered to me? Surely I was about to be drawn into a romantic fantasy realm where I would pledge to rescue from an evil fate some analogue of Thuvia, Princess of Mars. Obviously, Edgar Rice Burroughs and Frank Edwards had marked my subconscious more deeply than I knew. Or possibly I suffered from incipient schizophrenia.

At three-thirty, when school let out, I would amble part of the way home with a classmate or two. One day I told Charles Bertolami, in later life the dean of the dental school at the University of California at San Francisco, that he should henceforth be known as Pablo. "Yes, you are definitely a Pablo, not a Charles." And thus I called him ever after. When Dennis Delfino announced that he wished to become my Boswell, I thoughtlessly said okay. Dennis was convinced of my incipient greatness—if alive, how disappointed he must finally be—and wished to record for grateful posterity my observations, witticisms and offhand remarks. What inanities, I wonder, may yet lay preserved in some forgotten notebook? At any event, after a few days I persuaded him to stop this nonsense by presenting him with the holograph of my epic dramatic masterpiece, *The Wheat Farmer*, a searing indictment of governmental injustice and the evils of agricultural subsidies. At the tragedy's end the hardscrabble family inevitably loses its farm and all that they've worked so heartbreakingly to build.

The Wheat Farmer was performed as "reader's theater" in a class at Admiral King and reveals a hitherto unsuspected penchant for naturalism and even some political insight. Yet seldom during my school years did I ever think about the issues that would preoccupy me and my classmates in college: oppressive government, civil rights, the war in Vietnam, the whole social/sexual/psychedelic revolution that was about to make life so interesting (though mine in only a very tangential way). Instead I produced a play that could have been some newly unearthed juvenilia by a fourth-rate Arthur Miller or even Upton Sinclair, one of whose Lanny Budd novels I happened to pick up about this time.

Upton Sinclair! Lanny Budd! Not only eager to read apparently anything at all, I was also constantly on the lookout for ways to absorb prose and poetry more effectively, more professionally. I am, for instance, a relatively slow, if persistent, reader. Much of the time I move my lips while silently sounding out words and sentences. So, when AK—how I later longed for a jersey with the number 47— offered an extracurrricular speed reading course, based on the Evelyn Wood methods, I immediately signed up. Here I was taught to scan a text for verbal units, shifting the eyes down the page in little skips, like a chamois of the Alps leaping from crag to crag. In fact, we were taught to bounce a pencil from eye-unit to eye-unit.

My basic speed for enjoying light fiction waffled between three hundred and four hundred words a minute. By consciously pushing myself, I could raise this to seven hundred or eight hundred, even to twelve hundred words per minute for short bursts, though the eye tracking tended to bring on a violent headache if persisted with for any length of time. As a test I did zip through Ray Bradbury's *A Medicine for Melancholy* in forty minutes. Certainly speed-reading can be a useful skill, worth acquiring, and in a pinch I can now harvest mere information almost as fast as I can turn pages. But I soon revert to my usual slowpoke, meandering pace. The pleasure of reading wasn't speed, I decided, it was sound, the resonance of a narrative voice in your head. One wanted to listen with appropriate deliberateness to the author's sentences, to savor the nuances and admire the flourishes. Wasn't it Thoreau who claimed that books should be read as deliberately as they are written?

Still seeking to better myself as a reader, one day I bought a remaindered education textbook called *Keys to Learning*. Among its essays by Emerson and Santayana, its extracts from Rabelais and Montaigne, was an article by Mortimer J. Adler entitled "How to Mark a Book." Over the years, I must have returned to this overtly inspirational polemic twenty times. In it Adler asserts that to honor a book one must destroy it: The crisp, mint copy on a shelf is simply an *objet d'art* or consumer artifact, without inner significance. The books that matter are those we have wrestled with, like Jacob and the angel, those we have questioned and argued with and been persuaded by. The best way to create a proper agonistic encounter with any text is to mark it up.

In the course of his article Adler describes his own system for interrogating books and I soon adopted aspects of it. I started making lines in the margin next to quotable sentences, scribbling comments (dutifully sophomoric) at the top or bottom of the page, sometimes listing key points on the endpapers. I couldn't, however, bring myself to dog-ear pages, and after a few years I gradually gave up pens and switched entirely to pencils. Was it George Steiner who claimed that an intellectual was someone who couldn't read without a pencil in his hand? For me, it had to be a Ticonderoga No. 2—Nabokov's choice, I later discovered—or even the darker, softer, harder-to-find No. 1.

Naturally, I soon looked for other books by Mortimer J. Adler and eventually plowed through parts of his youthful opus, *The Mansions of Philosophy*. So far as I know, I got absolutely nothing from it. Eventually, I acquired a fat paperback copy of Adler's amplified treatise *How to Read a Book*, but found it diffuse and disappointing. His mind was simply too dry and Cartesian for a youthful follower of Rousseau. What I liked best were the reading lists at the back. These naturally resulted in a more-than-casual interest in the Adler-coedited series, *The Great Books of the Western World*.

It's hard to resist poking fun at *The Great Books of the Western World*. The first edition, published by the Encyclopedia Britannica and edited by Robert M. Hutchins and Adler, appeared in 1952 and quickly passed into American folklore as a symbol of 1950s intellectual kitsch. Marketed door-to-door like encyclopedias or vacuum cleaners, it was Chicago's updated answer to Charles Eliot Norton's Harvard Classics—once a mainstay of libraries and famous for its advice to read fifteen minutes a day. Hutchins and Adler promulgated reading as a "great conversation" and sold the sets to earnest, well-meaning parents who were talked into the rosy notion that an investment of $375 (and up) just might deliver instant culture. Naturally, the kids would Do Better in School. The set itself would look really spiffy in the living room, where it would also impress the neighbors. And, of course, the family would start to spend long evenings over steaming mugs of cocoa discussing whether man is by nature good or evil, why Plato banished poets from his ideal state and just what the heck Ptolemy was driving at in the *Almagest*.

Still, after culture vulture Dwight Macdonald delivered his slash-and-burn critique, "The Book-of-the-Millennium Club," you would have thought no one would ever again consider buying *The Great Books*. Not surprisingly, though, the young salesman, in short-sleeved white shirt and dark tie, who called at my parents' house one afternoon neglected to mention the outmoded translations, the ugly double columns of type, the lack of explanatory notes and the 102 arid essays (by Mort) in *The Syntopicon*, that wrong-headed index to the so-called "Great Ideas" (among them Love, God and Truth). Instead he offered the kind of snake-oil enticements common to all door-to-door fast-talkers: easy monthly payments, a handsome bookcase thrown in, a free dictionary. I admired his patter and remembered it, a few years later, when I took a summer job selling Fuller Brush products.

Still, none of these "special gifts" would have counted much with my father, or my mother, who was working part-time on the floor at Grant's department store. These serious books cost serious money. Of course, to me at sixteen, *The Great Books* sounded like heaven in fifty-four volumes. But I knew that my folks would never plunk down nearly four hundred dollars to buy them.

Then the salesman delivered his final pitch:

"And, besides the books and the dictionary and the bookcase, each of your children is eligible to compete in *The Great Books* essay contest. One child per year. First prize is five thousand dollars, second a thousand and third five hundred. Oh, yes, a set of *The Great Books* is also donated in the winning child's name to his or her school."

My mother's eyes lit up at the mention of contests. She understood about contests. Hadn't she just sold more Grant's blankets, during some nationwide competition, than anyone else in the district? With sudden inspiration, I took my parents aside.

"Mom, Dad, if you buy these books for me, I guarantee that I'll win at least the five-hundred-dollar prize. We'll come out a hundred ahead. And, who knows, maybe the girls might win too."

My dad looked at my mom. They both looked at me.

"Really, I promise I'll get the money back. I know I can do it."

They swallowed hard and ordered the books.

Need I describe the exhilaration of opening the two huge cartons that arrived a few weeks later? Still, even in my besotted state, I recognized that there was something sanctimonious about the set: The Great Authors looked official, approved, not so much enshrined as embalmed. These were not the sort of books one read under the covers with a flashlight. For all of Robert Hutchins's humanistic vision of famous writers and thinkers talking to one another across the ages, the presentation and design of *The Great Books* set invited worship rather than discussion. And even though Mortimer J. Adler's most famous essay encouraged people to read with pencil in hand, it would obviously feel like sacrilege to doodle on the thin Bible-paper pages of this costly investment.

Investment indeed, for I had a serious job to do. And one I couldn't mess up on or play around with. After duly passing several factual examinations, I earned the chance to cogitate about some of the less lofty of the Great Ideas, answering questions like, "What is the role of the gods in *The Odyssey*?" and "Does tragedy require sympathetic characters with whom we may identify?"

I won five hundred dollars. In the next six or so years my three sisters also passed through the *GBWW* gauntlet. Altogether the Dirdas took in twenty-five hundred dollars; four sets of *The Great*

Books of the Western World were donated to Admiral King High School. My youngest sister Linda—who picked up a thousand dollars—talked the AK library officials into letting her keep the volumes she won. At that point, the school didn't really want any more *Great Books*.

Nor did I—at least not all the time. For some reason—my increasingly acute interest in girls? a desire to shock my teachers as in the days of Miss Raymond?—I decided to write my junior year's major English paper not on, say, W. C. Bryant's "Thanatopsis" or *Huckleberry Finn*, but on *True Confessions* stories.

All my life I'd stealthily checked out the covers on these lurid magazines, but had never actually read any of them. So I gradually gathered a stack of issues from thrift stores, settled in for a long afternoon and whipped through a dozen, employing all my newly tested speed-reading skills. The grainy illustrations—disheveled beds, women with pageboy haircuts and blouses open to show off white brassieres, ferrety-looking boyfriends—promised more graphic sex than the stories delivered, but after several hours I began to detect recurrent narrative patterns and motifs. Perfect. For English I would set forth what Vladimir Propp might have called "The Morphology of the Pulp Romance Story."

Years earlier, I had wondered about girls and reading. What did they find appealing in novels written by men or focusing on heroes like Tarzan and Sherlock Holmes? How did they engage with these books? Wanting to be a Compleat Reader, I needed to better understand both women readers and the kind of stories so many of them apparently cared for.

Like my Rousseau monograph, this masterpiece of structuralist criticism disappeared many years ago. But what I remember is the recognition that a *True Confessions/Modern Romance* plot drew on some basic wish fulfilments, not unlike the louche paperbacks I occasionally found abandoned at job sites or in the steel plant's locker rooms. In my favorite *TC* story a tenderhearted young girl is burdened in life with a harelip—or was it a cleft palate?—and distorted facial features. Despite these drawbacks, Mary falls in love with a penniless young student who hopes to pursue a medical career. He seems genuinely interested in her, despite the disfigurement—until some misunderstanding compels Mary to believe that he simply feels sorry for her. So she disappears from his life, moves to the big city and spends the next ten years washing floors and cleaning apartments, carefully saving all her wages. By her late twenties Mary has accumulated enough to afford surgery on her face, surgery that may completely correct her defects and even, quite possibly, make her beautiful. Or at least as beautiful as a nearly thirty-year-old drudge, with callused hands, red knees and stringy hair, can be. Mary lacks self-esteem.

Any reader past the age of eleven can see where this will end. In the hospital the night before the operation our heroine finally meets the wonder worker who is to perform her life-altering procedure. It is, of course, the young man, now an eminent surgeon. When he realizes just who lies there in the bed, he breaks down in front of the bewildered scrubwoman. For all these years young Dr. Kildare has loved her, has never forgotten the kindness she showed him when he was poor, has tried for years to find her again. He will perform the surgery the next day and exert all his powers, but he tells her it doesn't matter: I love the person inside you and always will. The story ends with Mary leaning back into her hospital pillow, indifferent now to the operation that will alter her features. She has found true love.

This structure—essentially that of the fairy tale, in this case bits of *Beauty and the Beast*, the medieval legend of the Loathly Lady and *Cinderella*—was repeated in numerous stories. I carefully prepared an elaborate grid of possible narrative options, a kind of hypertext flow-chart. It was, I thought, an impressive and original piece of research. I hope I got an A.

An aside: Many years later, as a grown-up book reviewer, Michael Dirda, Ph.D., spent several months reading romance novels—Harle-quins and Regencies, both innocent and saucy—partly in homage to this early fascination with love stories and to learn how the genre worked at longer stretches. Though formulaic still, I found many of these books—especially Georgette Heyer's—hallmarked by consider-able wit, cleverness and narrative care. Not only did I enjoy them, but I also started my Valentine's Day essay about romances this way: "Here is where I finally lose all my credibility as a critic. . . ."

Chapter Eleven

Every angel is terrifying.
—Rilke

One evening at M&M Home Improvement, in the summer before our senior year, Ed and I were unloading tools and coil from the bed of the pickup truck. We had our shirts off, and as this was late in the summer our torsos were brown and muscular. All at once I glanced up and noticed a slatternly young woman with dark brown hair and high cheekbones gazing at me from one of the balconies of the back apartments owned by old man Muzick.

She was, I later learned or guessed, the swamp-angel wife of a middle-aged drunk who sometimes worked with us to pay off rental debts. The intentness of her staring eyes, the way her cheap white cotton blouse hugged her breasts as she leaned over the railing and the tightness of her jeans—"painted on," as we used to say—struck me like a blow or a revelation. Here was the kind of woman it would be mad, bad and dangerous to know. And yet . . .

I suppose she was in her early twenties, and I never saw her again. But this displaced Eula Varner, as Faulkner calls the irresistible honeypot of his Snopes Trilogy, long troubled my nights as the alluring incarnation of the innately, ineffably sexual: "At first sight of her you felt a kind of shock of gratitude just for being alive and being male at the same instant with her in space and time, and then in the next second and forever after a kind of despair . . . because forever after nothing less would ever do."

Back in ninth and tenth grades I had gazed from afar on the beauties of my class—Lois Gradisek, the blond All-American cheerleader; the dark-haired and sultry Angela Ortenzi; the flirtatious, knowing Linda Wearsch. But these sirens sang not for me. They dated club presidents and fashion plates like Dennis Savinsky. No, I would need to wait awhile for my first date, for my first kiss.

In the meantime I had discovered that certain books and magazines encouraged reveries of sweet sensual abandon. My dad had a stash of *True* and *Cavalier*, hardly erotic but definitely suggestive. For truly racy material, though, you needed to brave Rusine's Cigar Store (and illicit betting parlor) up on Broadway. Crammed with "books," including essential instructional manuals—*Hypnotism Made Simple, How to Pick Up Women, Mastering Judo* and *Streetfighting with Razors*—even many of its ancient paperbacks were sealed in cellophane, like the hardcore girlie magazines. As a result, you couldn't read the texts, but you could stare at the book covers: Teenage sluts in stiletto heels cocking their miniskirted hips while a caption announced, unnecessarily, "They couldn't say no"; errant wives in negligees enticing youthful grinning handymen up the winding bedroom stairs; drugged blondes with red, red lips, torn white slips and wrists shackled to the metal posts of a cheap hotel bed; titles such as *Sex Slave* and the even more laconic *Nympho*. At my bravest I could just drum up the courage to buy Aldous Huxley's *Those Barren Leaves*; I knew it was literature, but the cover—two lovers, swooning in ecstasy, naked splendor in the grass—made this witty novel about country-house intellectuals look like Grace Metalious's notorious *Peyton Place* or Jacqueline Susann's best-seller *Valley of the Dolls*.

For no one could ever actually read a truly dirty book, right? Such filth was only for grizzled, shambling guys of about fifty-seven, smelling of drink and drooling as they leered. Right? Not for a smart kid who read classics. Right? Right?

One Sunday morning I decided to take a walk up to Central Park, probably intending to jog around the baseball field during one of my periodic efforts at self-improvement. The morning was cool and damp, for a thunderstorm had raged the night before and the grass and rocks still glistened with rain. After I reached the park, I began to cross a gravel lot—a favorite trysting spot for local teenagers—when I noticed a white splotch on one of the big boulders along its edge. I strolled over and discovered that the splotch was a paperback, turned face down. I flipped it over with my foot. Its title was *Candy*.

The book was entirely soaked through with rain and its pages were a solid brick of wet pulp. Softly parted red lips graced the white cover and I recognized a seriously Dirty Book. This was confirmed by a bold statement that this paperback was an unexpurgated reproduction of the Olympia Press edition, first published in Paris. Those infinitely suggestive words, "unexpurgated" and "Paris," convinced me that here was a treasure worth saving.

To sneak the book past the vigilant eye of my mother required me to stuff the wet thing under my shirt. After a cheery, "I'm back," and a response of, "So soon?" I immediately scurried into my room. That door, of course, couldn't be locked—we never allowed that sort of thing in my family and it would have aroused immediate suspicion that Something Improper was going on—so I proceeded immediately to my little bathroom. This door could be locked, and I did so, yelling out that I was going to take a quick bath after my exercise. While I ran the water into the tub, I pried off the metal vent to the heat register with my pocketknife, then carefully wedged the book inside. Not only an ideal hiding place, the register would also provide the means to dry out the soggy pages. I need only wait a few hours for the furnace to do its work. I thumbed the thermostat up to eighty.

Later that afternoon, when my parents and sisters had gone out, I retrieved my treasure, only to discover that it had accordioned out to three times its normal thickness. The pages were rippled and the binding loose. However, the text was dry and, most important of all, completely readable.

Nowadays, *Candy* is regarded as a sixties semi-classic: a comic novel that uses, exaggerates and undermines many of the conventions of pornography; in short an updated *Candide*. Doubtless university classes study the textual variants among early editions—when did Maxwell Kenton disappear and Terry Southern/Mason Hoffenberg acknowledge their authorship?—while professors and students chuckle over the darling girl's encounter with her schoolteacher ("the burdens—the needs of a man are so deep and so—aching"), the hunchback ("Give me your hump"), and the Swami. The leitmotif phrase "Good grief, it's Daddy" has become, if not quite famous, then at least fondly recalled. But when I read the book, lying on a bathroom floor, while hot air blew on me from a ventless register, I utterly missed the humor. My blood was racing and my heart was pounding, my hands felt clammy and my face flush. Other parts of my body experienced comparable excitement. Here was the stuff that adolescent dreams were made of.

I raced through the novel, eyes growing wider and wider, all the way to Candy's erotic epiphany on the final page. Finished, I slipped the sinful book back into its hiding place and immediately surrendered myself to shame and guilt. It was one thing to glimpse a bare-breasted pinup, like those on the Ridge Tool calendars in Max's garage. But to read, indeed to see quite vividly in one's mind's eye, sexual acts of unspeakable deliciousness, was quite another. What should I do?

If I kept the book around, eventually I would weaken and reread it. That would obviously never do. Yet I couldn't destroy a book. Maybe I should just return it to the park. But what if a younger, less iron-resolved kid found it, and embarked on a life of depravity as a result? God, what if a girl found it! Or even one of my sisters! No, the book just had to go. I would give it to Tom.

Who, of course, read it and passed it on to Ray, who read it and handed it to Ed, who read it and lent it to Lance . . . Eventually, everyone in my circle had read *Candy*. Tom alone thought it quite funny—in retrospect, he must have been considerably more sophisticated than I was as a teenager.

Soon thereafter rumors proliferated of other Dirty Books, usually to be found down in the dark corners of dank basements. Piled under old issues of *Argosy* and other male magazines, their covers picturing big-breasted, come-hither babes in fishnets and garters, these 1950s and 1960s paperbacks are now highly collectible. For their cover art. They may seem tame compared to the photo spreads in today's *Cosmopolitan* or *Maxim*, but as surely as any madeleine they will induce languorous thoughts in almost any middle-aged heterosexual male. Back then, somebody once handed me a cheap novel—was it called *Big Sister?*—about how an innocent sorority girl is transformed into a sex-mad lesbian. I didn't dare to even open that: One had, after all, to preserve some standards or civilization would fall prey to ravaging maniacs, slavering with unrestrained lust. A terrible thing, obviously, though my uneasy dreams suggested that I might secretly feel somewhat differently. I couldn't help but recall again those troubling horror movies in which the innocent heroines were drugged, hypnotized or brainwashed into seducing whomever their master told them to.

And they did it. Gladly, grateful to serve as a luscious sexual plaything. Good grief!

Shortly after discovering *Candy*, though I doubt any causal link, I was elected my high school's representative to Boy's State. At this "mock" state government "youths" run for elected office, establish laws and generally learn about how our legislators supposedly work. Honored to be selected, I nonetheless judged it of paramount importance to prove that the emissary from Admiral King, the roughest and meanest high school in Ohio, was no sissy nerd in glasses. So along with my clothes I clandestinely packed (1) a bottle of elderberry wine, courtesy of my friend Ray, who swiped it from his father, and (2), a copy of *Fanny Hill*, more accurately titled *Memoirs of a Woman of Pleasure*.

After so many years, I can no longer recollect where I acquired that softcover edition of John Cleland's eighteenth-century erotic classic. I would never have had the nerve to buy it at Rusine's: "And along with the Milky Way and the Chiclets and the blue ballpoint I'd like that, uh, paperback way up on the rack there. Yes, that one with the girl lifting up her petticoats. . . ." No, impossible. I probably found the novel on one of my periodic visits to Clarice's or the Salvation Army; it seems unlikely that the St. Vincent de Paul charity shop would have allowed it on their discriminating shelves. Doubtless, I hid the book among a stack of Perry Mason mysteries (*The Case of the Curious Canary, The Case of the Careless Cupid, The Case of the Very Nervous School Boy*) or other even more innocuous paperbacks, all priced at a nickel or dime apiece.

Boy's State took place in Athens, at Ohio University—notorious as a party school ("If you kick the bushes, the bushes kick back"). I soon settled into its freewheeling spirit. On my second day there, my roommate—an earnest goody-goody student with, as he reminded me, quite serious political ambitions—wearily returned from a hard day on the convention floor to find me sitting, at my collegiate ease, sipping red wine from a jelly jar and studiously perusing Miss Hill's autobiography. This young Dan Quayle, or whatever his name was, reacted with a satisfying gasp, and immediately began to foam and sputter that I would be immediately thrown out of Boy's State if discovered. Moreover, he felt morally obligated to turn in such a miscreant as myself, obviously not of the mettle or principles appropriate to our juvenile government.

By this time, however, half the dorm seemed to know that Dirda possessed both alcohol and filth, so my room quickly filled with model students eager to sin with Fanny Hill or sip some homemade wine. Seizing my chance, in the best can-do spirit of Boy's State, I sold shots of red for fifty cents and ten minutes with the *Memoirs of a Woman of Pleasure* for, appropriately, a quarter. (I had grown up hearing, from older female relatives, the melodious phrase, "She's nothing but a two-bit chippy.") Had I been even smarter I should have swapped my contraband for votes and, like a northern Huey Long, gotten myself elected Boy's State governor. That, after all, is the American way. Ultimately, my week in Athens—for no one blabbed on me and I escaped expulsion—left me with a rather jaundiced view of our political process: Every person and principle was for sale, like any eighteenth-century whore. It was just a matter of finding the right price.

I must confess, however, that Miss Fanny proved rather a comedown erotically after the gladsome delights of Ms. Candy. Cleland's formal and somewhat euphemistic language struck me as tiresome, while the brutally frank presentation of various sexual tableaux lacked what one might call, strangely enough, romance. I never even finished the book, finding it, all in all, repetitive and boring. Like bad sex.

Still, dirty books might indeed be found anywhere, not that I, a sensitive moralist by nature, ever went looking for them. But they were there, on the periphery of my reading life. One summer I was working at a construction site and unearthed, near some railroad tracks, half hidden in a pile of slag, a copy of a particularly trashy paperback in which a daughter deliberately, rather than accidentally (as with Candace Christian), seduces her father. I read a few pages, finding the story repulsive in content, poorly written and utterly arousing: I tossed the book into an open coal car without any hesitation—after I'd finished it. Sad to say, while I've forgotten most of the details in even favorite novels, I can still recall with sharp vivacity the breathless fervor of the heroine when she achieves her goal. Truly, our hearts are as dark as the pit of Acheron.

Though I first experienced the conscious twitchings of inchoate desire in elementary school when I beheld Phyllis Armelie, romance had arrived back in eighth grade with Paula Shagovac. Paula was a snubnosed, slightly freckle-faced girl with light brown hair and the best figure in the Advanced Class. I would hold her tight at parties as we shuffled in dark basements to the sounds of *Dream Dancing* by, I think, Ray Conniff and his orchestra. For hours we would lock hands behind each other's waists and slowly sway to the music, our bodies hot and tight beneath our clothes.

For some reason, though, Paula's didn't seem quite the right lips, albeit full and probably willing, upon which to expend my precious first kiss. I should save myself for just the right girl. Such priggishness and moral vanity is more common than sometimes imagined among adolescents. But then my father never spoke to me about any aspect of sex—a failure for which I was grateful—and my mother only warned me, time and again, to be a "good boy."

At any event, Paula and I drifted apart, leading me to spend the first three years of high school aching with unappeased lust.

There were, of course, tentative minuets around one girl or another. I once rode my bike over to Nancy Cadwallader's and sat down on the side of the road to talk with her. My sister Pamela, visiting a friend, glimpsed me and immediately made up a taunting song about "sittin' on the curb with Nancy." Another time I visited Leslie Popa at her house up near Goldberg's and wasted an hour leaning on my handlebars before she glanced out the window and noticed me. But only when I started wearing contact lenses at sixteen—after much pleading—did I gain any real confidence that I might not be utterly repulsive to the female sex.

In my sophomore year I impulsively joined the "popcorn crew" for the Admiral King home football games. This elite culinary team consisted largely of students who were neither athletes nor members of the band yet who wanted to be part of the "excitement of the fall sports season," as the principal announced on the public address system. Essentially, we ran the concession stand under the cement bleachers at George Daniel Field, selling Coke, candy and popcorn. It probably sounds like Nerd's Corner.

I can vividly recall my first afternoon on the crew, leaving school early to hustle over to the stadium to set up our equipment. As a bunch of us popped our very first batch of corn, one of the senior girls started singing folk songs, to which we all joined in. "Michael, row the boat ashore . . ." Then somebody launched into a humorous ditty, which I have, alas, never been able to entirely expunge from memory. It began "Boil that cabbage down, boys, turn the old keg 'round" and gradually built to the elegantly concise yet heart-rending chorus: "Workin', workin', workin', workin', / Workin', workin', workin'." We belted out this nonsense in harmony as we heated oil and connected the CO_2 canisters for the pop machines.

One senior treated me with particular kindness. Tall, with short blond hair, Margaret almost quivered with playfulness and vivacity. I always tried to hang out as near to her as possible, yet couldn't of course aspire to be anything but her puppy-dog admirer. I was, after all, only a sophomore. Moreover, we only saw each other amid chaos: At halftime Coke and Seven-Up would slosh everywhere, the cry of "Hot stuff" would resound, and people would bump into each other as we hurriedly slung together hot dogs and buns, handed out boxes of popcorn and collected dimes and quarters.

Still, Margaret inspired me to write a poem called—what else?— "Unrequited Love":

When I think of her, my heart begins to beat once more;
When I say her name, my whole being is delighted;
When I see her, life begins anew.

Ah, to hold her hand would be my greatest thrill,
But that shall never be for it is not within Thy will;
For she is older by two years than I can ever be,
And so my love can come to naught but misery for me.

And although I know it's true,
There is nothing I can do,
For still—
When I think of her my heart begins to beat once more;
When I say her name, my whole being is delighted;
When I see her, life begins anew.

This sentimental effusion was not only embarassingly bad as poetry, but, more suprisingly, inaccurate as a description of God's supposed will.

About a third of the way through the season Admiral King played its big game against rival Lorain High. We triumphed (as was only right), and after the victory the AK band marched through the streets to the school parking lot. Ecstatic students and teachers followed. As I hurried along next to Margaret, elated at the game's outcome but even more delighted to be at her side in the dark, she impetuously, unexpectedly seized my hand. We promenaded, fingers interlaced, all the way to the school and my feet never quite touched the ground. When we reached the brightly lit band room, she ran off to find some girlfriend.

And that was that. Though we worked side by side till the end of the football season and then again at the indoor concession stand for basketball games in the winter, Margaret never again took my hand. She remained friendly and flirtatious, and nothing more.

Perhaps I should have been more assertive? I don't think so. Camaraderie, enthusiasm and a collective abandon led to a single moment's awful daring. For me, it was a perfect five minutes of innocent bliss, a gift of the gods. Even now I am grateful for that generous impulse, one that Margaret has no doubt forgotten, though I never will.

Still, my junior year passed and my senior year started and I had yet to do anything more than hold hands with a girl. Was I frightened? Fearful of being rejected? Hah! I sneered at teachers, laughed at D's on my report card, proudly called myself a nonconformist. Impossible. I was just waiting for the right moment and person. Well, maybe I really was a little afraid, and, like Hamlet, simply needed to act, to screw my courage to the sticking point? I vowed to kiss some sweet-fleshed young thing on the lips before my seventeenth birthday on November 6.

But how to accomplish this impetuous deed? I reflected on various strategies and finally settled on what I called Plan A. Somehow this outline of dating tactics, clearly influenced by my study of Dale

Carnegie, has survived to this day and I transcribe it for the possible use of younger readers:

PLAN A

Dress and Appearance: White shirt, burgundy sweater, black pants, dark socks, cordovan loafers. Also, Old Spice, mouthwash, mints.

Attitude: Pleasant, conversational, smooth.

1. Flatter girl. Use her name. Praise something that she is proud of and something she'd like to be proud of. Don't be bashful. Be profuse in your compliments, but credible.

2. Encourage her to talk about herself. You do little speaking. Subtle comments.

3. At the movie: Take a side seat, in a deserted area. After show has started, say about 15–30 minutes, take her hand. If she withdraws it, use arm approach. If she welcomes hand, continue. Use all the handholding techniques. After a while, take hand away. Put arm around her. Wait for response. If not satisfactory, just leave arm there lightly. If she snuggles, hold her tighter and get as close as possible. Work the head-together bit. Hold her hand with your other hand. Use all techniques.

4. After show: Hand in hand to car, if practicable. Talk of how pretty etc. she is. Must be credible. Ask if she is hungry. Go to a nice place. Joke with her. Make her laugh etc. Work at it. After snack, get serious again. More praise, but subtle. If mood is right, ask if she would care to take a look at the lake (submarine watching).

5. Lakeview: Be more masterful. Put arm around her. Admire lake and stars. Whole bit. Then when hand caressing is done and arm is set, turn her face toward you and quickly kiss her lips. Check response. If

satisfactory, again. Sigh slightly. Kiss her on neck three or four times.
Stop after this abruptly. Loosen hold on her slightly. Watch reaction. If
she wants more, tighten up and kiss her on lips again, twice. Let her do
a little kissing. No more than 45 minutes of this. Don't make it boring.
Leave her wanting more; craving, if possible.

6. After Lakeview: Encourage talking of how great evening was.
Make her more light-headed; laugh; joke. Take her home. Be sad to
part. If practicable, kiss her once on porch and say you'll call her some-
time. Leave quickly.

7. On way home: Examine evening. Review any mistakes made.
Possible corrections. Think about it. Relish every moment.

8. At home: Record impressions of date in journal.

Ah, such naïveté! Such earnestness! Such would-be sophistication! "Must be credible." And what could those hand-holding techniques have been? Oh, I felt on such shaky ground—for all I really
knew was how to read. Little wonder that I had started surreptitiously studying the sex manuals of Dr. Albert E. Ellis, noting down
such sentences in my journal as: "The woman's emotional and physical sexuality must be awakened by the demanding desire of the man.
Once awakened, it fills the woman's whole being and tends toward
permanence."

Certainly, if study was what it took, few young men could have
been better prepped for teenaged romance. But would I actually fulfill my vow to kiss a girl before I turned seventeen?

The leaves had fallen, the days were growing short and time had
almost run out when I asked vivacious, dark-haired Judy Bachman to
the Admiral King–Sandusky football game on November 5, a Friday
night. We boldly walked into the stadium, hand in hand, quarreled
during the first quarter, eventually made up, went to an after-game
party—kids were doing a line dance called "The Elyria"—and ended

up parked on a dark street at one-thirty A.M. I had been born around ten A.M., leaving less than seven hours till I turned seventeen. I wrote in my journal the next day:

Then we talked at great length about kissing. Judy said she'd kissed two boys in her life. . . . She felt a kiss was something special, something that meant I love you, and shouldn't be given lightly, citing certain girls. I answered that I wouldn't know, never having kissed anyone on the lips. To my surprise, she then said I could kiss her, just to know, and turned toward me. But I hesitated because suddenly a kiss had become a formal arrangement, a commitment. I didn't kiss her. We talked on until just before I started the car to take her home. At that moment she leaned up forward from her seat and put her hands around my neck. I said No, Jude, not this way, not after all you've said. But she answered that it was all right. So we kissed. Actually it was more that she kissed me. . . .

My first thought after kissing her was this: I thought it would be wetter; I always imagined the girl's lips or your lips were moist all back. Maybe ours were dry because of talking. I don't know. I took her home.

So much for my long-awaited rite of passage. As Julien Sorel might say—I'd been reading *The Red and the Black*—"Is that all there is?" I saw Judy one or two times more after that historic night. Sad to say, I can now remember almost nothing more about her. But there would be other girls, better kisses. And soon.

That winter, following one of my usual whims, I joined Junior Achievement, a program in which local businesses sponsor student companies, hoping to pass on to the impressionable young the elements of modern-day capitalism. Elected president of Simco Enterprises, manufacturer of car litter bags, I soon established a rather socialistic worker-owned enterprise that, to the chagrin of our gray-flanneled masters, made more money than any other JA company. Simco met on Thursdays from seven to nine and one evening I remarked a pretty, rather busty girl from Lorain High who worked at another JA company. Vicki possessed a gypsyish character—sultry, wild, a little flamboyant, very sexy. During one of our breaks she and I took a stroll and may have even dared to enter Rusine's, which was only a few doors away. At nine that evening I asked if she could use a lift home. She telephoned her father that she was getting a ride and might be just a little late.

When I started the car, she slid right over to the driver's side, to sit closer to me, and boldly said, her eyes glistening like those of a New York divorcee, "We don't have much time." Clammy with anticipation, I drove to Lorain High and parked in a shadowy corner of its lot.

We were clawing at each other as soon as I turned off the key. Her lips, as wet as I had imagined, jammed against mine, her tongue jetted into my mouth, she sighed and groaned with pleasure. I pulled her tighter to me. My hands ran up and down her back, as she hiked up her skirt so that I could knead and caress her inner thighs. I unbuttoned her blouse and kissed her skin and then pushed my fingers under the bra. Her own fingers played up and down my arms, between my splayed legs. The car windows steamed.

But after ten minutes she said, "We need to go. I have to be home already." Then added, "My dad's a cop." Readjusting our clothes and our breathing, we drove slowly to her house. No fool, I asked her if we could go out on Saturday. She said she'd let me know. Her folks were "pretty strict."

When Vicki called later, she explained I should visit her at home that Saturday. "My folks want to meet you." So that evening, dressed in my Plan A burgundy sweater, navy pants and cordovan loafers, I rang her doorbell, introduced myself to her pleasant housewifely mom and her easygoing, beer-barreled dad. They seemed to approve of me—"Such a smart, well-mannered young man"—and I was invited to stay awhile. The house must have dated from the 1920s: old dark armoires, vases on lace doilies, creaking wooden floors. It felt warm and inviting. Presently Vicki's mother left to go upstairs and her father abandoned the dining room, where we'd been chatting at the big mahogony table, to watch a ball game in the TV room.

As soon as good ol' dad rounded the corner, Vicki started climbing all over me. Her father was sitting no more than twenty-five feet away and could come waltzing through the doorway at any moment, and yet we ended up rolling together in passionate embrace on the worn dining room rug. We were both mad with desire, or perhaps just really, really stupid. But somehow we weren't caught. After a few minutes, we finally stopped our torrid petting and I genteelly kissed her good night.

And then she vanished from my life, as unexpectedly as she had appeared.

I called once or twice, but she was always busy, and then I heard she'd found a steady boyfriend. After a while, I again rationalized that this was all for the best. Our encounters had been white-hot, a supernova that couldn't be sustained. And I knew that I wasn't ready to go further than second base. Or maybe third.

A year later—if I may look ahead—my senior year was electrified by two great passions, first for my classmate Karen Staskiews and then for my beautiful, my lost Caroline. Sleekly seductive, with long dark tresses artfully framing her face, Karen was playful yet enigmatic, like the possessor of some delicious secret that made her coyly smile but that she would never reveal. KDS, as I called her, was a consummate flirt—dating a gang leader, going out with me, then briefly ensnaring Ed and Tom. For months we exchanged notes in class and gossiped about other couples. Of Serbian descent, KDS even taught me some Serbian curses, one of which goes something like, "*Yah Bahvahtz Kooratz Te Yebuh.*" We deeply liked each other—and had I gone to the senior prom, I would have gone with her—but somehow we never quite generated the right sexual chemistry. Friendship and a certain similarity of outlook interfered, I think, with the necessary fantasizing and self-abandon of passion.

After Karen and I drifted apart, I one day noticed a beautiful, somewhat gawky sophomore with black hair, full breasts and, as I wrote at the time, eyes "like soft summer skies with brilliant suns at the center." My infatuation with Caroline lasted through the summer, though it was fraught from the start. At first Caro was recovering from a stormy connection with a basketball player. Then her sister Anne fell for me, which complicated matters considerably for a while. But eventually the two of us just surrendered to an insatiate attraction. We would make out on her family couch whenever her parents left the living room, whether for five minutes or two hours. Sometimes we waited for the Canadian invasion fleet in the parking lot at Lakeview. We embraced on blankets in the weedy grass behind George Daniel Field while the Fourth of July fireworks burst in the night sky.

At Oakwood Park, near her house, Caroline and I would kiss until our ravaged lips hurt. I recited poetry to her—"Leda and the Swan"—and she would unbutton her blouse and pull me into her arms. "Don't stop, please keep kissing me, yes, please, harder. Don't stop yet, it's not so late. It'll be okay. Just a few more minutes. Oh, Mike." She never wanted me to take her home at night. Nor did I ever want to.

But in late July I borrowed Ray's motorcycle and drove over to Caroline's in the early evening. We took a walk around the block and, after a few minutes of meaningless chat, I just went ahead and broke her heart. It seemed to me the only honorable course: I was about to go off on a long summer trip, then to college. She had begun to talk about marriage, but I knew she shouldn't wait for me, or expect me to be true. Still, it was awful. "Oh, Mike, how can you do this to me? Why? Why?" The tears flowed down both our cheeks. "Caro, I'm sorry, I'm so sorry. But I'm not ready to settle down. Oh, I hate to do this to you. I just hate it. And I miss you already. But there are so many things I want to do, places I want to go, and I just can't be thinking about you and Lorain all the time. Please try to understand." We kissed a last time, and she looked positively stricken as the front door slowly closed and she disappeared from view. I rode back lonely and depressed to Ray's and I never saw her again.

Chapter Twelve

Reading is an abyss; you don't emerge from it.
—Flaubert

Throughout the emotional turmoil of my senior year, I was already looking forward to life after graduation. Back in seventh grade Mr. Latsko had convinced me that if I were to go to college—by no means a certainty—I would be happiest in a small liberal arts school. So that fall I quickly researched various institutions: Reed, Carleton, Swarthmore, Grinnell, Williams and a few others ranked high on my list, but so did nearby Oberlin College, a mere thirteen miles away. I had passed through the town a couple of times, usually while on my way to the county fair in Wellington (corn dogs, sheep, Hurricane Hell Drivers), but—aside from the afternoon I biked over to work on my Rousseau project—had never set foot on campus nor spoken to any of its students and teachers.

But I liked the sound of the place. It was reputed to be a haven for beatniks, radicals, musicians and East Coast intellectuals—just those sorts of unconventional identities I myself yearned after. Without further thought I elected to apply for an early admissions decision, figuring to hold Ohio University as my backup. Before I sent in my application, however, I exacted a solemn pledge from my parents never to come visit me, at least not without my express permission.

Even though I recognized that the competition for Oberlin might be fierce, I had scored well on the various standardized tests that burden the life of the high school student (and was in fact Admiral King's only National Merit Semi-Finalist for 1966). I never seriously doubted that I'd be accepted. Mostly I worried about the financial aid package, which needed to be substantial.

As part of the application, OC required any prospective student to enclose an essay about his or her life, hopes, dreams, ambitions. As had been my typical practice when faced with such assignments—"if they give you lined paper, write crosswise"—I chose to veer off onto a more appealing topic. In this case, I decided to discuss the five books that had most influenced my recent life.

It didn't take me long to settle on the titles: *The Odyssey, Walden, Atlas Shrugged, Zorba the Greek* and *Heart of Darkness*. With a little more space I would have squeezed in *Crime and Punishment, Immortal Poems of the English Language, The Count of Monte Cristo* and quite possibly Dale Carnegie's *How to Stop Worrying and Start Living*. I no longer possess my original essay—perhaps it molders in the Oberlin archives—but here are some of the reasons why I selected these particular five books.

Obviously, *The Odyssey* stood for my childhood dreams of adventure. In the days when my father would sing to me about Marianne down by the seashore sifting sand or Abdul Abulbul Emir and Ivan Skavinsky Skavar, he would also tell me what he could remember of the exploits of Ulysses (as Dad, like James Joyce, preferred to think of the epic's hero). Later in childhood I read several different retellings of the epic, and eventually studied with care W. H. D. Rouse's translation, in a Signet paperback. As a boy, I had yearned to sail the wine-dark sea, endure hardship, battle monsters, face up to witches, enjoy the sensual delights of Circe and Calypso, talk with spirits and destroy my enemies. Alas, the only part of the Greek hero's character that seems to have stuck with me in later life is his restlessness, best memorialized in my then-favorite poem, Tennyson's "Ulysses":

> *Yet all experience is an arch wherethrough*
> *Gleams that untravelled world, whose margin fades*
> *For ever and for ever when I move.*
> *How dull it is to pause, to make an end . . .*
>   *Come, my friends,*
> *'Tis not too late to seek a newer world.*

As I have earlier explained, *Walden* represented my first taste of philosophy, a more protracted inquiry into the proper way to live. Thoreau's prose impressed me with its gnomic economy and austere beauty. I agreed with the doctrines of simplicity, high-minded civic purpose, reverence for nature and personal seriousness. Moreover, Thoreau stood out as the most famous nonconformist in American literature, and wasn't I just such a person? How fateful are even the casual remarks of our teachers!

But how does one reconcile Thoreau with Ayn Rand? It now feels embarrassing to remember my onetime excitement over *Atlas Shrugged*, but the early 1960s marked the great heyday of Rand's popularity. Late one afternoon when I was fourteen, a few weeks before I ran off to Pittsburgh, I stopped at the branch library in Lorain Plaza, hoping as usual to find something good to read. Maybe I'd heard that *Atlas Shrugged* was exciting. Or maybe I picked it up because of its title and because of my penchant for long novels. At any event, I sat down at one of the library tables and was immediately caught up in the story by its celebrated hook, the enigmatic first sentence: "Who is John Galt?"

I kept on reading, as the setting sun burned through the library windows and eventually compelled me to change tables. At seven-thirty Lance or Ed came by and forced me to look up from the page, asking if I wanted to play some baseball. "No." I read until the library closed at nine, then checked the book out and rushed home, periodically stopping under street lamps to run my eyes over another couple of paragraphs—something I hadn't done since reading Sherlock Holmes and Father Brown stories.

That night I stayed up until two A.M. utterly enthralled by this philosophical work of science fiction. Such melodramatic energy! *The Count of Monte Cristo* had long been one of my touchstones; *Atlas Shrugged* possessed something of the same mix of cinematic flourish, conspiracy and revenge. A scientific genius working as a day laborer vows to stop "the engine of the world." The greatest living philosopher roams the seas as a pirate. Businessmen, inventors and original thinkers pass an hour with a quiet stranger and then suddenly disappear. I had once speculated that my buddies and I could conquer the world, were we to stick together—and in *Atlas Shrugged* I found a tale in which a trio of friends did just that.

I finished the novel in three days of continuous reading, some of it in math class. John Galt's ninety-page radio speech, clarifying his economic program, I found pretty much a bore and wrong-headed. Ayn Rand's utopia might be a great place for the gifted and talented, for people who double-majored in physics and philosophy like the visionary Galt, but what about a more ordinary Joe? After all, the heroine Dagny Taggart's devoted and sympathetic assistant ends up abandoned in the desert, wandering alone in the night as he watches her train recede into the distance.

Shortly after returning the book to the library I heard Rand expound her views on the radio. She refused to argue or debate her libertarian capitalism; she would merely explain knotty points to the sympathetic or, better yet, obsequious inquirer. Her voice was husky, Russian-accented and peculiarly hypnotic. I was later astonished to learn—could it have been mentioned in *The Virtue of Selfishness?*—that her husband, named Frank O'Connor like the short story writer and one of the dedicatees of *Atlas Shrugged,* had grown up in Lorain. I naturally assumed that the novel's graphic steel mill scenes were based on the National Tube.

In retrospect, my enthusiasm for Rand's magnum opus indicates my usual criterion for judging fiction: I love books that excite me in some way, for isn't reading essentially mental adventure? When young, I found that charge in actual adventure stories, especially those with a romantic, even melodramatic swagger. In later years, distinctive prose styles—Dunsany, Lovecraft—delivered a slightly more refined *frisson.* But I was still always looking for kicks.

While the philosophy of life in *Atlas Shrugged* ultimately repelled me, that in *Zorba the Greek* was liberating. Nikos Kazantzakis's novel may seem an odd favorite for a teenager, especially since I've never even seen the celebrated film with Anthony Quinn. As so often, I simply picked up a used paperback one day and skimmed the first pages somewhat distractedly—until reaching the words that, at least temporarily, altered my life. A young Englishman, having just met Zorba, the life force incarnate, is reflecting on his own character: "I had fallen so low that if I had had to choose between falling in love with a woman and reading a book about love, I should have chosen the book."

I stopped, went back and slowly pronounced aloud each word in the sentence, then looked up from the page. Here, in a single observation, Kazantzakis had described my own miserable condition. I was sixteen years old at the time, had never been on a date, never really been out with a girl. The adolescent Dirda needed to change, to get his nose out of books at least a little. I finished *Zorba* first, though, paying close heed to its exhortations to a fuller, more sensual life: "My boy, if a woman calls you to share her bed and you don't go . . . your soul will be destroyed! That woman will sigh before God on judgment day, and that woman's sigh, whoever you may be and whatever your fine deeds, will cast you into Hell!" Cue the dance music. Two weeks later I kissed Judy Bachman. Or she kissed me. Whatever.

And so we come to Joseph Conrad. As a young teenager I plucked from our family bookshelves an anthology called *The Golden Argosy*, supposedly the best stories of all time. I passed happy hours with O. Henry's "The Gift of the Magi," W. W. Jacobs's "The Monkey's Paw," Saki's "Tobermory," Frank R. Stockton's immortal "The Lady or the Tiger?" (such a deft playing with reader expectations, such postmodern undecidability), and many others. But they all seemed flat, mere trick stories, before the thickened prose and magnificently oratorical flourishes of Conrad's "Youth." Even though a youth myself, probably fifteen or sixteen, I was already susceptible to any hint of wistfulness and regret, to the sense of having missed out on life:

And we all nodded at him: the man of finance, the man of accounts, the man of law, we all nodded at him over the polished table that like a still sheet of brown water reflected our faces, lined, wrinkled; our faces marked by toil, by deceptions, by success, by love; our weary eyes looking still, looking always, looking anxiously for something out of life, that while it is expected is already gone—has passed unseen, in a sigh, in a flash—together with the youth, with the strength, with the romance of illusions.

On the strength of this masterpice I bought a paperback—fifty cents, new—of *Heart of Darkness*, which entrapped me in its even more luxuriant, curling sentences—like lianas, like pythons—and for several years, or at least months, it served as my favorite model for a serious work of fiction.

What did I so admire? First, the dense lyrical prose. Conrad's sentences mirrored that threatening sense of the jungle slowly encroaching on the soul, his syntax so tangled a reader could almost lose his way. The frame—Marlow talking to a group of friends—invested the narrative with both verisimilitude and a welcome tinge of the fantastic; it was almost a club tale. And, of course, I thrilled to hints of unspeakable sexual practices and forbidden rites, all of them summed up in Kurtz's dying ejaculation: "the horror, the horror." Above all, my growing taste for the cynical quickened at the final twist, when Marlow lies to Kurtz's anguished fiancée and says that, yes, of course, Kurtz spoke her name with his last breath.

These days, *Heart of Darkness* has drawn intense scrutiny for its depiction of colonialism, imperialism and racism. But for me, as a callow self-centered adolescent, Conrad's novella offered a report from the darkest corners of the soul. Even more intensely than my old favorites *Crime and Punishment* and *Hamlet*, this great patterning work of modernism showed me that books could be something other than stories or lessons, they could be verbal re-creations of roiled human consciousness. For a long time henceforth, my truly great adventures in reading would be found in the masters of the psychological novel—not only Dostoyevsky and Conrad, but also Stendhal, James, Proust and Joyce. Their complex books are best loved by the young. As we grow older, our tastes turn back to the spare, the classical and the merely delightful.

Such were the books, I informed the officials at Oberlin College, that had most influenced the eccentric young scholar applying for a place in the class of 1970. To me they represented aspects of my character as I perceived it or wished it to be. Restless, independent, with a penchant for the melodramatic gesture, wistfully romantic and almost debilitatingly introspective—this was Michael Dirda, or so I believed.

Apparently, Oberlin either approved my essay or my choice of titles, for I was admitted late in the fall with an acceptable scholarship, a good-sized loan and the promise of a four-hour-a-week job in the school laundry: collecting dirty linen and handing out fresh sheets, towels and pillowcases.

Chapter Thirteen

After all, they knew that to be real each had
To find for himself his earth, his sky, his sea.
—Wallace Stevens

On the day I graduated from high school my father left the ceremonies early to attend a funeral: A childhood friend's son—just a little older than I—had been killed in Vietnam. For me the sixties were finally about to begin and the very real specter of that stupid, hateful war would haunt my generation for the next half dozen years, and more.

But that summer of 1966 I had planned a great road trip to the "wild, wild West" and then on to Mexico and Guatemala. My companions were a teenage boy from France, a community college reading instructor and my high school French teacher. This last, William Briola, taught me during my final year at Admiral King, but he himself, in simply being Bill, taught me a lot more than a foreign language. He will forever represent the kind of intellectual suavity that I admire and envy—in part because I know that I will never possess such dash, such poised insouciance.

Picture the first day of French IV in the fall of my senior year. Entering the classroom, with its rows of one-piece student desks, I see, to my surprise, that our teacher isn't Judy Brown, to whom I owed most of my then-feeble understanding of French. Back in ninth grade she had introduced me to the language: "*J'entre dans la salle de classes. Je dis bonjour au professeur. Je prends ma place.*" During our junior year she guided me and Tom through a slightly simplified version of Jules Verne's *Tour du Monde en 80 Jours* (*Around the World in Eighty Days*). Then, on my own, I struggled with my first real novel in French: Saint-Exupéry's *Vol de nuit* (*Night Flight*).

But this year the kinetic, excitable Miss Brown isn't waiting for us in French IV. Instead I find a tall, black-haired young man, slender, with bushy eyebrows and long lashes, at ease in a well-cut suit. He moves with precise, fluid motions, and speaks English just a little slowly, as if he were addressing foreigners or the mentally incompetent.

I can remember being dispatched to a supply closet to fetch our textbooks, which through some bureaucratic miscommunication, had never been delivered to the classroom. When I returned pushing a cart of grammars, Mr. Briola—as we discovered he was named—was asking each student to read a paragraph of French aloud, to test his or her accent and pronunciation. I had a cold with phlegm in my throat, so my voice sounded particularly low, syrupy, like Maurice Chevalier's when he thanks heaven for little girls. "It's just like being in Paris," said the new teacher.

Everyone soon agreed that Bill was a little unusual. He appeared slightly foppish, meticulous, almost too agreeable. He taught French well enough, but was obviously a man who didn't belong in a high school, especially in a rough high school like Admiral King. Here, it struck me, was an emissary from the more refined, glamorous worlds I had long dreamed about. For instance, Bill was always reading a Livre de Poche, actually preferring these cheap paperbacks to ritzy, Bible-papered Pléiade editions. These latter, he would complain, were frustrating: "You read two hundred pages and it looks as though you've hardly started on the book." Once I noticed a thick volume tucked under his arm, one of four, I later learned: Jules Romains's *Les hommes de bonne volonté* (*The Men of Good Will*). For Bill no book was too long or too daunting. "I just don't feel right unless I've read for at least a couple of hours each day." His voluble mother, a subscriber to the Book-of-the-Month Club, would start and finish an entire novel every afternoon.

Surprisingly, Bill quite liked Lorain. He explored the city with an anthropologist's eye and an epicure's taste. Having grown up in a middle-class household in the Cleveland suburb of Bay Village— given unwelcome notoriety by the recent Sam Shepard murder case—he loved to investigate my hometown's exotic and alien cultural system. For instance, he enjoyed playing bingo in church halls. He got a kick out of the kitschiness of it, yes, but would always throw himself into the spirit of the game. He even acquired the special markers that dedicated bingo junkies prefer, and would oversee four or five boards at once. There was no superciliousness to him, none of what the English call "side." For a while he bought his sports jackets on clearance at Ontario's or Elyria City—two big discount stores— and wore them with such panache that you'd think they were bespoke fashions from Savile Row or a men's boutique on the Champs-Élysées. "A really good tie," he once told me, "is the secret." Once or twice a week he stopped at little Hispanic restaurants and *bodegas* in South Lorain, or contrived to be invited to students' homes to eat beans and rice or potato pancakes, or maybe to sample a homemade tomato sauce and taste a proud mother's nut roll.

Already by mid-September Bill recognized that I was a fellow reader and soon began to shower me with books. At first he lent or gave me French paperbacks—Camus' *L'Étranger* (*The Stranger*), novels set in Provence by Jean Giono and Henri Bosco, Marcel Pagnol's plays about Marius, César and Fanny—but gradually he began to pass on all kinds of castoffs, everything from Henry Miller's *Tropic of Cancer* to René Wellek and Austin Warren's *Theory of Literature*. Meanwhile, in class he would regale us with anecdotes about his night-school French courses at Western Reserve University, with special attention paid to a female Zorba, a buxom Greek woman who, he claimed, had done everything and been through more. Eventually, he invited me to come sit in on this class, with the promise of stopping at a restaurant or bookstore afterward. My parents said fine.

Nowadays, people would be suspicious of such personal attention from a teacher, but over the years Bill never behaved toward me as anything other than a mildly amused mentor or rather superior friend. On evenings when we sped down Lake Road in his canary-yellow Mustang, he would relate anecdotes, stories and prejudices: He admired Lincoln Town Cars because their front and back doors opened in opposite directions like a book; he felt Samuel Beckett had gone too far toward a musical impenetrability in his later style; in Guatemala, he had heard, everyone carried a gun. It is notoriously difficult to reproduce spoken charm, and I won't try here, but in my experience Bill remains one of the two most enchanting conversationalists I have ever known. There were times, as we drove to or from Cleveland, when I genuinely wished I could listen to him all night.

Wherein lies the magic of a voice? Like the sound of the ocean, a certain diction, a certain timbre may suddenly soothe, almost salve one's entire being. Is there a release of endorphins or serotonin in the brain? Many of the peak experiences of my life, it's now clear to me, are little more than a few minutes, at most a few hours, of vocal lullaby. My mother's voice telling me a story, Charles Laughton reading from the Bible, a pseudo-British accent discoursing about words, Ayn Rand explaining her philosophy on the radio, a young teacher speaking in the Ohio dusk about the *roman fleuve*—all these have flooded my grateful soul with an oceanic feeling of inexpressible contentment.

Bill smoked Camels with a 1940s movie-star flair, and all his clothes and books soon picked up the faint acrid fragrance of tobacco. Even now, I will sometimes take up a paperback that once belonged to him and smell its pages, remembering his soliloquies about life and literature as we raced along the shores of Lake Erie.

Bill took me to my first opera —the Met performing Gounod's *Faust*, with Nicholai Gedda, Gabriella Tucci and Cesare Siepi under the baton of Georges Prêtre—and, though the actual music and production bored a philistine me, I delighted in gazing at Cleveland's elite decked out in tiaras, lavalieres and evening clothes. Beforehand, we stopped at my very first sit-down restaurant, a small Italian place in Shaker Heights; it was dark and quiet, but the white tablecloth sparkled with silverware. I remember asking Bill which fork or knife to start with and my urbane guide answered dismissively, "It doesn't matter. If you're paying for the dinner, you can use any utensil you want."

Once or twice during the year I drove up on a Saturday to Bill's parents' house in Bay Village, where I met his mother, his well-meaning and slightly bemused father and his hippieish sister Louise who, a year or two younger than I, revered John Sebastian of the Lovin' Spoonful and wore long flower-print Laura Ashley dresses and cute granny glasses. She adored her brother, who was nearly as devoted to her.

After talking for a while with his family, Bill and I would climb the stairs to his small attic bedroom, which was lined with three-by-three-foot wooden bookcases, all painted a dull orange. In retrospect, I don't suppose my new mentor could have owned more than a thousand books, but unlike most of us he had read them all. He would order French novels from Guy Boussac in Paris roughly once a month, and even acquired a few titles for me that way. One afternoon I was visiting his home when a package arrived from France: What pleasure just to observe his excitement in opening the tightly packed parcel and then stacking up, in a neat pile, the various treasures therein. Shades of the TAB Book Club! He could hardly wait to start on the collected poems of the nineteenth-century romantic Alphonse de Lamartine or the black-humored plays of Jean Anouilh. Unlike many bookmen, Bill had no interest in first editions or fine printing: He simply wanted to read the works of the authors who interested him. And when he found somebody he liked, he would methodically, steadily absorb his or her *oeuvres complètes.*

Around this time I had been reveling in the archaic biblical syntax and nameless horrors of H. P. Lovecraft. The teenage Bill, it turned out, had also gone through a Lovecraft phase and had actually ordered books from Arkham House, some of which, he told me, were now worth a considerable sum. Yet he allowed me to borrow whatever I wanted and so I finally read all about the Elder Gods and Miskatonic University, as well as the great essay on supernatural horror in literature: The truly weird, I copied into my journal, may be characterized by "a subtle attitude of awed listening, as if for the beating of black wings or the scratching of outside shapes and entities on the known universe's utmost rim." I coveted Bill's attic bedroom, with its crisp tidiness, colorful bedspread, an old French tapestry hanging on the wall and books precisely ranged in serried rows. It was just what I wanted my own to look like.

When I graduated from Admiral King, Bill dropped by my family's open house, bringing a gift of two books: Ovid's *Metamorphoses* and Thomas Mann's *Buddenbrooks.* Oddly, I resisted reading both for many years, and even now have never opened Mann's novel. Yet the paperbacks have traveled with me as totems or charms ever since that sunny afternoon, when Bill lounged dapperly in the backyard, sipped a drink and bathed in the admiring glances of my female relatives. Even my mother said, "Doesn't he have the most wonderful eyelashes?"

That summer of 1966 Bill announced that he was planning a car trip to Guatemala and was actively seeking travel companions. A former student named Gérard, with whose famly he had boarded in France, was coming to visit and he had promised to show the boy the American West and Mexico. A young woman teacher—of reading!—from Lorain County Community College was also debating the merits of tagging along. Might I be interested?

And so I worked for only two months at the steel plant that summer and then joined these three on the great adventure of my youth. Each of us was permitted to pack a single suitcase, in part because a Mustang grows seriously crowded with four people in it. Bill installed an air conditioner and bought new tires, as he made a point of telling my concerned dad, who had given me permission to go on this trip as my high school graduation present (along with a pair of binoculars). On July 29, 1966, my fellow travelers pulled up in front of our house and we took off toward Chicago and beyond.

I kept a record of our journey, but, like so many early papers and notebooks, it must now be at the bottom of a lost cardboard box. I do remember toting along a couple of spy novels, Donald Hamilton's Matt Helm thriller *The Ambushers*, and Philip Attlee's *The Paper Pistol Contract* featuring the Nullifier, Joe Gall—my Fawcett Gold Medal edition carried an enthusiastic endorsement from Raymond Chandler. Later, in Mexico City, I bought an outrageously expensive paperback of Conan Doyle's *The Poison Belt*, a further adventure of Professor George Edward Challenger of *Lost World* fame. In the glove compartment Bill stashed a leatherette Nelson Classics edition, for himself, of *Nicholas Nickleby*.

During our first day we drove without stopping to Davenport, Iowa, just on the western side of the Mississippi. That evening I walked out of the Fall Corn Motel with Gérard and we ambled over to peer at the broad expanse of slow-moving water. After uttering grunts of praise for the original Great Brown God—I was something of a connoisseur of rivers since my adventures at Pittsburgh's Golden Triangle—I expressed real admiration for Gérard's khaki military shirt and his canvas shoes, both of which struck me as deeply cool. He asssured me that their duplicates were to be had for mere *centimes* in Paris flea markets. "In fact, Michel, I will give to you my shoes and *chemise* before returning to France." But he didn't, alas.

Most mornings Bill would rouse us early from our beds, aiming to clock up a couple of hundred miles before lunch. Afternoons were reserved for serious sightseeing: Bill would assiduously compare guidebooks, maps and brochures and would cram as much culture and scenery as he could into any given day. We gawked at Mount Rushmore, the Badlands, the Great Salt Lake, the Grand Canyon and other points of natural interest, not to mention all our rushed visits to historical societies and roadside attractions like Wall Drug (home of the buffalo burger). In the evenings we would check into a motel, eat a good dinner and then, more often than not, play bridge.

One night at the card table, I fondled a bottle of Seagram's 7 whiskey, about half full, and proposed finishing it by myself during the next hour or so. Before long, I was as drunk as I ever expect to be. The former president of Admiral King's first bridge club—its members few but choice—grew loud, boisterous, began reciting verse, and eventually threw up. Copiously, several times. But I refused to go to sleep. Stripped of my clothes, I wrapped myself in a bedsheet and made my way via the fire escape to the roof of the motel, where I read aloud from the Gideon Bible and gesticulated like an ecstatic television evangelist, doubtless hoping to effect the immediate conversion of the tractor-trailer drivers barreling along on the highway below. Somehow Bill and Gérard finally manhandled me back into bed.

The next morning a pitiable creature, vaguely humanoid, awoke nauseated, filthy and hungover. Plunging its aching carcass into a cold bath would surely clear the head or soothe a stomach that, oddly enough, seemed to be mine. I promptly vomited in the tub. Who would have thought there was so much bile in me? Nonetheless we were soon driving and looping and climbing up and down through the Rocky Mountains on our way to Salt Lake City. Scarcely alive anyway, during the next several hours I prayed for death as a blessed release from my undeserved earthly suffering. When we finally stopped in Salt Lake City at the Mormon Tabernacle, Bill insisted on us all trooping in to an organ concert: The rolling boom and thunder of Buxtehude made my head throb in timpanic sympathy. Several years passed before I again drank whiskey, and not until graduate school would I ever be so deeply sickened by liquor again.

After we crossed the border from Arizona, we drifted south, like modern cowboys, toward Durango. There I wandered around dark backstreets, asking young Mexicans where I might buy a switchblade: I had promised to bring one each to Ed and Ray. Later, in another small town, I slept in a peso-a-night flophouse rather than an expensive hotel: It wasn't half bad, otherwise I would probably remember it better. I do recall awakening at one or two A.M. in a fancy establishment in Mexico City and discovering a four-inch-long cockroach blithely sharing the pillow next to me. I flicked it away with my index finger and went back to sleep. Where could I have found such aplomb? Or even foolhardiness. In yet another town I shot pool for money in a late-night honky tonk—look to your laurels, Fast Eddie and Minnesota Fats—and was probably lucky, in more ways than one, to lose.

Like generations of tourists before us, in Guadalajara we bought jewelry and souvenirs. Here I acquired a plain striped brown and tan pot and a wooden mask reminiscent of an ancient Aztec god or a figure from Easter Island. I could never locate just the right serape, one like that worn by Clint Eastwood in *A Fistful of Dollars*. In another town I paid a shoeshine boy to polish my loafers, and cajoled him into climbing up into his platform chair while I knelt down and went to work on his worn leather sandals. Smiling children gathered around to watch the crazy *norteamericano*. In Guanajuato I roamed the hilly streets at night, raucously singing, with students from the school of architecture.

Near Mexico City Bill insisted that we climb the steps of the ancient Pyramids of the Sun and the Moon. In the capital itself we were driven by a crazed cabbie at seventy miles an hour through narrow avenues to a noted French restaurant. I suppose we were tired of enchiladas and Dos Equis. It was, of course, on this very trip that I learned my two key phrases of Spanish: "*Te quiero mucho*" and "*Cerveza, por favor.*"

Once out of Mexico City, we drove farther south along the Pacific, still aiming to reach Guatemela, an imagined El Dorado of jungle and ancient ruins. On a mountain road we stopped at an inn so that I could use the WC: This consisted of an outhouse, near the edge of a cliff, with a long trough. Any human waste simply rolled down this wooden slide and then fell through the humid air into the lush valley far below.

Somewhere south of Mexico City we calculated that we were running out of time, money and car insurance. The expedition needed to turn around, start heading back; Guatemala would have to wait for another year. Rather than retrace our Pacific route, we impulsively decided to follow a primitive mountain road—so marked on the map—and travel across a narrow strip of land to Vera Cruz, before heading north along the Gulf Coast. "Only seventy miles as the buzzard flies," said Bill.

It took us more than ten hours. As we drove up the narrow mountain track, hardly wider than our Mustang, with deep ruts everywhere, Gérard and I would periodically leap out to clear brush, logs and fallen trees from the roadway. By the time night fell, we realized that we had made a serious mistake and began, for the first time on our trip, to be genuinely worried, even afraid. When night descends in rural Mexico it grows very dark indeed. We crawled slowly down from the heights, hoping that the Mustang wouldn't break a hose, get a flat or spring a leak. Unfortunately, the mountain road led directly into a dense tropical jungle. Insects buzzed loudly. Large creatures moved in the distance, and then a little nearer. No longer did any of us dare to leave the car. And then miraculously we picked up the cheery backlights of an old bus and we followed it into Vera Cruz.

The next morning was glorious: sunny and warm, a pale blue horizon, a faint sea breeze. I lounged outside our hotel with my traveling companions at a table underneath a big umbrella and devoured fresh fruit cocktail—the most delicious of my life—and stared out at the Gulf of Mexico. It felt as though my life were finally about to begin. A few days later we crossed the U.S. border—one of my three switchblades was found and confiscated—and began a winding journey home. In Texas we spent two hours loading our trays with American food at an all-you-can-eat Wyatt's Cafeteria. Chicken-fried steak! Apple pie! In Illinois we detoured to see Lincoln's Springfield home; Bill never could resist any tourist attraction. Finally, on

August 22, after twenty-seven days and 8,350 miles, we glimpsed again the smoky sky above Lorain.

Eight or nine years after our epic journey, Bill headed south to Mexico once more. I never saw my friend again. On a desert road a speeding truck rammed into his new Shelby Cobra Mustang and my kind, amusing mentor died in the hospital, a young man still in his early thirties. That summer, when I returned from graduate school, Mrs. Briola gave me most of Bill's French books. A few years later I dedicated my Ph.D. dissertation (on Stendhal) to his memory.

Can an unabashed heterosexual male love another man? Then I certainly loved Bill, and miss him to this day. Even now I sometimes glance up at what is now my set of Jules Romains's *Les Hommes de bonne volonté*—and remember the day when I first saw my dapper French teacher reading volume one, in a classroom at Admiral King, so long ago.

Part Four

A LIBERAL

EDUCATION

Chapter Fourteen

Passion is our ground, our island—do others exist?
—Eudora Welty

For some reason, I didn't take any books with me to Oberlin, not even a dictionary. The place had a library, didn't it? All I can remember packing are some khakis and sweatshirts, a portable record player and a few Peter, Paul and Mary LPs. In that fall of 1966 I was tanned and exultant after my adventures in Mexico, and stoically resigned to the breakup of the old gang. Ed and Ray were heading off to Case Western Reserve in Cleveland, while the ever-savvy Tom had been admitted to M.I.T. Apparently we weren't going to conquer the world together after all. Like most seventeen-year-olds starting college, I was nervously on my own.

Arriving in Oberlin after driving down Route 58, one passes from surrounding farmland into tree-lined blocks of old houses leading to the leafy quiet of Tappan Square. Except for a row of shops, the park is surrounded by college buildings: the Renaissance-style Allen Art Museum, the somewhat vorticist Hall Auditorium, the Conservatory of Music (resembling an old-fashioned radiator painted white), a gothic folly called Peters, where administrators worked, the sternly upright Finney Chapel and, yes, the ivy-covered Carnegie Library. A little beyond these a new undergraduate or his tearful parents might just make out the massive, nineteenth-century

Wilder Hall (home to the student union and Rathskeller), the Kettering science building, some three-story dorms, playing fields—a timeless-seeming world of grass, trees and old stone.

But Oberlin is more than just an idyllic college town. Its conservatory is world-famous and the art museum ranks among the best for its size in the country. I had not thought much about music and art when I'd applied for admission, but they were to prove the revelations of my first semester at Oberlin. When I think back to the great awakenings of that early fall, I remember concerts and paintings and a lynx-eyed girl from Tennessee.

As an incoming freshman in the class of 1970, I'd been assigned a double in 2-C Burton—this meant the second floor, center section of Burton Hall. (I later learned that my old pals Alfie and Sonny had installed its windows.) My roommate turned out to be a laid-back Oklahoman from Tulsa named Mark Wattman. With light brown hair and a wide streak of zaniness, Mark possessed the rare gift of an irresistible amiability. He was just impossible not to like, no matter how great his family's wealth. In his closet I first glimpsed alligator-skin belts and crocodile-skin shoes and tailor-made jackets—all of which he urged me to borrow: "Anything you want, Dryden. Just take it. But how about letting me wear those gym shoes of yours in return? I like the look of them." Finding Dirda just too strange a name, Mark had soon started calling me Dryden—wasn't he a poet or something?—and the nickname stuck with me for years. As the semester went on, I did sport his fancy duds on special dates, and he sometimes padded around the campus in my old Keds. Nonchalant and feckless, he was half courtly gentleman, half good ol' boy hell-raiser—and seemingly altogether happy in his skin. I, by contrast, felt very unsure of myself.

Among my section-mates, two, living in undergraduate squalor at the opposite end of the hall, would prove especially influential during my collegiate life: Clint Vose and Roger Phelps. They became my closest Oberlin friends, and there will be more about them shortly. Yet another guy, Todd Newmark, I never knew very well, but he possessed a greenish/brownish Harris Tweed jacket that he wore with casual prep-school panache. I coveted that coat. And its owner's sleek, aristocratic finesse.

Todd revered Mahler and early that September introduced me to *Das Lied von der Erde* and the *Symphony of a Thousand*. He would trot down to my room in the evening with his arms full of records, gently place one on my turntable—"Dirda, are you sure this needle isn't going to ruin my record? You really should get yourself a proper stereo system"—and crank up the volume to ten. I'd lean back on my bed and he'd pace the floor, caught up, ecstatic, in the Niagara of melody.

Seeing such passion, how could I fail to envy it? These big-band sounds, with Christa Ludwig doing the vocals for the mournful *Lied*, awakened a hunger for more of such soul-stirring and soulful classical music. That appetite soon grew ravenous after I attended an orientation concert in Finney Chapel: George Szell and the Cleveland Orchestra performing Sibelius's Second Symphony.

This was quite honestly a life-altering moment, on a par with my discovery of *Crime and Punishment* in seventh grade or the confusing pangs of first love. Hitherto I had reckoned that classical music sounded like either Lawrence Welk's champagne orchestra bubbling along or like the screeching arias belted out by the Miss America finalist from South Carolina. Even Gounod's *Faust*—with Siepi!—had somehow, despite a glittering audience, bored me. But the Sibelius Second, especially its last movement's ziggurat of crescendos building to the blast of triumphant horns, left me swooning like a Jamesian heroine. Each time I thought the movement—all passion spent—must surely end, the music would drop back to a lower register and remount once more its melodic staircase, until it finally reached a sinew-shattering climax. I thrilled to the transparently manipulative way Sibelius built up the tension, deferring resolution in a manner that seemed vaguely—no, make that definitely—triumphalist and sexual.

Shortly after that epochal evening I ran into a Conservatory student who sat me down over coffee and informed me precisely which composers and works I just absolutely had to listen to immediately. "Really, my dear, how anyone can be so ignorant, I just can't imagine. But it's never too late to learn." So on gray, rain-swept October afternoons I soothed myself with the limpid piano pieces of Debussy and Ravel, surrendered to the melodramatic, almost mawkish sentiment of Tschaikovsky and Rachmaninov and tried to determine whether the Third or the Seventh was Beethoven's greatest, most perfect symphony. Eventually I went back to my Conservatory friend— a composition major—and asked him to recommend an opera. He looked me over carefully. "Wagner, definitely Wagner. You, my dear, are just going to adore *Tristan und Isolde*."

Over three successive evenings I rushed out after dinner to play another couple of discs from Wilhelm Furtwängler's classic recording with Kirsten Flagstadt. The Conservatory's music library provided so-called listening rooms—small soundproof closets with state-of-the-art acoustical equipment. Here I would lie back on a kind of love seat, big earphones wrapped around my head, electrified by the aching, yearning chromaticism of Wagner's doomed illicit lovers. When I finally reached the final side of the final disc—Isolde's "*Liebestod*," that musical analogue to Bernini's statue of the ecstatic St. Teresa—I was myself enraptured. As Flagstadt's voice whispered "*Mild und Leise*" I could feel my palms break out in a sweat. My heart seemed to float upward in my breast, as her transports became mine. I sat staring, scarcely breathing, while the last chords gradually ebbed away after that long-awaited final cadence. I was not surprised to learn later that at the end of the nineteenth-century, conscientious mothers refused to allow their daughters to listen to this opera. It was a celebration of physical love.

Not that I yet knew about such things from personal experience. Early in the fall I started dating a girl from Massachusetts, but we somehow never fully clicked. I then cast my eye on a blonde named Mary Callahan, who went out with me just once—and thirty years later I still remember the extraordinary good-night kiss she gave me. When I eventually read Joyce's *Portrait of the Artist as a Young Man*, I recognized Mary's kiss:

He closed his eyes, surrendering himself to her, body and mind, conscious of nothing in the world but the dark pressure of her softly parting lips. They pressed upon his brain as upon his lips as though they were the vehicle of a vague speech; and between them he felt an unknown and timid pressure, darker than the swoon of sin, softer than sound or odour.

That I only felt Mary's collagenic mouth against my own for a second or two, and never again, remains high among those unexpected regrets I will carry to the grave.

Plato says that we are meant to fall in love with the people who complete us, with whom we make up a single, ideal being. One day, about halfway through that fall semester of my freshman year at Oberlin, I noticed a strawberry blonde with slightly freckled skin and a faint Southern accent: Alexandra Stanton.

She first attracted my attention by prancing in front of me in the cafeteria line, sporting a high-buttoned white blouse and a severe dark skirt: "This is my New York secretary look," she announced with a bob and a smile. Before long, I was helplessly smitten with her—and I do believe, even now, she with me. We dated seriously for almost two years, a merry, tempestuous whirl of kisses, jealousy, violated social rules, heavy petting in the study parlors of Wilder Hall and visits to each other's families—I was in Nashville, her hometown, on the day in 1968 when Martin Luther King, Jr., was shot.

In everything that happened to me at Oberlin as a freshman and sophomore, she should be remembered as the ground bass, the central background element, the most important person in my life. Alexandra could be, by turns, girlish and corny (she had a penchant for greeting cards decorated with Joan Walsh Anglund kittens playing with skeins of wool), as fiery as Scarlett O'Hara when crossed or as coldly disdainful as a dowager in a Tennessee Williams's play. In fact, sometimes I think she regarded her Lorain boyfriend as a kind of low-life Stanley Kowalski—a "ruffian," as she once called me, her eyes shining with ardor. But this cat-eyed, elegant southern belle also believed I would accomplish great things. And knew just how to flatter: "You will grow more and more handsome as you age, Michael. You will be quite irresistible in your forties and fifites." During one semester she knitted me a sweater, as we sat together week after week in Finney Chapel listening to noonday lecturers and visiting musicians; another time she embroidered my three initials (MDD) on a bath towel and washcloth. And one night she even gave me some of her hair, wrapped in a pale blue stocking; it glinted like old gold, like the tresses of Botticelli's Venus. How could I not worship such a woman?

I wrote constantly about Alexandra in my journals, ceaselessly memorializing our conversations, analyzing my feelings, recording her very sighs: "Tonight Alex said that I kissed her once and that was nice; then I kissed her twice and that wasn't so nice, I kissed her three times, and oh dear. After that she didn't think about it." When we finally broke up in our junior year, after tempests of misunderstanding, after tsunamis of tears, I set down a rather forlorn, Proustian summing-up: "I might maintain I loved Alexandra, but perhaps what I really loved was a certain vision, not even, alas, of Alex, but of myself." Was that true? I don't know. I hope not. Even now, decades since we last glimpsed each other, she still occasionally troubles my dreams and for a nocturnal moment I am again eighteen.

Since Alex played the piano and took private lessons in the Conservatory, I found myself spending even more time there. After *Tristan* I listened to Georg Solti's *Ring* cycle, which took nearly a month, and then branched out to Bach cantatas, Haydn string quartets and the lieder of Schubert and Hugo Wolf. I checked out books from the music library: Shaw's *The Perfect Wagnerite*, Mozart's letters, B. H. Haggins's *Music for the Man Who Enjoys Hamlet* and Virgil Thomson's smart, witty reviews. Sometimes I would sit in the Conservatory lounge—pencil in hand, a poem by Paul Valéry or Andrew Marvell in my lap—and watch, with astonishment, as composition majors scribbled away at their chamber pieces, oblivious to gossip and distraction.

Thus Warner Concert Hall and the Conservatory's warren of listening parlors came to be crucial to my education. During any random week I'd drop by Warner to listen to a student recital, more often than not, staying for only a number or two, usually something performed by a friend or a piece I'd been longing to hear live, such as Ravel's *Gaspard de la nuit*. How agreeable just to slouch down in a seat, wearing jeans, gym shoes and an old sweatshirt, and simply soak up twenty minutes of melody or counterpoint before going off to study at Carnegie. Sometimes the playing and singing might be glorious, occasionally lackluster or even embarrassing, but the ready availability of the music and the easy manner in which it could then be integrated into daily life still strike me as enviably civilized.

Of course, established virtuosi would schedule performances in Oberlin too. I remember concerts or master classes by singer Gérard Souzay, pianist Rudolf Serkin and cellist Mstislav Rostropovich. Szell and the Clevelanders appeared regularly in Finney Chapel or the concert hall. One Saturday in late fall Alexandra—breathtaking in a white cocktail dress and iridescent gold stockings—took me to hear them play Beethoven's Ninth. "The music was tremendous," I later wrote fatuously, "and there I was, surrounded by some of the most educated people in the world with a lovely girl on my arm." Sigh. Even my youthful shallowness can't wreck my memory of the beauty of that evening, of that music, of that girl.

My new friend Roger Phelps worshiped Mozart, and could even whistle impressive chunks of Wolfgang's youthful opera *Bastien und Bastienne*. He would regularly invite me into his room to savor Rita Streich performing the Queen of the Night's two arias from *The Magic Flute*—"highest note in opera," Roger would exclaim—or to listen to the Twenty-first Piano Concerto (its second movement made famous as the theme to the film *Elvira Madigan*). Both Todd and Roger admired Stravinsky too, so I acquired a recording of *The Rite of Spring* and learned just where the most pagan, frenzied sections were located on my disc, mainly so that I could play them at full volume, suddenly and earthshakingly, in the middle of otherwise quiet evenings. Sometimes I'd open my windows and really wake up the quad. But over time I settled down to the more meditative works that to this day remain my favorites—Haydn symphonies and Beethoven string quartets, Bach chamber music, most of Mozart, Ravel, Debussy. "Music, when soft voices die, lingers in the memory." Oberlin was laved in gorgeous melody.

In my father's view I was attending college so that I might one day land a white-collar job that pulled down some serious money. "Just get that diploma in your hip pocket," he would say, imagining that chimerical house on a hill. But here I was constantly mooning over classical music and, in my mother's opinion, a nice but rather hoity-toity girl. "Maybe you should take accounting instead of European history," Dad would suggest. But there was no use in talking to me. "No, Dad, I want a liberal education." He would shake his head. "What's that?" "Oh," I'd answer, "literature and languages, philosophy, history and music. And, of course, art."

I had discovered the Allen Art Museum that same fall of my freshman year, and regularly sought refuge for serious reading or study on a bench of its inner courtyard, where small fountains plashed or, more accurately, dripped.

Allen was the quietest building in Oberlin. After admiring, as one always did, its Cass Gilbert Renaissance-style façade, one entered a large exhibition vestibule, with smaller separate galleries off to each side. In my day one would be immediately confronted by Rodin's statue of the Prodigal Son, his arms reaching out, forever imploring forgiveness from his unseen father. I, for one, knew just how he felt. Along the perimeter of the main hall display cases showed off old porcelain, Chinese bronzes, glassware, jewelry and other objets d'art.

In the smaller galleries hung the main paintings, including several masterpieces: Terbrugghen's Caravaggesque *St. Sebastian Tended by Irene*, with the female saint (and her maid) tenderly drawing out the arrows from a corpse-white, lifeless body; a number of dark-glazed landscapes by Ruisdael, Cuyp and other Dutch masters (the great authority on the northern Baroque, Wolfgang Stechow, was then a member of the Oberlin faculty); Bartel Bruyn the Elder's egg tempera portrait of a stern elegant lady with a high, domed forehead and Mona Lisa smile; an early sixteenth-century *Fountain of Life*; and lustrous work by Modigliani, Canaletto, Matisse, Cézanne, Picasso, Monet and the Hudson River luminists. There was even that student favorite, the sixteenth-century *Madonna dell Suffragio* in which a teenage Mary wears a kind of Frederick's of Hollywood gown with cutouts to expose her full and erect breasts, one of which she squeezes with her long delicate fingers. You couldn't ask for a better small museum—a serene outpost of the humanistic vision, inviting in size and scope.

If you climbed its stairs to the second floor you would find yourself in a print gallery and library, where an art major might be allotted a reserved desk. I would sometimes wander along the walls and pluck out big albums—Cézanne, Monet, Rubens, Titian—and settle myself beneath a green-domed study lamp and turn their pages, just looking at the pictures, usually searching for melancholy landscapes or naked Olympias. Ingres' photo-realism and Renoir's frank sensuality particularly appealed then, and I lingered long over Delacroix's *Sardanapalus*, in which the slaying of the satrap's courtesans was so resplendent with rumps and breasts and languorous postures that it might have been an orgy of sex rather than of killing. Eventually I decorated my Burton Hall quarters with cheap reproductions of a Renoir nude, *La Baigneuse Endormie*—her reddish hair reminded me of Alexandra's—and of Van Gogh's picture of his room at Arles. Such sensual and domestic quietude were, however, gainsaid by the ambitious words I posted on the other wall: "Give me an armor of eternal steel./ I go to conquer kings."

Much to my chagrin, I never found the time for a studio art class—even now I daydream about learning to draw well with pencil or chalk—but did take Introduction to Art History and later audited courses on baroque painting (taught by the brilliant young Richard Spear) and on modern art. This latter survey was conducted by the feisty Ellen Johnson, who knew personally many figures of the New York school (and herself owned and restored Oberlin's only Frank Lloyd Wright–designed house).

Johnson maintained that young people should be encouraged to live with actual paintings and drawings, not reproductions. So she established a lending library of original artwork—prints or watercolors by Picasso, Sol Lewitt and Claes Oldenburg, for example—that students might borrow for a semester. For some reason, I always missed the sign-out day for these pieces, maybe because you had to camp out early in the morning to be assured of acquiring a popular work by, say, Chagall. But, like the music that wafted from open windows, among the pleasures of life at Oberlin was the subtle yet pervasive presence of art: You might even stop by a friend's room just to visit her Warhol *Marilyn Monroe*, coyly smiling down from the wall over the bed.

Chapter Fifteen

There comes a time when you realize that everything is
a dream, and only those things preserved in writing
have any possibility of being real.

—*James Salter*

Much as I loved the Con, the art museum and my southern girlfriend, my greatest passion at Oberlin might well have been for Carnegie Library. Kitty-corner from Finney Chapel, Carnegie (est. 1908) was puffing through its last years, and shortly after my graduation closed (as a library) with the advent of the ultrabright Mudd Learning Center. But between 1966 and 1970 the old vine-covered building encompassed the only universe that mattered.

On the ground floor, toward the parking lot at the back of the building, lay the utilitarian reserved reading room, where teachers set aside recommended texts that would permit eager learners to augment their understanding of the ontological proof of God or the history of sprung rhythm. Busy, often noisy students jostled here for the books they wanted to consult, or, more usually, absolutely needed that very night—only to discover that someone else had invariably checked them out for the evening. Those crowded tables remain particularly dear to me, however, because while sitting at one on a "study date," I first discovered the songs and sonnets of John Donne. I had opened my copy of Witherspoon and Warnke's *Seventeenth-Century Prose and Poetry* and, all at once, a hot-blooded young man was blurting out his desires and sexual frustrations, as though four hundred years hadn't gone by: "For God's sake, hold your tongue and let me love!" "He is starke mad, who ever sayes,/ That he hath been in love an hour." "License my roving hands, and let them go,/ Before, behind, between, above, below./ O my America! My new-found-land." Such passionate avowals were as much a revelation as Wagner's *Tristan* or Caravaggio's dark sensualism. How had I missed them in Oscar Williams's anthology?

While the reserve room felt as pragmatic as a beehive, Carnegie's main reading room, lined on one side with tall windows, frequently glowed romantically in the soft autumn twilight. To reach it you would climb the wide staircase off to the left of the ground-floor entrance hall, then turn right, passing the circulation desk. Low wooden shelves held dark-hued reference books, including the thirteen volumes of the *Oxford English Dictionary* (much resorted to in working out the word- and idea-play in metaphysical poetry), while high above peered down the oil-painted faces of stern Oberlin notables. Staring up at Fairchild, Mahan, Finney—elders of unshakable moral rectitude and unflinching idealistic vision—one could hardly wonder at the no-nonsense college motto: "Learning and Labor." For such nineteenth-century men, education wasn't something you got into for fun. It was a vocation, a duty, a religious calling.

As all undergraduates soon realize, no nonprescription sleeping aid is more effective than fifty pages of required reading in an overheated library after a big evening meal. Many's the time even I would doze off while hunched over my biology or econ textbooks. Still, here I also read, for the first time, T. S. Eliot, W. B. Yeats and Wallace Stevens.

Because of Oscar Williams's anthology, which reprinted "The Hollow Men," I did know some Eliot, but had never encountered "Prufrock" or *The Waste Land*, let alone *Four Quartets*, all of which were reputed to be largely incomprehensible to anybody without an advanced degree from Göttingen or Heidelberg. Was it Roger—he had, after all, gone to Andover—who urged me to check out the collected poems anyway? Like Antony Blanche in *Brideshead Revisited* or many another undergraduate of the 1920s, I was bowled over by the verbal music of Eliot's simple, perfectly balanced lines; no individual word was in the least "poetical" yet their combination produced unforgettable phrases: "I have heard the mermaids singing each to each/ I do not think that they will sing to me. . . . Footfalls echo in the memory/ Down the passage which we did not take/ Towards the door we never opened/ Into the rose garden."

Before long Donne and Eliot had edged out Housman and Hopkins as my favorite poets in English. Except, of course, when I was actually reading Yeats. Who could resist the creator of lines as Celtic twilighty as "The silver apples of the moon/ The golden apples of the sun" or as swift and brutal as "Nymphs and satyrs copulate in the foam"? While Yeats's approach to life veered between the wistful and the pontifical, insurance executive Wallace Stevens enjoyed being funny in a dandiacal way. Just scanning the contents page of his *Collected Poems* could elicit smiles, if not outright chuckles of Dadaist pleasure: "The Revolutionists Stop for Orangeade," "Disillusionment of Ten O'Clock," "Mrs. Alfred Uruguay," "A Lot of People Bathing in a Stream." And his lines! "It was evening all afternoon. . . . A great disorder is an order . . . For the listener, who listens in the snow,/ And, nothing himself, beholds/ Nothing that is not there and the nothing that is." As the French say, such semantically shifty phrases cause you furiously to think.

Besides genuflecting before the poetry of Eliot (and I went so far as to check out several of the books he mentions in his notes—Jesse Weston's *From Ritual to Romance*, J. G. Frazer's *Adonis, Attis, Osiris*), I soon bought paperbacks of his critical prose as well, *The Sacred Wood* and the *Essays on Elizabethan Dramatists*. I revered the poet's persuasive literary intelligence, even when perplexed by the density, or diffuseness, of his thought and peculiar syntax—the man really needed a couple of weeks with Miss Raymond. Most of all, though, I relished the quotations with which he would illustrate his essays, highlighting thrilling blank verse from what were to me obscure Jacobean dramatists. Who was John Webster? Cyril Tourneur? Thomas Heywood? This last composed two lines that, as Eliot says, "no men or women past their youth can read without a twinge of personal feeling": "O God! O God! That it were possible/ To undo things done; to call back yesterday . . ." My sentiments exactly, though what I had to regret back then remains a little vague. The bitter and macabre poetry of Webster forced its way deep into my private pantheon, especially after the Oberlin theater department mounted a coloratura production of *The White Devil*, while early on I copied Bosola's majestic death speech from *The Duchess of Malfi* into my commonplace book. The murderer is asked, "How came Antonio by his death?" and replies in these weary, somber phrases:

> *"In a mist: I know not how*
> *Such a mistake, as I have often seene*
> *In a play: Oh I am gone—*
> *We are only like dead wals, or vaulted graves*
> *That ruined, yeildes no echo: Fare you well—*
> *It may be paine: but no harme to me to die,*
> *In so good a quarrel: Oh this gloomy world,*

In what a shadow, or deep pit of darknesse,
Doth (womanish, and fearful) mankind live!
Let worthy minds nere stagger in distrust
To suffer death, or shame, for what is just—
Mine is another voyage."

Mine was another voyage too, and it led me deep into the Carnegie Library stacks, a vast, low-lit realm of books that one entered through a dark and Dantesque portal near the circulation desk.

Within, industrial-strength shelves were ranged across floors constructed of translucent plastic blocks intended to maximize illumination. While browsing the fiction—Henry Green, Gerald Green, Graham Greene—I would sometimes hear the tap-tap of a girl's heels on the floor just above: Could one possibly see up her legs to a rounded thigh or the pale silk of a panty? Squint so hard as one might, the plastic, like those frosted windows in bathrooms, distorted the image for the hopeful voyeur. Still, it was bruited that the moans from serious make-out sessions might sometimes echo from distant corners of the stacks, and lovers be discovered in dishabille among volumes of medieval philosophy. Some winking seniors even hinted that actual intercourse had been engaged in and consummated down where the scientific journals grew musty in the basement, moldering in their grave like John Brown's body. I suspect that all undergrads are encouraged by these hopeful rumors. In the nineteenth century Oberlin did allocate stack access according to one's sex, setting aside, say, the hours between one and three for men only and those between three and five for women. One could never be too vigilant. What, after all, is more seductive than the prospect of sinning in libraries?

Indeed, for a young man or woman between the ages of eighteen and twenty-two Oberlin possessed just one drawback, but it was a doozy: Aside from the Apollo Movie Theater and the shadowy recesses of the more obscure letters of the Dewey Decimal System, there was almost nowhere to be safely alone with one's sweetie. When I matriculated as a freshman, dorms were still single-sex. One might only enter a young lady's room legally during Sunday afternoon "visiting hours" when Junior Residents diligently patrolled the hallways and manually verified that doors were unlocked, occasionally peering in to be sure that their charges had not cast aside all propriety, and most of their garments, in answer to some Maenad-like fury in the blood. During the week women were due back in their dorms by midnight and by two A.M. on weekends, these later hours usually requiring the acquisition of a special "two o'clock key," to which freshman women had limited access (six a semester).

I am now glad to have caught the tag end of a vanishing era. By the spring of my sophomore year most of the traditional social rules had been discarded, and by my senior year a couple could flagrantly cohabit in French House and, to the embarrassment of their parents and the envy of their friends, wake up one morning to find their smiling faces on the cover of *Life* magazine. But in 1966 and '67, men still wore ties to dinner on Wednesday "dress-up nights" and women put on makeup and skirts. Come the weekend, however, quietly desperate couples roamed Tappan Square or North and South Quads searching, panting for a place to be alone together. Any out of the way or dimly lit corner—say, the tiny lounge near the mailboxes at Dascomb, really just a couch and a lamp—might for an hour become a hotly contested love nest. After nine or ten even the vestibular recesses, perhaps three feet deep, in front of the interior double doors of Kettering Science Hall would be draped with amorously entangled couples, all of whom were, by convention, utterly invisible to their chattering classmates passing through the corridor.

There was, in fact, only one place where a modicum of privacy could be legally found: Wilder Hall. The upper floors of this labyrinthine building contained some thirty or so rooms designated "study parlors." On Saturday night, after the concert or the movie let out, the waiting line of the ardent young in one another's arms would snake down the hallway. Of course, even if one were fortunate enough to secure a parlor, say Room 328, this was no assurance of absolute seclusion. Monitors sometimes wandered the corridors, making sure lights were on and, according to the rule, that at least three feet remained on the floor. But these roaming lictors were generally lax, and I suspect the college understood and forgave a certain amount of passion in its students.

Chapter Sixteen

Remember that every life is a special problem, which is not yours but another's; and content yourself with the terrible algebra of your own.

—Henry James

The sixties may arguably have suffered their excesses, yet no one can dispute that those years remain the *anni mirabili* for public forums, angry debates, spoken rage, in short for real participatory democracy. Back then, new journalists, meganovelists and beat poets played with language in innovative and unexpected ways. At Oberlin students argued about ideas, politics, books, everything. It was a great age for talk.

On my second day as a freshman I actually overheard a couple of students vociferously questioning a professor about Kierkegaard: "Why is despair the sickness unto death?" Not in the King humanities building, by the way, but on the sidewalk in front of the Co-op Bookstore—just an ordinary boy and girl with green book bags slung over their swamp-coated shoulders arguing about philosophy. In the Con people would vociferously debate the merits of Bruckner or Stockhausen. On any given evening the SDS (Students for a Democratic Society) might stridently meet, or war resisters rally, or black undergraduates insistently demand.

Words rang out everywhere. On warm afternoons smaller classes often spread out under the shade trees. Walking across Tappan

Square, the sharp-eared might catch the occasional phrase from a half dozen different groups scattered around the park: "What do we make of Bismarck's . . . *Existentialisme est un humanisme* . . . Why does Gatsby . . . the moral imperative . . . Can you logically defend. . . . What does Talcott Parsons mean by . . ." At lunchtime on Thursdays, Finney Chapel hosted full-blown, sometimes overblown, addresses by distinguished lecturers, and you were expected to attend; I remember a celebrated biologist explaining why mortality might be bad for the individual yet good for the species; on another occasion Allen Ginsberg performed "Howl" to a standing-room-only crowd. "I saw the best minds of my generation destroyed by madness. . . ." Earth Day brought symposia on whales and forests, while "Black Week" offered a memorable series of talks and harangues: In a dark suit and subdued tie, the novelist Ralph Ellison eloquently preached an inclusive view of American history and literature—and was politely ignored; poet and playwright LeRoi Jones, not yet Amiri Baraka, appeared in a black dashiki, with three unsmiling bodyguards, and sounded a wildly applauded call for revolution.

Argument, discussion, sermons, lovers quarrels, political symposia, chants and jeers, erotic confessions, late-night bull sessions, oral presentations—Oberlin resounded, a sea of many voices. Couples studied together, then over coffee, their fingers intertwined, would probe each other's views on Milton or anarchism or women's liberation. Guys sprawled in dorm lounges and munched on tuna fish sandwiches while debating the existence of God, the Domino Theory in Southeast Asia and whether sex without love was okay. In the Burton lounge one night a rather mousy section-mate declared, "I don't know if God exists and I don't care. Either way, it makes no difference to my life." A week later I heard the most promiscuous Don Juan in our crowd murmur, with infinite sadness, "You know,

men, sex is the greatest thing in the world. But it just isn't that great."
He is now a gynecologist in Southern California.

No one then ever brought up making money, or landing a job on
Wall Street, or becoming a CEO, or retiring at forty. What did such
things matter? The world needed changing; the poor and disenfran-
chised needed help; the war in Vietnam had to be stopped. "Hey, hey,
LBJ, how many kids did you kill today?" One aspired to be either an
artist or an activist—hadn't Oberlin been the first college in the
United States to go co-ed, the first to admit blacks and whites
together? An Obie aimed to live a life of consequence, of service and
noble ambition. In the 1960s the whole college crackled with passion
and energy. "Bliss was it in that dawn to be alive/ But to be young
was very heaven." Even though I often stood slightly apart from my
classmates, I still miss those days of honorable rage, I still mourn that
visionary company of the sixties.

For, much as I admired my more engaged comrades, I resisted
joining any kind of cadre or group action. My political principles
tended toward gradualist socialism: No one, I maintained, should be
permitted to inherit more than, say, a hundred thousand dollars,
adding that "trash collectors, coal miners and public school teachers
ought to be the highest-paid members of society." But, being more
self-centered than many of my friends, I first wanted to understand
the world before transforming it—and I yearned to experience some
of the privilege they were blithely renouncing. Besides, I did know
how completely the actual workingmen of the world, or at least those
at National Tube and M&M Home Improvement, disdained "student revolutionaries" and "outside agitators": "Those damn kids
should get a haircut and a job. They've probably never worked a day
in their lives." As a result, my own preferred style of conversation
veered away from the political to the intensely private. I especially
liked to listen, sometimes with secret amusement, to Clint Vose or

Roger Phelps. Both these gifted, eccentric friends churned with ideas and theories about everything from games and homework to art and human psychology.

Clinton Pembroke Vose III had grown up in Cleveland, the smart, athletic son of a well-to-do businessman who packed him off to boarding school at Phillips Andover. There, to his parents' ultimate chagrin, he met Roger Phelps, who one afternoon taught the Ohio innocent the fundamentals of chess. "I played Phelps a hundred games before finally beating him. But after that . . ." After that, Clint metamorphosed into an unstoppable chess juggernaut. Soon nothing other than the game of kings seemed to matter very much. Dismissed from Andover, Clint returned to Cleveland, but kept pushing pawns and advancing bishops, slowly mastering the intricacies of the Ruy Lopez and the French Defense, studying the games of Capablanca, Lasker and Alekhine. By the time I knew him, he had started to fantasize about working as a psychologist at some asylum to which the unstable chess legend Bobby Fischer had finally been committed: He and the grandmaster would spend all their remaining days playing chess together. To some, this would sound like Hell on earth, reminiscent of the fate of Tony Last—in Waugh's *A Handful of Dust*—who found himself trapped for the rest of his life into reading aloud from the works of Charles Dickens to an illiterate madman. But for Clint Vose Heaven itself will be laid out in black and white squares.

In fact, Vose drove himself to win at all games. In the evenings he would often play bridge or poker (and later supported himself for a year on his nightly earnings). During his senior year he whimsically decided to go out for soccer—and was named the varsity goalie. He regularly bowled 200 or better and could beat the women's national table tennis champion at ping-pong. On principle, he almost never wore a jacket and in the dead of winter would dismiss a freezing, snowy day as merely "no-coat zippy." Built like a boxer, his fair hair worn in a crew cut, with a bit of heft to his middle, Clint could hardly boast the rip and cut of an athlete's physique, but he did possess to the highest degree one formidable trait: the ability to focus. He would practice a game or a sport hour after hour after hour, slowly improving, growing in understanding, never giving up, gradually mastering whatever he needed to know to excel, all the while concentrating all his physical and mental powers, blocking out the rest of the world from his consciousness.

For Clint really lived in his mind, loved ratiocination, and to this activity which most of us strenuously avoid, he brought a childlike naïveté and enthusiasm. In the middle of the night he might shake my arm, whispering, "Dirda, Dirda, wake up." "Huh, what is it, Vose?" He would pause and then announce, with unironic solemnity, "Do you want to know why Freud was wrong about the death wish?" I would murmur, "Vose, do I?" And he'd say, "Yes, you do. Get your clothes on and let's go for a walk." And so, at one or two in the morning, we'd shuffle along in the velvety darkness and my eighteen-year-old classmate would explain to me why Freud was absolutely, utterly mistaken about the death wish.

Clint was, inevitably, a brilliant and terrible student. At the beginning of each semester he would coolly figure the precise combination of C's and D's that would allow him to earn the lowest possible grade-point average and still remain in school. His view of homework was simple, like my old friend Tom's: "If you can do it, why do it?"

Years later Clint flew out to the Philippines with Korchnoi for the World Championship chess matches against Karpov, then eventually settled into a job with Hewlett-Packard as a computer wizard. Of all my friends, past and present, he remains, with Ray, the most perennially youthful, and though I've only seen him three or four times since our Oberlin years, I always count those visits among the red-letter days of my life.

While Clint bubbled with the springlike genius of a child prodigy, our friend Roger Phelps paced and brooded, altogether a darker, more complex and troubled soul.

"Roger Dodger" was wiry, black-haired and, before long, heavily bearded. Like Clint, Rodge cut classes and ignored assigned homework, often passing long periods reading purely for his own edification and pleasure. I remember the afternoon I found him curled up on his bunk with Henry Green's *Loving* and was thus introduced to one of the modern novelists I most admire. The two of us signed up together for a Russian literature in translation course—a class I gobbled up, if only for the chance to read Lermontov's *A Hero of Our Time*, Goncharov's *Oblomov* and Tolstoy's "The Death of Ivan Illyich." After the first week Roger never went back. Something about the young teacher annoyed him.

Now and again Phelps would still play some pickup chess with Vose, but much of the time he preferred to lie around, listen to Mozart and write in his journal. Even though I worked in the laundry and could have supplied him with all the sheets and pillowcases anyone could ever want, he somehow decided that bed linens were unnecessary, mere clutter: For a whole year he slept on a prison-gray mattress and covered himself with a ratty sleeping bag.

What Roger lacked in focus, he made up for in passionate intensity. Like a Turgenev hero, like Bazarov in *Fathers and Sons*, he was always eager to talk about Life, Literature, Art, Music, the Soul. He scribbled out his random thoughts and entire philosophical systems, then stayed up half the night reading, sometimes Sherlock Holmes, sometimes Freud. Avoiding the classroom, he chose to shine in the section lounge, where he might inaugurate an after-dinner bull session that would carry over into his room when he needed to illustrate a point by playing a bit of *Don Giovanni* or quoting a passage from Jung on the collective unconscious. To me Roger burned not with a hard gemlike flame, but with a deep spiritual fire, one that might readily lead on to madness or crime. Not illogically, Dr. Roger Phelps now works as a psychologist and mental health counselor.

Ralph Waldo Emerson once wrote, "I pay the schoolmaster, but it is the students that educate my son." In fact, much of my Oberlin education took place outside the classroom: Dazzling chess lessons with Clint and musical afternoons with Roger; figuring out how to waltz with Alexandra to the strains of "The Blue Danube" at a spring "cotillion"; Mark Wattman explaining to me about proper dress clothes. I remember learning how to carry on polite conversation when professors sat down at my dinner table—and to admire my classmates who stood up for what they believed was right, no matter the consequence. In my freshman year at Oberlin I studied not only Erwin Panofsky's history of art but also Emily Post's guide to etiquette. Both had their place. I took my inspiration from W. E. B. Du Bois: "We call higher education that part of human training which is devoted specifically and peculiarly into bringing the man into the fullest and roundest development of his powers as a human being." There were a lot of powers I hoped to develop.

All this said, I nonetheless found myself growing increasingly solitary during my first year at college. Part of me yearned to be more frolicsome and lighthearted, but I just couldn't risk it. Oberlin was my big, perhaps my only, chance to make something of my life. And I was in serious trouble.

Chapter Seventeen

*It is a rule of God's providence that we succeed by
failure.*

—John Henry Newman

Despite the intellectual and erotic excitement of college
life, excitement that started from my very first week as a
freshman and never abated, it nonetheless came to pass
that in the middle of the journey through my first semester at
Oberlin, I sank into the Slough of Despond. I was working hard in
all my classes and doing poorly. I felt dwarfed by friends immea-
surably superior to me in talent and charisma—chess champions,
Mozart experts, urbane preppies and committed revolutionaries. I
was surrounded by kids who could play the piano like Sviatoslav
Richter or the violin like Heifetz; I could play the accordion. More
and more I was growing secretly convinced that I should have gone
to work in the steel plant or taken a full-time job hanging Nuprime
windows at M&M.

Worse yet, I kept remembering Admiral King and the election of
the students meriting "senior superlatives." My graduating class had
voted on the twelfth grade's "most intelligent," "best-looking," "most
athletic" members. As it happened, I placed second in several of the
dozen or so categories, leading one of my more waggish friends to
award me a special citation: Most Likely to Just Miss Succeeding.

That jape seemed to be coming true. I had gotten to college, I was eager to learn. But my half-term grades were terrible.

As a freshman, I had registered as a biology major, imagining that I might specialize in botany. To be a naturalist in the mold of Thoreau, to walk through the woods and identify all the plants I surveyed—a patch of *Orchidaceous espinosa*, some night-blooming, rosy-speckled bloodwort, fungi from Yuggoth—this was my dream. But like James Thurber I soon discovered that I could never see anything in a microscope but my own eyelashes.

So I switched to economics. In the 1960s everyone majored in government, sociology or econ—these civic-minded disciplines would bring the revolution. Alas, microeconomics required arcane math skills I didn't possess, as well as an interest in guns or butter, while grand economic theory proved all too seductive for one of my dreamy temperament. I produced a paper on Henry George and the Single Tax, which came back with this penciled comment: "Mr. Dirda, like Henry George, you write fairly well. But neither of you really understands economics at all."

And so I thought about a major in European history or possibly French. Or, if nothing else worked out, English. But here too were . . . difficulties.

During registration week I had signed up for the Introduction to English Literature class, having scored well enough on my verbal SATs to place out of freshman composition. But one could only be excused from the mandatory introductory class by exceptionally high marks on the AP test in English—and I had never received my results.

I had taken the test in Elyria, shelling out my own hard-earned cash for the opportunity to drive to another city and make a fool of myself. Not many kids from Admiral King bothered with the AP program exams back then, but—cocky little snot—I fancied that I knew as much as my teachers, probably more, at least about books. I can still remember that Saturday's first essay question: Analyze the following sonnet—not identified as Shakespeare's, though I guessed he was its "onlie begetter": "Like as the waves make towards the pebbled shore/ So do our minutes hasten to their end. . . ." My kind of poetry.

For some reason, that morning I felt especially smart-alecky, even a little manic. Flipping ahead through the exam, I soon recognized that my antic temperament would blithely thwart any effort to answer questions in the earnest, pontifical way the AP honchos almost certainly expected. So my only hope, and a wan one at that, lay in really showing off, in pulling out the old Dirda razzle-dazzle. Answering the Shakespeare question, I boldly declared that most of the essays would present such and such an explication, but a few would suggest another, somewhat deeper interpretation. But, I continued, both views were sadly incomplete and utterly superficial, the true significance of the poem being . . . Well, who knows what I might have said? Could well have been any sort of blather. I do vaguely recall some theory built on the cash nexus (I'd been reading more Marx), possibly that the sonnet was a verbal scam to attract patronage from a rich aristocrat (hardly what you'd call insightful). For the next two hours or so I was similarly outrageous, dismissive and, to my shallow mind, terribly, terribly clever. But secretly I knew I'd blown away the exam and so wrote off my twenty-five dollars as a total loss.

I was wrong. At the registration desk a bespectacled lady almost prissily disclosed that OC had awarded me nine hours of semester credit in English and that I didn't need the Intro to Lit course. "So," I quickly inquired, taken aback and sensing restlessness behind me in the long queue, "what's available Monday, Wednesday and Friday at, uh, eleven?" "Hmm. Just a moment. Oh, yes: Seventeenth-Century Metaphysical Poetry." "I'll take it."

It was a surprisingly large class, maybe fifty students. Someone mentioned that its instructor, Professor Andrew Bongiorno, was retiring at the end of the year and this would be one of the last courses he taught. "A living legend," another someone added.

At precisely eleven the door opened and a bald-headed, small-boned man, with the face of an El Greco saint, and a particularly ascetic one at that, walked briskly to the front of the room, a clutch of papers and books under his arm. He wore a shapeless dark suit, with a dull white shirt and a skinny black tie, and looked as though he never dressed in anything else. When he spoke, the voice was deliberate and precise, and all his sentences emerged in orderly progression, enriched with literary allusion and biblical quotation, all knowledge seemingly his to command.

Many years later, I acquired a copy of *Louis Agassiz as a Teacher*, a slender volume of essays compiled by Lane Cooper, Bongiorno's mentor in grad school at Cornell. In one evocation of the great naturalist I glimpsed my old professor:

> *No philosophical conception was too general for him, and no detail of observation or inference too small. No fact could appear too slight for his intense and comprehensive scrutiny, and his memory for minute resemblances and differences was vast; yet the enduring quality of his work arose from his sense of order, and from the soundness and rigor of his principles. . . . His power of working was enormous, for he made virtually no false motions, but proceeded silently, swiftly, with no apparent effort, and for long periods without interruption.*

This was, Professor Bongiorno explained to our class, Seventeenth-Century Metaphysical Poetry and we should all acquire a copy of Witherspoon and Warnke's anthology. Together we would read the work of Donne, Herbert, Marvell, Crashaw, Herrick and Vaughan. Each week he would administer a fifteen-minute quiz, a single question requiring a one- or two-paragraph answer, no more than a handwritten page. The final examination would be rigorous and demanding. The more poetry you could quote from memory, the better you would do.

He then added the astonishing sentence: "Once I used to insist that my students learn by heart many of the poems we are about to discuss." But he added, "About twenty years ago, undergraduates began to complain about this practice and so I no longer insist on memorization." At the end of the first class he requested that we start reading John Donne, paying special attention to "Go and Catch a Falling Star," "The Undertaking," "The Good Morrow" and "Air and Angels."

Andrew Bongiorno had arrived at Oberlin College as an undergraduate in 1918. Except for six years spent studying under Lane Cooper at Cornell, where he took his Ph.D. in English (with an annotated edition of *Castelveltro on Poetry*), he had passed his entire adult life at Oberlin, even marrying Laurine Mack, daughter of an Oberlin prof (and sister of Maynard Mack, the distinguished Yale authority on Shakespeare and Pope). Over the years Bongiorno had undertaken many different courses, but now in his mid-sixties he preferred to teach Dante (using, *faute de mieux*, the Sinclair translation) and the School of Donne. For pleasure he read Trollope, for his spirit he studied the New Testament. Poetry, in his view, approached meditation and even prayer; its beauties might lead one to self-understanding and spiritual growth. "I firmly believe with Emerson that all men are poets and mystics," he said. "Therefore, I would urge every serious student of literature to acquaint himself with the nature of mysticism."

In a typical hour Professor Bongiorno would begin by scribbling on the blackboard, often some lines from classical poets. "These verses of Donne will doubtless call to mind Horace's famous . . ."—and he would recite the Latin he had chalked up behind him. He spoke softly, without supericiliousness, genuinely believing that we would recognize the echo, indeed were probably just about to point it out ourselves.

Such unassuming, almost saintly wisdom left me abashed and envious. Here was a true Master. Yes, of course, I should be able to recognize that allusion to Juvenal or Propertius—hadn't Robert Hutchins emphasized that canonical writers conducted a Great Conversation with one another down through the ages? As the semester progressed, I vowed to acquire the kind of learning exemplified by this modest, deeply Christian humanist.

For my first essay, my very first grade in college, Bongiorno awarded me a D. I was dumbfounded. And humbled. At long last the nightmare was over! I had been exposed for the intellectual charlatan I knew myself to be. But I could, would study harder and try to redeem myself. The next week I received a D+, and an invitation to chat after class.

"I believe, Mr. Dirda, that you have enrolled in the wrong course. Metaphysical Poetry is restricted to junior and senior majors only." But by then the semester had advanced too far for me to change my schedule. "If it makes any difference," I broke in hopefully, "I'm thinking of majoring in English." Professor Bongiorno looked gently pained, like St. Sebastian receiving a last, unexpected arrow: "Perhaps you should consider other possible majors."

Well, what other major? I was taking French 311–312—a year-long introduction to French literature—from Professor Vinio Rossi. A wry, quick-witted New Yorker (whose father had been an anarchist associate of Sacco and Vanzetti), Rossi had written a study of the youthful André Gide, earned a Ph.D. from Columbia and possessed a high forehead, sleek black hair, a growing potbelly and a liking for the word "*Tiens,*" (meaning essentially "Now, then"). In his classes, he rambled and digressed—all in French, of course—about books, movies, campus life. He was intellectual bonhomie incarnate.

For his course we were required to hand in a weekly *explication de texte*. He'd distribute a photocopy of a lyric by Baudelaire or Villon and we'd dissect the poem and explain how it worked. Early in the semester, as Rossi passed back papers, he idly asked, "What's the worst grade you can get?" Somebody hesitantly answered F; one or two others said A—because that meant you were a goody-goody or a brown-noser. "No," thoughtfully concluded our genial professor, "the worst grade you can get is C+. Because that means you're mediocre."

I always received C+.

With my permission, Dad—always dressed in neatly pressed khakis and a button-front short-sleeved shirt—had taken to stopping by my room at ten on Saturday mornings. I never felt any of the embarrassment that scholarship boys are supposed to feel about their blue-collar parents, but Dad's dreams were never mine and we had less and less to talk about. We'd stiffly exchange inanities for a few minutes, and he'd look uncomfortable, sitting bolt upright, fiddling nervously with his hands. Shallow youth that I was, I failed to grasp that he might actually miss me. Sometimes he did bring fresh-baked cookies or even take some clothes home for my mother to wash. One Saturday—did I remember when I'd told him years before of my harassment by the school patrol?—I broke down and confessed how hard everything was for me and that I wasn't sure I belonged at Oberlin.

Never in his life did my father pay me a compliment or congratulate me on any accomplishment. Nonetheless I always knew he loved me, even if he could never bring himself to pronounce the actual words until, two decades later, he lay dying. But throughout his life he would always do whatever possible to protect me or make me strong:

"Kid," he told me after a minute, "a lot of these guys here have had advantages that you never had. They've traveled to Europe in the summertime, or gotten jobs in Washington, working for big-shot congressmen. They've gone to ritzy private schools. A few might even be smarter than you. But you have two hands, two arms and two legs just like them. You're as good as they are. This place gave you a scholarship, didn't it? You know how to work, right? Just work harder than anybody else. If you do that, everything will turn out fine."

Would it? There was only one way to find out. And so, in an existential moment of decision, I irrevocably altered my life: I cast off the Wild Ginger Man and vowed to become a grind, a nerd, a true geek. Farewell, glad animal spirits! Hail, studiousness! Meet thy new possessor! From now on, I would, Carnegie-like, fire on all my mental cylinders as a 'round-the-clock study machine. At the same time, I resolved that it didn't matter whether I received A's or C's: I would take classes simply because I felt determined to know something about philosophy, music theory, the Bible. I was here for a liberal arts education and, by God, I meant to get it.

When Rossi passed out a sonnet called *"La Dormeuse"* ("A Sleeping Girl") for explication, I set out to tax and display all my powers. First I copied out Valéry's languorous, evocative poem, paying close attention to its punctuation, line breaks and rhymes. Then I memorized it, from the evocative opening, *"Quel secrets dans son coeur brûle, ma jeune amie"* ("What secrets in her heart is my young friend burning"), to its final phrase, *"et mes yeux sont ouverts"* ("and my eyes are open"). As I walked about campus, I recited the verses to myself—

and thought and thought about what the words meant, how the sounds of the syllables interlaced, why these particular images had been selected. I looked for alliteration, assonance, symbolism and unusual diction. And then I carefully wrote my paper, marked it up and wrote it again.

The following week in class Rossi stared at me in a strange new way. He handed back our essays and I quickly turned to the final page of mine, where he had scribbled in French: "Too many language errrors—badly structured, poorly developed exposition. But . . . you have inserted into this explication original IDEAS, ideas that seem to me occasionally brilliant . . . or at the very least intelligent—something almost unique in this course. B++++++." "Brilliant"—he had written that my ideas were brilliant. To correct the faults in language and usage, Rossi suggested that next year I sign up for an advanced grammar and stylistics course. I could hear Miss Raymond chuckling with satisfaction.

Meanwhile, I kept working harder and ever harder in seventeenth-century poetry, now earning C's and the occasional C+ on my weekly quizzes. Not good enough. Remembering that Bongiorno had once required students to memorize poetry and that apt quotation would support arguments on the final, I recklessly dog-eared pages of Donne, Herbert and Marvell and, in the spirit of my morning walk to Admiral King, began to learn poems, stanzas and key lines by heart. I reviewed my class notes again and again. I read all the criticism in the reserve reading room. I reflected on every poem's meaning and machinery. And then I sharpened my pencils and sat down for the semester's one all-important test.

I received a B- for the entire course and was ecstatic. But the final-exam blue books hadn't yet been returned when Bongiorno bumped into me in the hall at King and gently asked me to stop by his office. What could this mean? Was there a mistake? Was I supposed to get a C-? No. "I just wanted to congratulate you privately, Michael, on having written one of the three best finals in the class. A really remarkable piece of work." And then he added: "You know, you might consider becoming an English major after all."

Chapter Eighteen

The only morality for a writer is knowledge.
—Hermann Broch

By the beginning of my second semester at Oberlin in the spring of 1967, I had hesitantly begun to think of myself as an English major. But not an entirely conventional one. I was interested in literature, no matter what its nation of origin, but also in intellectual history. I yearned to be—as should be clear by now—cultivated as well as erudite, at ease with the world's art and music as well as familiar with its books. How I would make a living didn't cross my mind then. Perhaps I'd become a professor.

Certainly I was lucky enough to attend a college where captivating teachers set the norm. Sometimes you didn't even need to take a class to be inspired by them. The retired and distinguished Professor Frederick B. Artz, author of standard works on medieval history and revolutionary Europe, resided in an ordinary-looking house behind Carnegie Library. I met the man very briefly, only once. But I have never forgotten his study. Dark bookshelves along the walls. Worn volumes—hardcovers, sets—standing in hushed rows. The kind of antique globe Prince Henry the Navigator might have daydreamed over. Oriental rugs, of course, and Renaissance prints, even a green-globed library lamp in the center of a massive desk. I decided that I'd rather have that room than Bill Briola's.

European history, of the kind Artz once taught, particularly appealed to me, as I insisted on better understanding the course of Western civilization since the ancients. So I signed up for one course after another with Barry McGill, Robert Neil and Marcia Colish.

Sandy-haired, tall and thin, McGill would stride into the lecture hall and immediately begin talking. He invariably wore serious, crisply pressed three-piece suits; favored dashing rep ties with quietly assertive stripes of burgundy; and always kept his dressy black wingtips polished and spotless. There was no nonsense about him. He lectured, we took notes. But such a mind! Such clarity in his exposition of anything from nominalism to the course of the Thirty Years War to English parliamentary law! As he spoke, in crisp, Gibbonian sentences, one felt awe at the precision of his intelligence. Imagine Sherlock Holmes as a history prof and you will gain an inkling of McGill's charisma.

After my graduation I never saw McGill again, but there was obviously far more to the man than an Ohio college instructor with the dry manner of an Oxford grandee. Somebody did tell me that, following the death of his wife, the long-retired McGill, restless and lonely, spent some hours each week shelving books in Carnegie. A former colleague asked why and he reportedly answered, "I began my academic life as a student working in the library, and I can think of no better way to end it." I hope this story isn't apocryphal.

In those days Oberlin swarmed with professors who poured their energies into the classroom and never quite got around to producing that long-deferred major work of scholarship. Bongiorno, Rossi and McGill were of this company, and we students benefited. So was Robert Neil, who specialized in German history and sometimes wore suspenders and lederhosen to class and a smoking jacket while he smartly typed away in his book-lined office. Funny, worldly and very quick-witted, Neil had studied with Crane Brinton at Harvard and, according to rumor, had there dispensed fabulous sums on wine for his college dining club. He directed my research on socialist thought in the nineteenth century—Herzen, Marx and, my personal favorite, the anarchist Bakunin ("The passion for destruction is a creative passion"). It was the sort of thing one studied in the sixties.

In their different ways, all these were men were classroom wizards, whether wise as Gandalf (I had discovered *The Lord of the Rings*), rigorously analytical or digressively anecdotal. But Marcia Colish wasn't only a great teacher, she was a great scholar too.

Colish taught the richest, most mind-expanding course of my entire academic career: The Intellectual History of the Middle Ages. Many people know a little about the thought and literature of the modern world, but Colish introduced her students to Augustine's apologetics and philosophy, Bede's *Ecclesiastical History*, the educational achievements of Alcuin, the soaring theological intellects of Anselm and Bernard of Clairvaux, the romances of Chrétien de Troyes, Abelard's razor-sharp mind, the ecstatic visions of the Victorines, St. Thomas Aquinas's rigorous scholasticism and that *summa* of medieval culture, Dante's *Divine Comedy*.

I realize now that she could scarcely have been more than thirty, but there was no doubting her vast learning even then. (She was later elected president of the Medieval Academy of America.) Colish spoke machine-gun fast in a brassy New Yorky voice—she was a Jewish convert to Catholicism—and one had to listen sharply to keep up with her plum-packed lectures. Gnosticism. Avicenna. The Other World. Universals. Andreas Capellanus's *Art of Courtly Love*, Hrosvitha's plays. And her assignments: Read E. K. Rand's *Founders of the Middle Ages*. Read M. L. W. Laistner's *Thought and Letters in Western Europe, A.D. 500–900*. Read Charles Homer Haskins's

Renaissance of the Twelfth Century. Read *The Divine Comedy*—all of it—by next week.

"Exhilarating" hardly describes this class, and Marcia Colish must be held largely responsible—along with my genial Chaucer teacher Robert Longsworth—for my eventually starting graduate school in medieval studies. Might Colish have also steered me to fulfill my religion requirement with Old Testament Literature? Having gone through the Bible once for a hundred dollars in the Douai version, I reread Genesis to Zechariah and Malachi all over again in the Revised Standard Version. As my teacher was the translation's general editor, Herbert Gordon May, his closely analytic and authoritative lectures appeared to emanate from God himself.

Over time I checked off not only the college's required classes, but also those I'd set up as essential in my own mind. For instance, Rossi agreed to direct an independent reading course on Montaigne and later led a dozen students through Proust's doleful human comedy, *À la recherche du temps perdu.* So during 1968 when riots swept the nation and protests rocked the Oberlin campus, I would often wearily retreat to Carnegie for sessions of sweet, silent reading. Bent over a table for hour after hour, I would lose myself in the *Arabian Nights* transformations of Swann, Odette and Charlus. And if I wasn't tracking Proust's lovers and *arrivistes* I might instead surrender to the swaggering defiance of Milton's Satan—"Better to reign in Hell than serve in Heaven"—or to the urbane skepticism of Hume and the double entendres of Restoration drama.

A true teacher, the classicist William Arrowsmith maintained, embodies his subject. Certainly this seemed true and important at Oberlin, where professors and students interacted outside the classroom as much as they did in it. Nearly all my instructors inspired me by their example, by becoming human advertisements for the kind of mental excellence they most admired: Christian humanism, razorlike intellection, vast learning, Renaissance *sprezzatura*.

Or intensive factual mastery. In his class on Shakespeare's tragedies and final romances, the fiery, Lear-like Warren Taylor, then a year from his retirement, maintained that interpretations of the plays changed like hemlines, but that there was no substitute for simply knowing them inside out. (As indeed there isn't.) So his tests were rigorous, and exactingly detailed. "What happens when Hamlet visits his mother in her bedroom? Quote as much dialogue as you can in your answers." My flair for memorizing obviously stood me in good stead.

For a semester's study of Yeats and Stevens—under the direction of the sensitive, sensible David Young—we discussed not only all the verse of two of my favorite poets, but also whole volumes of their prose: Yeats's *A Vision*, Stevens's *The Necessary Angel*, raftloads of miscellaneous essays, criticism and letters. In Dewey Ganzel's elegant, wide-ranging class in American fiction we read the work of Clemens, Crane, Howells, Dreiser, Anderson, Hemingway and half a dozen others. And often very long books too, like Frank Norris's *The Octopus*, a grandly melodramatic epic about wheat farming (my old subject!), and *The Ambassadors*, in which I first heard the sinuous, hesitant, punctilious and compassionate voice of Henry James: "Live life, live all you can. It's a mistake not to."

For a couple of classes in German—I'd worked on the language for two years in high school instead of taking 11th- and 12th-grade math—I turned to poet, critic and translator Stuart Friebert. Friebert introduced me to such modern German poets as Karl Krolow and Hans Magnus Enzensberger ("*Lies keine oden, mein Sohn, lies die Fahrpläne*"—"Don't read odes, my son, read the train schedules"), but above all he showed me the wonders of Kafka: "*Ein Käfig ging einen Vogel suchen*"—"A cage went in search of a bird." The oily, social-climbing Rilke, who was achieving virtual godhead at the time, was difficult to warm to, but there was no resisting the sad-eyed "Panther" or the the final exhortation of the "Archaic Torso of Apollo": "You must change your life."

Certainly, my favorite teacher of all, Mathis Szykowski, an expert on the nineteenth-century novel, knew all about changing one's life. A Polish Jew in World War II France, the neglected child of divorced parents, he lost most of his family to the Holocaust, emigrated to America, married a black woman, spent several years as a socialist in California and New York City. He arrived in Oberlin on a short-term appointment with only an M.A., and seven years later, well into middle age, was granted tenure. Without a Ph.D. The college didn't really have a choice: Anyone with a smidgen of French scrambled for a place in his courses just to experience, as one student evaluation had it, "a genius in action." When Szykowski spoke about violence or politics or art or ideology, about Life, you could look into his eyes— unnervingly large and probing behind his thick glasses—and know that he wasn't just getting this stuff from books.

Szykowski also taught the French stylistics course, the one Rossi had recommended I take to improve my grammar. In class Professor Szykowski would distribute a mimeographed page of French prose—no author or work identified—and ask for comment on its character, idiosyncrasies and special effects. We would do our best, and then after a quarter hour of our laboring explanations, our teacher would himself slowly dismantle the passage— from Balzac or Flaubert—before our wondering eyes. He made me realize that prose not only should be written as carefully as poetry, but that it could also be read with the same rewarding attentiveness. Little wonder that one of the best-known "readers" of literature in our time, Barbara Johnson (now of Harvard), sat next to me in this and several other Szykowski courses.

Class assignments, like the man himself, were appropriately challenging. For instance, "Write a story that is comic and pathetic at the same time." I thought about this paradoxical balancing act, then related my encounter with the school patrol. Write a story set in the country. I made up a Maugham-like tale about a sensitive young man who goes to work on a farm and there falls for the farmer's daughter. In a moment of passion the two young people sleep together. Being morally upright, our hero is immediately consumed by guilt and swears never to commit such a terrible act again. But the girl wants to have more sex. He refuses, pleads with her to wait till they're older. Irked, she spits out, "If you won't, I'll find someone who will," casting a lascivious glance at one of the other farm hands, a loutish, vulgar redneck. What can the boy do? His rash act has corrupted a girl he once revered into little better than . . . Against his principles he has sex with her for the rest of the summer. But—the story is told retrospectively—we learn that the experience poisons his entire life. He never marries. The girl, of course, is perfectly healthy and normal, while the boy's spirit has been insidiously stunted by received ideas about morality.

I worked enormously hard on these French compositions, often spending half my study time on them, driven to write something artful and worthwhile. Szykowski corrected our papers with microscopic attentiveness, emending grammar, questioning word choice, pointing out felicities, thinking aloud in the margins about what we were saying or trying to say. In essence, he addressed a student paper with the same sensitivity he brought to a paragraph by Flaubert. And this example—that every word should be deliberated, that every sentence should be weighed—carried over into all my subsequent writing. In Mathis Szykowski's French class I learned to write English.

Chapter Nineteen

Careful reading should precede all writing. The object
of each paper or report should be thoroughness and
truth. Literary finish is desirable.

—Lane Cooper

As a boy I'd devoured crateloads of adventure stories and biographies, as a high school student I'd picked my way through established classics under the partial guidance of Carnegie, Fadiman and Adler. In college I discovered "criticism."

I'd always been interested in learning to read better, more efficiently. My thrift-shop paperbacks bore pencil notations in the margins and I knew how to look for word units and skim my way down a page if I had to. But my classes at Oberlin and the constant discussion of ideas, politics and life in its hallways compelled me to start thinking about literature in a more serious, even philosophical fashion. What, I wondered, is the best way to read a poem, a novel, anything? Could I be too absorbed in the beauty of sentences or the turn of events and so be missing the real meaning? Is there a real meaning? Back then, some kids used to end every argument with the phrase, "Oh, that's just your subjective opinion." Was that all liking or not liking a book meant? That couldn't be right, could it?

All my course syllabi suggested various secondary readings, but these tended to be geared to specific problems or texts. So, on my own, or through the recommendations of teachers and on the advice of classmates, I was slowly guided to a half dozen books that formed and corrected my taste while demonstrating what R. P. Blackmur defined as "the critic's job of work." Even now, in this age of theory, I regard their authors as some of the best instructional guides to the deeper enjoyment of literature.

One afternoon in the Oberlin Co-op Bookstore, I glimpsed a trade-sized paperback from New Directions with a huge "7" on its otherwise white cover. What could this be about? I picked up William Empson's bluntly titled *Seven Types of Ambiguity* (1930) and read some of the opening chapter, bought the book and soon covered nearly every page with underlinings and Adlerian marginalia.

Empson's diction was so peculiar—loosely jointed sentences, coupled with a casual, even chummy voice that could be oddly humorous, all the while inviting the reader to assent to propositions because they seemed commonsensical or obvious. "Unexplained beauty," wrote the twenty-four-year-old prodigy from Cambridge, "arouses an irritation in me, a sense that this would be a good place to scratch; the reasons that make a line of verse likely to give pleasure, I believe, are like the reasons for anything else; one can reason about them."

Despite this conversational nonchalance, Empson's razorlike intellect could delaminate the shiny veneer of any poem or line of verse, uncover its true makeup, plunge into the eddies of meaning beneath the placid surface. Not only did he practice close reading that approached Louis Agassiz–like dissection, he showed a preternatural sensitivity to the undisclosed, even the unacknowledged: This couplet may seem to say that, but if we look more closely, feel more finely the tiniest calibrations, we can see that it actually means this instead. Or as well. Or even both—at the same time.

Most people who've read *Seven Types* remember the analysis of Shakespeare's "Bare Ruined Choirs" sonnet, but I was most struck by Empson's general ability simply to see without blinkers, to become almost as a little child again. The first line of Keats's "Ode to Melancholy"—"No, no; go not to Lethe, neither twist"—"tells us that somebody or some force in the poet's mind, must have wanted to go to Lethe very much, if it took four negatives in the first line to stop them." Of a Crashaw poem, he writes, "a saint is being adored for her chastity, and the metaphors about her are veiled references to copulation." When Faustus exclaims, "Ugly Hell gape not; come not, Lucifer," he shows that the necromancer, crying out against his impending doom, may be secretly welcoming it. Following initial imperatives, those unaccented "nots" seem almost halfhearted. Something in Faustus's restless, questing spirit looks forward to death as what has been called (by Peter Pan) "a very great adventure."

Such unexpected readings made me realize that the effects of poetry arose from just such richness of signification, that lines could be powerful because of the multiple fields of meaning they created. More practically, Empson's book taught me to reflect on every word in a text, to trust none of them and suspect them all and to welcome the plurality of poetic worlds that the simplest words might give rise to.

Throughout my college years it was my habit to wander about the Co-op at the start of each semester to see what teachers had ordered for their classes. In the fall of 1967 I noticed, next to a stack of Theodore Roethke's poems *Words for the Wind* ("I knew a woman lovely in her bones"), a paperback of Randall Jarrell's *Poetry and the Age* (1953). Jarrell soon reinforced the lessons of Empson. That collection of essays includes two famous reappraisals of Robert Frost, pointing out that the "Kris Kringle" of American poetry harbored a more complex, darker and even sexier side than most people—especially kids—realized. He wasn't just a swinger of birches or a guy who spent a lot of time cleaning brooks.

In "Design," for instance, Frost could view a spider, flower and butterfly as "assorted characters of death and blight," transmute the color white into the chilling hue of predestination and shiver at the utterly alien, unfathomable darkness of Nature. A poem like "Provide, Provide" disclosed a bitter wisdom—about reputation and the need for accommodation to life's harsh unfoldings—that once read is impossible to forget. Beauty, says Frost, won't last, power can be lost, the wheel of fortune always turns, and, most painful of all, "No memory of having starred / Atones for later disregard." The poet then concludes by coolly suggesting that "boughten friendship" is better than none at all. "Provide! Provide!"

No cynical French aphorist of the seventeenth century could be more gimlet-eyed about the way of the world.

Like Eliot in his early essays, Jarrell knew how to quote brilliantly, then segue into a brief paragraph or two of his own that, without any belaboring, detailed how the passage worked its particular magic. To show the sensual Frost, Jarrell reprinted a chunk of "The Pauper Witch at Grafton" in which a woman ensnares a man by making him gather wet snow berries from beside a waterfall "up where the trees grow short, the mosses tall." Not only that, she adds: "I made him do it for me in the dark./ And he liked everything I made him do."

As Jarrell observes, the way Frost's poem almost coerces you into reading those last two verses conveys more about the power of sexuality than all of Dylan Thomas, or Dr. Kinsey's report, for that matter. (Yet much as I quicken at those lines, I find an earlier one— "Only bewitched so I would last him longer"—even more darkly evocative of female sexual power.)

As incisive as Jarrell could be in his revaluations—the other great triumph in *Poetry and the Age* is the revisionist appreciation of Whitman—I learned as much from his style as from his critical intelligence. He unashamedly displayed an almost fannish enthusiasm, cheerleading for the neglected and unfashionable throughout this and his other books: He praised Kipling's short stories and Chekhov's, Robert Graves's White Goddess poems ("There is one story and one story only/ That will prove worth your telling"), Christina Stead's *The Man Who Loved Children*, Turgenev's *Sportsman's Sketches*. He was fearlessly personal—these, he proclaimed, are the poems and stories I truly love.

But Jarrell wasn't just a soft and fuzzy *littérateur*, his soul adventuring among the masterpieces. His sentences often cut and drew real blood, neatly skewering the pretentious, vulgar and inept. The poetry of my poor Oscar Williams "gave the impression of having been written on a typewriter by a typewriter." Criticism, he observed, was "the poetry of prosaic natures (and, even in our time, of some poetic ones); there is a divinity that inspires the most sheeplike of scholars, the most tabular of critics, so that the man too dull to understand 'Evangeline' still can be possessed by some theory about 'Evangeline.' . . ." After reading Jarrell, anyone's critical writing aspired to be lively, shrewd and passionate.

In some ways, *The ABC of Reading* (1934) took liveliness almost too far. Ezra Pound was a whirling dervish, a carnival barker, a one-man band for the study of the books that mattered most. Read the inventors of new forms, he shouted, the truly original, not the palely imitative. And then he held up passages, with preacherly commentary, from the most far-flung and unlikely authors: Gavin Douglas, Arthur Golding (whose translation of Ovid was "the most beautiful book in the English language"), George Crabbe, Walter Savage Landor.

As the impresario of literary Paris and London, ol' Ez declaimed—in CAPITALS—and coined sentences that sounded as definitive as Aristotle's: "Great literature is simply language charged with meaning to the utmost possible degree. . . .The way to learn the music of verse is to listen to it. . . . Incompetence will show in the use of too many words. . . . More writers fail from lack of character than from lack of intelligence." Pound embodied pure iconoclasm, asserting that France had regained the intellectual dominance of Europe by reducing the academic hour to fifty minutes. Above all, though, "*Il miglior fabbro*," the better maker—as Eliot called him in the dedication of *The Waste Land*—didn't just enjoy books or love them, he reminded you that real poems, real authors MATTERED, that they were vital to the life of the mind and the humane culture of the world. Reading Pound at nineteen left me feeling as if I had encountered Prometheus, the Fire-Bringer, and that my soul had been set ablaze.

Back in the 1960s the notion of "commitment," that an intellectual should participate in history and act to change it, troubled anyone of a scholarly bent. Its chief exponent, Jean-Paul Sartre, still reigned from the Left Bank—simultaneously existential philosopher, cultural provocateur and impolitic activist. His polemical *What Is Literature?* (1948) impressed me because it foregrounded questions about value: Why do we read? What function should literature exercise in society? For whom does a writer write? Practicing explication and stylistic analysis by inclination, I needed to think beyond the page to the public who would actually react to a text. Literature ought to be more than a graveyard or a Pantheon: At its best, it could and should be a mode for engaging with the world, with History. To matter, as Sartre exhorted, a writer needed to address the present moment, else be found irrelevant.

Shortly after discovering *What Is Literature*, I picked up some Lionel Trilling and Irving Howe, eminences of the era. But their worthy, somberly intelligent essays failed to awaken the least correspondent breeze in my soul. I admired the earnestness and devotion to the life of the mind, yet never closed their books hoping to grow up and be like them. These dour New York intellectuals preferred the pontifical to the passionate. R. P. Blackmur, by contrast, appealed to me far more—"Criticism is the formal discourse of an amateur"—yet even in his youthful *Language as Gesture* (1952) and *The Lion and the Honeycomb* (1955) his style made for hard slogging, while in later books he grew rebarbative and impenetrable. Similarly, Kenneth Burke I learned from most when he avoided grand theorizing—his very *raison d'etre*—and instead stuck to analyzing the semantic displacements or dramatistic undercurrents in "Kubla Khan," *Mein Kampf* or the first three chapters of Genesis.

W. H. Auden had blurbed my paperback of Burke's *Philosophy of Literary Form* (1941), and so I naturally went looking for the poet's own essays. In Auden's *The Dyer's Hand* (1962) and his later nonfiction I discovered neither a kindred soul nor a goad to increased social consciousness, but rather a clever, austere critical mind in action. In an essay like "Making, Knowing, Judging" the poet freewheels on the page before our eyes, spinning off dazzling aperçus, ideas and speculations:

> *To say that a work is inspired means that, in the judgment of its author or his readers, it is better than they could reasonably hope it would be, and nothing else. . . .*

Elsewhere Auden might address philosophical matters—the relationship of Master and Servant or of Christianity and art—and then jump immediately to what he would outline as the essentials or even essences. Sentences could be compact aphorisms, essays grand schemas—sometimes with grids or charts. To me Auden represented a slightly reprobate Anglo-American Paul Valéry (whose own fictional alter ego M. Teste famously asserted: "Stupidity is not my strong point"). In the end, I revered Auden's intellect, even though it was too diagrammatic and surgical for mush-minded me to emulate.

Still, Auden inspired one to reread fairy tales, to listen to operas, at least to attempt to grasp the interconnections and commonalities among artists, composers and writers. He made one pay heed to larger patterns and archetypes, especially in *The Enchafed Flood* (1950), his three brilliant lectures on "the romantic iconography of the sea."

What one might call this macroscopic view of literature drew forth its greatest champion in Northrop Frye. If Empson brought your nose right up against a poem, then picked apart every word, Frye made you stand back and survey a work's whole shape and form. Like Auden, he taught a kind of reading without walls, revealing that, say, *The Big Sleep* conformed to the model of the chivalric romance—detective Philip Marlowe, like knightly Parzival, can restore the polluted waste land by asking just the right questions—while the chivalric romance in its turn obliquely reenacted the Fall and Christ's blood sacrifice.

Besides underscoring the crucial importance of great patterning works and templates drawn from myth, ritual and Scripture, *Anatomy of Criticism* (1957) was engagingly lively, even dryly witty. Rousseau, remarks Frye of my old high school favorite, "says that the original society of nature and reason has been overlaid by the corruptions of civilization and that a sufficiently courageous revolutionary act could reestablish it." Certainly, a view to which many in the sixties would assent. But the Canadian critic adds almost with an ironic smile, "It is nothing either for or against this argument to say that it is informed by the myth of the sleeping beauty."

Frye also helped define my understanding of liberal education, which he characterized as "the fertilizing of life by learning, in which the systematic progress of scholarship flows into a systematic progress of taste and understanding." A noble ideal, one to which Cardinal Newman himself would assent. For myself, though, I was coming to recognize that my memory could marshal all sorts of facts from my reading and that I could focus obsessively on a poem or problem, but that the truly "systematic" might be alien to my nature. Still, I couldn't help but envy and want to learn from such a mighty intellect as Frye's, one that could look out on all the world's art and literature and see, beneath the hurly burly, the hidden engines. Years later, I encountered this sort of encyclopedic understanding at its most magnificent in the great German émigré scholars Erich Auerbach (*Mimesis: The Representation of Reality in Western Literature*, 1953), Leo Spitzer (*Linguistics and Literary History*, 1948) and E. R. Curtius (*European Literature and the Latin Middle Ages*, 1948).

At his worst, Northrop Frye could seem merely nimble-witted, like Empson, oddly enough: Both, you felt, could work their interpretive legerdemain on anything and be convincing. But *Anatomy of Criticism* repeatedly confirmed the value of my own greedy reading habits: "The first thing the literary critic has to do is read literature to make an inductive survey of his own field and let his critical principles shape themselves solely out of his knowledge of that field."

Outside the academy no one ever displayed such omnivorous reading habits as the preeminent literary journalist of the twentieth century, that patron saint of the profession, the rotund, jowly and prickly Edmund Wilson. I began to read Wilson as a college sophomore and now own virtually all his books. In my youth I particularly envied the clarity and force of his prose—a reflection of the masculine, slightly imperious nature of his character. Yet, surprisingly, he never taught me much about how to interpret a poem or novel. Stanley Edgar Hyman (in *The Armed Vision*) notoriously, perhaps jealously, dismissed him as a popularizer, a mere paraphraser of other authors.

Ultimately, though, I came around to Wilson out of admiration for that unflagging appetite for books. More than anyone I knew or knew about, he really did seem to have read everything, from Persius to Pasternak, Mary Chesnut to Agatha Christie. So much industry taught one the virtue of thoroughness and the unassailable authority that resulted from knowing a writer in his or her entirety. In various essays Wilson safaried his way through an *oeuvre complète* and set down the strange sights he found along the way. "My purpose," he wrote at the beginning of *The Triple Thinkers* (1938), "has always been to try to contribute something new: I have aimed either to present some writer who was not well enough known or, in the case of a familiar writer, to call attention to some neglected aspect of his work or his career." Such honest reportage was hard to come by among strictly academic scholars, while other critics espoused the cardinal virtues of their pet theory, practice or school of thought. They were partial critics, while the all-too-human literary journalist struck me, for all his crotchets, as an impartial one.

Not least, however, Edmund Wilson lifted the writing of reviews and literary history into a real, if secondary, art form. Some chapters in *To the Finland Station* (1940), such as "Karl Marx dies at his desk," possess the rhythm and beauty of a novella by Turgenev or James. A writer, Wilson showed, could impart to even casual journalism an elegance, shape and dramatic energy that would make it rereadable and memorable. As a student, I returned to *Classics and Commercials* (1950), *The Bit Between My Teeth* (1965) and his other collections again and again. I still do.

Chapter Twenty

Cultivate what the public reproaches you for—it's you.
—*Jean Cocteau*

Near the end of May 1968, I finally met my first real writer—and the last great personal mentor of my life.

I had promised my friend Roger Phelps that I would stop and visit him for an afternoon in New York City, where he lived in the summers. "Come on, Dirda. I'll show you the Met. You can say hello to Robert and Becki." The sophisticated Roger called his parents by their first names. "It'll be fun. We'll be sure you don't miss your flight." This was a chartered jet to France for the members of the Oberlin Summer Program in Aix-en-Provence and Paris. Since the plane didn't leave till late in the evening and I had daydreamed too long about New York to pass by the chance to see a little of it, I naturally said yes.

Following Roger's directions, I made my way to the Phelps apartment on East Twelfth Street just off Fifth Avenue—the edge of Greenwich Village. Emerging from the subway into Washington Square, I found myself cowed by the overcharged, over-the-top, overwhelming character of Manhattan—the crowded sidewalks and speeding taxis, the shrill pleadings of street vendors and panhandlers, the debilitating heat of the day. Before I had trekked a few blocks I had been subtly propositioned by one middle-aged gentleman and eyed by a couple of attractive thirtyish professional women. But then

I was nineteen, tan and even handsome, what Edward Gorey once described as a well-set-up young man.

And so was the slender guy who came bounding down the stairs, two steps at a time, after I'd rung the Phelps doorbell. Black tousled hair, white T-shirt, blue jeans, Clark Wallabys on his feet and a welcoming grin on his face—doubtless Roger's older brother. It wasn't.

I had never met an actual, breathing author before. A freelance literary journalist in and around New York for most of his adult life, Robert Phelps is usually remembered today for compiling *Earthly Paradise*, a selection of Colette's autobiographical writings. But he has other claims to literary fame, not to mention my own lifelong affection and indebtedness.

Born in Elyria, a dropout from Oberlin (he studied with Bongiorno and rebelled against that gentle soul's traditional Christian scholarship), Robert fled the cornfields of northern Ohio, first to Chicago (like Sherwood Anderson, his fellow Elyrian) and then to Manhattan. From an early age he revered books, the writing life, creative makers of any kind. (As a penniless young man he'd swiped Robert Lowell's first collection, *Lord Weary's Castle*, from a Cleveland bookstore. "A first edition too.") If he prized a novelist or poet or essayist, he accumulated everything the man or woman had published. "The test of one's devotion to a writer," my new mentor would tell me, "is the willingness to collect his journalism."

At the time we met, Robert lived mainly in a single thirty-by-thirty-foot room, with dark-stained floors and walls lined with bookshelves: a cave of making. The curtains were always kept drawn, blocking out the day and night. Pole lamps stood next to a slightly high-tech chrome and leather easy chair. Extension lights jutted from the corners of bookcases. On a coffeetable in the middle of the room there always lay page proofs, literary magazines, catalogues. Instead of a sofa, a daybed butted up against the back of a freestanding bookcase and was covered with pillows embroidered with scenes from classical mythology (the handiwork of Robert's wife, the painter Rosemarie Beck). Near the music corner—lots of Stravinsky, Poulenc and Ravel LPs—stood a long low set of white shelves on top of which rested more books, some heavy tumblers and a big bottle of Tanqueray gin.

Robert's work desk was simplicity itself: A sheet of painted plywood across two metal filing cabinets. Near at hand, reference books: a Larousse, the *Concise Oxford English Dictionary*, the *Annals of English Literature 1475–1950* ("the principal publications of each year together with an alphabetical index of authors with their works"). Above the desk hung a four-by-six-foot bulletin board adorned with notes, pictures, quotations, even hand-cast astrological charts. In the center the writer had pinned a photograph of himself strolling down a country road in tennis shoes with novelist Glenway Wescott; next to it an exhortation from Auden: "We were put on this earth to make things." Robert always typed on a portable manual typewriter, preferring yellow, green or pink paper, and on the day he first bounded down the stairs was finishing a review of Randall Jarrell's posthumous *Third Book of Criticism*. I picked up the page proofs—the first I had ever seen or touched.

Except for a few random English and American classics, this hero worshiper of the literary life kept no book or author he didn't deeply care about. And like Bill Briola he had read everything on his shelves. More than anyone I have ever known, Robert followed Mortimer J. Adler's advice and marked up his library—not with the abandon of a college freshman with a Day-Glo yellow highlighter, but thoughtfully, sparingly, almost poetically with black ink. Open his copy of Auden's *Enchafèd Flood* and you would find a small picture of the poet pasted on the flyleaf and passages from the text underscored, often in tandem with comments, source notes (Robert tracked the book's title to

"Othello, II, 1, 16") and even obstreperous questions: "On what principle," he demands of a ghostly Auden, "do you quote the Latin original for Horace but quote Dante only in translation?" Not only rubbed and worn, Robert's books would lie flat in their loosened bindings. "Well-loved" is the coy booksellers' term. They were.

Robert didn't care for dust jackets. They were too garish, and he preferred the muted hues of binder's cloth. "Books only look and feel like books without the jackets." Not that he threw the dust wrappers away. Instead he snipped out the author photographs and pasted them in a scrapbook, originally called "The Poet's Face." Into this, as he recalled later, "miscellaneous pictures and clippings were glued or Scotch-taped, with relevant dates, quotations and biographical details scribbled in the margins. When one volume was filled up, another was begun." Robert reveled in literary gossip and biographical anecdote, the kind of material celebrated in the *Paris Review's* Writers at Work interviews (but also much that was too scandalous to be printed there). Soon "the poet's face led to his desk, his family, his travels, finances, love affairs—anything germane to his vocation. In the same way, poets came to include not only writers but composers, painters, any expressive maker. It was all very personal and capricious, often indiscreet, and swaddled throughout in hero worship for the creative life."

Eventually this album would be expanded, reworked with the help of his friend Peter Deane, and published as *The Literary Life: A Scrapbook Almanac of the Anglo-American Literary Scene, 1900–1950.* I buy every copy I find in secondhand bookstores; it is, in the words of its preface, "a loving elegy, a larky swansong, a doting, dotty, but undaunted Souvenir Album for books, books, books, and for all the men and women who ever believed in making them."

Surveying his shelves that day, I soon identified my host's favorite writers, for he had searched out what bibliographers call the A, B, and even C items: all the books they had written, edited or contributed to. W. H. Auden and Colette owned entire bookcases all to themselves, but Robert also cherished the work of Jean Cocteau, Glenway Wescott, Marcel Jouhandeau, Henry James, Janet Flanner, Cyril Connolly, Paul Léautaud, Louise Bogan, Rayner Heppenstall and Brigid Brophy. He advised me to read Robert Craft's diaries and conversations with Stravinsky—Craft, I was assured, was "the Boswell *de nos jours*." He counted poet and translator Richard Howard, composer and diarist Ned Rorem, publisher Roger Straus and critic Susan Sontag among his friends. The novelist James Salter—who writes so tenderly of Robert in his brilliant memoir *Burning the Days*—expresses what many others must have felt: "He was one of the most important influences in my life and in whatever I have written. . . . Would this interest him I often wondered? Would he find it deserving?"

This transplanted Ohioan remains the most deeply literary man I've ever known. In his youth he cofounded Grove Press, brought out its first three books (Crashaw's poems, selections from Aphra Behn, Melville's *Confidence Man*), then sold the business to Barney Rosset. In *Love and Death in the American Novel* Leslie Fiedler praises his novel, *Heroes and Orators*, as superior to better-known work by Truman Capote and Gore Vidal. The younger Phelps edited an exemplary anthology called *Twentieth-Century Culture: The Breaking Up*, appeared as a regular book columnist for some years in the *Herald Tribune Book Week* and was acclaimed by Garry Wills—in *Confessions of a Conservative*—as having been in his heyday the best reviewer in the country.

In person Robert exuded an angelic generosity of heart and spirit, touched with a bit of malice and that almost fetishistic reverence for genius. "You should make pilgrimages to the writers you admire. Or to their graves." He himself had just recently visited Melville's tomb in the company of poet Louise Bogan. To my eye, his days seemed uncluttered by the normal burdens of life—he read, scribbled, gossiped, occasionally had lunch with editors over robust martinis. "Now how would you translate *L'Oeuvre au noir*?" he asked me once. I couldn't figure it out, nor could he, despite having spent the afternoon mulling over the expression, which derives from alchemy. (Marguerite Yourcenar's novel eventually appeared in English as *The Abyss*.) He regularly gave me books I coveted and couldn't quite afford: Stendhal's *Oeuvres Intimes*, Auden's commonplace book *A Certain World*, Gallup's bibliography of T. S. Eliot, Jules Renard's *Journal*. Once, when he returned from a trip to England, he brought back for himself the complete works of Ivy Compton-Burnett. "A little Ivy," he later told me with a shake of the head, "goes a long way."

Robert occasionally taught literary journalism—or "creative nonfiction," as he dubbed it—at the New School and literature at Manhattanville College. His printed syllabi carried titles like "Available Light" or "Oblongs and Squares" (a phrase from Virginia Woolf's *The Waves*: "We have made oblongs and stood them upon squares. This is our triumph, this is our consolation"). These course descriptions were often divided into elaborate grids and were invariably decorated with quotations: "The work of art is the death mask of its conception" (Walter Benjamin); "The hind that would be mated to the lion/ Must die for love" (Shakespeare); "The spirit afterwards, but first the touch" (Charlotte Mew). All these quotes immediately went into my own commonplace book. Touchstones.

He would send me advice over the years: "Try to write something of your own—something you have felt or seen. Try to work at it regularly, no matter how slowly. It will redeem those hours of Middle English. And try to remember that when you're finished with grad school you'll be equipped to eat without benefit of steel mills." Then he'd go on to describe some of his life, say at MacDowell colony:

I'm working on a memoir-novel this month, with a quiet cabin deep, deep in the birch and maple woods. I have a piano to bang on when I'm blocked and I croak Schumann and Poulenc to my own accompaniment. I'm here from 8:15 to four. Then I go back to my sleeping room, shave, nap and at precisely 5:30 mix myself a massive Tanqueray martini (6 parts gin, 0.1 part very dry vermouth and a twist of lemon peel over four cubes of ice). Dinner's at 6:30 and by 8:30 I'm in bed with my Garzanti dictionary or Valéry or Renard. The autumn colors are the most beautiful I've seen in 15 years. Yesterday I drove 6 miles to visit Willa Cather's grave in a tiny village called Jaffrey Center. . . . I think I have a review in next week's Life, *or the one after that. At least I wrote it and they paid me; of Forster's posthumous novel* Maurice.

With his lucky students Robert would reread his favorite texts: Cavafy's "The God Forsakes Antony" ("do not mourn . . . / your works that have failed, the plans of your life/ that have all turned out to be illusions"); Auden's "Thanksgiving for a Habitat" ("where I needn't, ever, be at home *to/* those I am not at home *with*"); Christopher Isherwood's *Berlin Stories* and Janet Flanner's Paris journals; D. H. Lawrence's Maurice Magnus memoir; Colette's midly shocking *Bella-Vista*; Mozart and Da Ponte's *Magic Flute*; Genet's *Our Lady of the Flowers*, and many others equally wonderful and unexpected.

I gradually acquired all these books, most of them at the Strand just down the street from 6 East Twelfth. For years I would study the acknowledgments at the back of *The Literary Life* and try to find the very same books, gradually building a library as much like his as possible—Ford Madox Ford's *The March of Literature* ("the book of an old man mad about writing"), Edwin Denby's dance criticism, Isaac Babel's short stories, Scott Fitzgerald's *The Crack-Up*, Cyril Connolly's *The Unquiet Grave*, a particular favorite: "The more books we read, the sooner we perceive that the true function of a writer is to produce a masterpiece and that no other task is of any consequence."

Over the years that I knew him Robert worked fitfully at a memoir called *Following*—and I wish he had completed it. He used to quote the religious thinker Simone Weil—"We really possess nothing on this earth but the power to say I"—and he himself loved best orts and fragments, anything that revealed the personal, the inner life of a creator, that made the writer present on the page:

Parable, fable, fiction are all fine. I want them. But whether I can gracefully justify it or not, I also want diaries, letters, marginalia, table-talk, all the nonofficial forms by which men have also revealed their mystery, disguises, wishes, feints. . . . Whenever a writer, any writer, uses some semblance of his own first person and tells me something about himself or the world around him which only he could have known, then a viable community of two is formed as I read. It can be a friend or a stranger. But more than the literary art is involved, and I must bring more than my safe aesthetic responses. The encounter may be joyous. It may also be maculate, messy, perturbing, as human relations often are.

For Robert, as he once wrote in a piece about Colette, "there are two classes of writers: those whose subject is the human heart, and those whose emphasis is upon all the other, perhaps more important possibilities in human experience. The latter include many of our most illustrious and bewitching contemporaries, from Valéry to Kafka, to Pirandello and Virginia Woolf. The former include all of my favorite writers, from Shakespeare to Jane Austen to Colette. Compare *All's Well That Ends Well*, *Persuasion* and *Julie de Carneilhan*. Does any writer know any more about love than the other? Aren't they in this respect peers, all three of them, for all the ages?"

Like any writer who must live by his wits and words, Robert took on a steady stream of projects. Yet he possessed a genius for discerning in the work of others those aspects of art and intimacy that he himself most valued. And so he edited Louise Bogan's criticism, James Agee's touching *Letters to Father Flye*, Ned Rorem's sometimes scandalous Paris and New York diaries, a selection from Jean Cocteau titled *Professional Secrets*, the journals of Glenway Wescott and keepsake volumes of Colette's letters and writings about nature. Most of these are enhanced by introductions and commentary—and in these pages I occasionally hear again his sly chuckle, his ingratiating, insistent voice:

This Almanac [The Literary Life] had better be owned, not borrowed; and its owner must use it possessively, aggressively, fountain pen in hand. He must cover the margins with further details, other titles, with events from political history, sports, movies, whatever obsesses him personally. He must thicken the plot, add to the soup, make his own copy unique, and thereby reclaim a little more of the total truth about our first half century's progress. . . .

Fountain pen in hand, indeed: "Here," he said, "you should have a real pen," handing me a blue Esterbrook with a medium nib. "It used to belong to Glenway Wescott. He gave me a couple of them." I have that Esterbrook still, a charm or totem of the literary life.

Not only the first real writer I ever met, Robert was also one of the wisest and dearest and most generous men I have ever known. Like my teacher Bill Briola, he should have lived on and on. But in his early sixties, after having already suffered for many years from a "shaky paw," as he called his Parkinson's disease, Robert was diagnosed with a fast-spreading cancer. When he died, as was said of Byron, a light went out of the world.

Yet on that first day, as Robert breathlessly ushered me into his apartment, past the bundles of *Partisan Review*s, *New Yorker*s, and *Books and Bookmen* piled high in the hallway, those future sufferings would have seemed impossible to imagine. He must have been in his mid-forties—a decade younger than I am now—but looked to be in his late twenties. For the next two hours he thrust books into my hands and practically chortled over outrageous stories about Christopher Isherwood, Cyril Connolly, Kenneth Tynan . . . "Charlotte Mew? She was a protégé of Thomas Hardy, who actually copied out some of her poems at the British Museum. She killed herself by drinking disinfectant, Lysol in other words, and the local paper referred to her as 'Charlotte Mew, said to be a poet.' Like us a Scorpio. . . ."

At five he offered me a drink, set out a board of Jarlsberg cheese and stone-wheat crackers, then leaned back and sipped from his own huge tumbler, before saying reflectively, "You know, Michael, if you're going to France, you really should have a love affair with a French girl. Best way to learn the language. When you do get back, I'll give you a copy of my friend Jim Salter's *A Sport and a Pastime.* Very sexy and beautifully written." He smiled angelically. "Now, where were we? Oh, yes. Auden. . . ."

By the end of that day, with my very first Tanqueray martini in my hand and marvelous talk of books and music and New York and Paris in my ears, I finally knew exactly who I wanted more than anything in life to be.

Chapter Twenty-one

The history of love is the history of absence, of arrival and departure.

—*V. S. Pritchett*

Our plane to Paris swarmed with laughing students from Oberlin and other colleges. The perky, blue-suited stewardesses, as women flight attendants were then called, served up canapés, soda pop flowed and young people swayed and danced in the aisles or chatted with seated friends. After a while, our faculty advisors insisted we settle down already and try to sleep: We would arrive in Paris early in the morning and wouldn't see a bed until we climbed into our *couchettes* on the train south to Aix-en-Provence. "You'll only have a few hours to look around"—enough time for a quick tour of the Louvre, a stroll along the Seine, a visit to a bouquiniste (where I bought a dictionary of French slang) and a *sandwich de pâté* in the Latin Quarter. But it was enough: All my days in Paris later in the summer—when we returned in August from Provence—would be roughly the same as this one, for I wanted nothing more than to be a romantic *flâneur*, a walker in the City of Light.

As is well known, Aix-en-Provence boasts the most beautiful main street in Europe. Plane trees form a canopy over a series of fountains. One side of the Cours Mirabeau emphasizes commercial buildings and confectionary shops, the latter selling *les callisons d'Aix* and other sweets. The other side is the busier and more endearing, with cafés alternating with *papeteries* (stationers) and bookstores. Veering off from the pedestrian-thronged boulevard ancient cobblestoned streets wend their way to the cathedral, the market square, the theater.

I was assigned lodging near the top of the Cours Mirabeau, on the block where Cézanne had been born. In their youth the painter and the novelist Émile Zola chummed around together and these two creative spirits soon presided over my explorations of Aix and its environs. I visited and climbed the Montagne St. Victoire; I read Zola's two early Rougon-Macquart novels set in a fictionalized Aix: *La Conquête de Plassans* (*The Conquest of Plassans*) and *La Faute de l'Abbé Mouret* (*The Sin of Father Mouret*).

My landlady, Madame Wytenhove, plump and somewhat prickly-natured, could have served as a model for one of those ceramic peasant dolls called *santon*. (Many years later, while reading M. F. K. Fisher's affectionate but somewhat saturnine portrait of Aix, *Map of Another Town*, I discovered that she too had roomed with Madame Wytenhove, albeit ten or fifteen years before me. We might well have slept in the same bed.) Madame's son, a college student whose name I have forgotten, was *sympathique* and generous. He spoke to me at breakfast—over big muglike bowls of *café au lait*—about Empire furniture and eighteenth-century art, drove me out to see the dam that Zola's engineer father had built and one evening told me the wonderful opening of Musset's *Confession of a Child of the Century*: The hero is celebrating his coming of age, in the company of his friends, mistress and well-wishers. He has never felt happier—until he accidentally drops his fork or napkin. When he leans down to retrieve it, the birthday boy detects his best friend and mistress playing footsies under the table. In that moment he realizes that all his happiness has been a sham, mere self-delusion.

An enthusiast of romantic excess, and as such a man after my own heart, Madame's son also encouraged me to read Flaubert's gaudy *Temptation of St. Antony*, pointing out the Queen of Sheba's litany of the sensual delights awaiting the chaste anchorite. "*Vous n'avez que toucher mon épaule* . . . You have but to touch my shoulder. . . . I am not a woman, I am a world."

The Oberlin program in Aix required attendance at two classes, one in literature and one on local history. The lit course was devoted to drama, and over six weeks we explicated our way through Camus' *Caligula*, Musset's *Lorenzaccio* (about the attempted assassination of Lorenzo de Medici), Sartre's *Le Diable et le Bon Dieu*, Beckett's *En Attendant Godot* and one or two others. Nearly all of the works addressed issues of personal identity and existential choice—in Sartre's play, for instance, the ruthless mercenary Goetz transforms himself into a kindly saint and then, after many years of holiness, back again into a soldier, simply because of the turn of a card.

The notion of existential choice—that action determines one's being—certainly fit the spirit of the times. Arriving in Paris at the beginning of the summer, my friends and I had just missed the "Events of May," when students rioted and took over the Sorbonne and the surrounding blocks. For a few days civil war seemed to threaten France and de Gaulle called for the military to go on standby and await his command. Eventually, "order" was restored without bloodshed, but the legend of that glorious May had been established: The young might somehow oust the old order and usher in a better, more just world. I did glimpse some of the revolutionary slogans posted on the walls—"*L'Imagination au pouvoir*"—and kicked aside a few remaining chunks of rubble from the street demonstrations.

As a result, early in my temporary expatriation I sauntered up a hill to the Université d'Aix-en-Provence to talk to students there about "*la révolution*." The young had camped out in the classrooms and still spoke fervently about Daniel Cohn-Bendit (a.k.a. Danny the Red) and subverting the current modes of production. But it was so hard, they admitted, to make revolutionaries out of workers, out of "*pères de famille*." Yes, indeed, I thought, remembering my clueless Oberlin classmates on their visits to the National Tube in Lorain. During that endless French summer I would repeatedly sit down with bearded young Maoists and seductive anarchists—in youth hostels, in cafés—and listen raptly as they recalled the already mythic "*événements*." All power to the imagination!

The first days in Aix drifted slowly by, in a mist, in a dream. Classes in the morning. A lunchtime pizza—even better than Yala's—from a small restaurant that cooked the pie in what looked like a medieval stone oven. Then a ramble through town, stopping perhaps to pick up a quadrille-ruled notebook from a *papeterie* or a second-hand *livre de poche*—I remember weeping over the sentimental classic *Toi et Moi* by Paul Géraldy, a lyrical account of a couple's love affair and breakup. In the late afternoon I might linger for an hour in a café, perhaps the Marxist one at the top of the Cours.

One afternoon, while I was sipping a coffee and watching the girls in their summer dresses, a ragged street accordionist struck up a tune. As a former virtuoso, Lorain's Myron Floren perused his technique with interest, partly because he was the worst accordionist I have ever heard. Not the least of his problems started with his strange fingering—he never used his thumb on the keyboard and must have learned to play on a concertina or button accordion. I nodded to the old busker, gave him a pocketful of change, then impulsively said, "Let me see your instrument." With a shrug he took it off, I slipped into the arm straps, immediately launched into "Boogie Woogie on the Squeeze Box." The old man's eyes lit up, as my fingers raced through the eighth and sixteenth notes. He slowly circulated among the café's other patrons and collected quite a hatful of money. As I returned his accordion, he made me the offer of a lifetime.

"*Jeune américain,*" he said excitedly, "I like you. I really like you. What do you say to a partnership? I know the begging routes from northern Italy along the Côte d'azur to the Costa del Sol in Spain. I'll show you all the ropes to this trade. You play the accordion and we'll split the take. *Que dites-vous?* How about it?"

For a moment I paused, remembering my bone-deep happiness on the road to Pittsburgh, on the backroads of Mexico. But finally I shook my head. "*Non, monsieur. Merci, mais. . . .*" I was in school, I had obligations. One couldn't just take off like that, right? To this day, that goliardic proposal—to travel the begging routes of Southern Europe—remains the youthful path not taken that I most regret.

I must have seemed an easy touch in those days, for a wrinkled and weathered old Gypsy used to approach me two or three times a week. The most haglike creature imaginable, she frequently towed along two sweet-looking urchins of four or five to help in her begging. After I'd handed the ancient crone money once or twice, she finally sidled up to me and whispered hoarsely, "Young American, you have a good heart. *Ça saute aux yeux.* So I want you always to be happy and have good luck. I wish for you to have this." She reached into the nether recesses of her garments and brought out a matchbox, opened it and showed me a human thumb. "*N'ayez pas peur.* Do not be frightened. This," she said, "was cut off a fresh corpse when the moon was full and all the signs were right." Rest assured: It would unquestionably bring me good fortune. And could be mine for a mere sixty francs.

I said No. Sixty francs was then worth about fifteen dollars, a hefty enough sum for me, especially since I was trying to save money for Paris. Besides, who wouldn't suspect chicanery—could that be her own thumb in the matchbox? Some kind of Gypsy bait-and-switch?

But a few days later she again materialized out of nowhere and this time allowed me to hold the matchbox in my hand. Its macabre contents did look real. And could I be feeling some mysterious mana flowing into my veins? Still, I said *"Non, merci, Madame."*

Of course, I eventually recognized my utter foolishness. When again in this life was I likely to be granted the chance—the rare opportunity—to buy a human thumb from a Gypsy, a thumb sliced from a dead man's hand when the moon was full and all the signs were right? How had the Frost witch-poem gone? "I made him do it for me in the dark." And so I went searching all over Aix for this antique Esmeralda, but naturally could never find her. Perhaps it was for the best, since I don't know what I would have said or done at customs. But many times, in years afterward, I was to rue my lack of the good luck that thumb would surely have brought.

Once a week students were required to turn in a paper for our drama course and here I truly surprised myself. Having labored so hard at Oberlin on my compositions, I resolved that—what the hey—this was summer and everyone deserved a break. Besides, I'd been reading Gide's *Nourritures Terrestres*, that call for a fuller, more extrovert, less intellectualized life: "Throw away my book," says its sensualist narrator.

So I dashed off all my essays early in the morning on the Friday they were due. To my amazement the first earned an A, the second an A+ and I eventually received an A+ for the course. This was unprecedented (for me, at least) but announced that my years of academic purgatory had come to an end. During my junior and senior years at Oberlin I recall nothing but straight A's.

My long paper for my course on the history and folklore of Aix dealt mainly with Zola's *The Sin of Father Mouret*. In this novel a young curate awakes from a breakdown with amnesia, remembering nothing of his priestly cassock and vows. Serge finds himself in the garden of a chateau called Le Paradou, where its kindly owner cares for him and he meets a delicate young girl named Albine. The two fall in love. The languorous musky garden, fragrant flowers, the birds and bees, everything seduces the pair into tender lovemaking. All Nature rejoices in their intercourse. And then the curate regains his memory, with tragic and bitter consequences.

Aside from my own "farm" story for Szykowski's class, one could hardly ask for a more obvious celebration of *la vie sensuelle* and a darker portrait of the stunting of the soul that results from narrow-minded devotion to religion. Appropriately, this sense of awakening, of liberation from the constraints of school and family, even from my own self-imposed work ethic, pervaded those sun-dappled weeks of May and June. Although I was writing to Alexandra every few days, I seldom heard back from her and was beginning to yearn for a romantic adventure of my own. In that pagan south the beneficent gods granted my wish.

One night in Aix I acquired a ticket to a performance of Verdi's *Falstaff*, the opera derived from the fat knight's amorous adventures in *The Merry Wives of Windsor*. Madame Wytenhove's son took one look at me in my casual American clothes and insisted that I borrow his tight-fitting black evening suit. So, turned out in a costume of continental elegance, the *jeune américain* suavely took a seat near the center of the crowded hall. While waiting for the overture, I surveyed the chattering audience. One row up, off to my left about six seats, a young woman was sitting with two older people—parents, no doubt. She was of medium height, with black hair, a sultry face—and she occasionally appeared to be glancing at me. I smiled with debonair nonchalance, she smiled back and then the music began.

After the last curtain call three hours later, the audience poured out of the opera onto the winding streets of Aix. The sidewalks were thronged, so I was cautiously walking along on the cobblestones in the direction of the Cours Mirabeau when a low voice at my side murmured, "*Ça vous a plu?*" That is, "You liked it?" meaning the opera. I answered, "*Oui, bien sûr.*" And turned to see the dark-haired beauty from the theater. The older couple hadn't been her parents after all.

We conversed idly for a minute as we strolled along, and then, as if it were the most natural thing in the world, she reached out and took my arm. Nothing could have been more delicate, more romantic. An ancient town, cobblestone streets, glorious music, a warm dark night, a breathtaking and unknown girl at my side and, best of all, the soft pressure of her fingers tightening around my sleeve. Allow me to pause from my writing and just sit here now and remember. We are young only once.

When I invited her to join me for a coffee, she answered in English, "You aren't French, are you?" "No, I'm an American student." She, it turned out, was Canadian, spending a year abroad perfecting her French and Italian. Her name was Renée Horvath.

In the overly bright café, the floodgates of English opened. I hadn't spoken the language in weeks and now happily babbled away. Renée was a year or two older than I, with a fiancée back in Montreal or Quebec, and had been living in Aix for six months. We talked of everything—school, books, France, travel, languages, Canada, each other.

When the café closed at one, I naturally escorted her home—a student apartment—and she naturally invited me in for a glass of wine. We sat on the floor—she put Indian sitar music on the record player—I can still visualize a candle, a single mattress—and still I rattled on and on. Finally, at three, we agreed to rendezvous for lunch the next day. As I stood in Renée's doorway to tell her good night, it occurred to me that just maybe I'd monopolized the conversation and should apologize for my garrulousness. "I think I may have talked too much tonight." Renée looked up, bowed my head down and kissed me hard on the lips, then said, as she slowly closed the door, "Yes, you did."

We met in a café the next afternoon, then for a picnic the following day—a blanket in a garden, wine, cheese, baguette. At the beginning of July the Oberlin program had scheduled a five-day break before our week in Avignon at a *Festival des Jeunes*. Renée suggested that the two of us hitchhike to Florence. "Afterward I'll go on to Rome and you can return to France. What do you say?" Utterly infatuated at that point, I would have accompanied her to Siberia or Tibet.

Of that road trip I only remember our first lift—two college girls in a Mercedes, the driver sporting a simple gold band high on her arm, like a barbarian princess. I couldn't take my eyes off it. So sexy.

We arrived in Florence exhausted. Since Renée knew Italian, I guarded our bags, while she found a suitable *pensione*. Did we pretend to be married? Was that whole issue somehow finessed at check-in? The two North Americans certainly never fooled the knowing landlady.

We fell asleep early in the evening from sheer fatigue and awoke at ten, found a little trattoria still open and after pasta and wine strolled around the city. We meandered through the still-noisy streets—and for the only time in my life I heard salacious comments directed not only to the beautiful girl on my arm but to the beautiful boy on hers. Somehow, we ended up at a park and, on the smooth unbroken surface of its lake, glimpsed a dozen sleeping swans. In the moonlight Renée leaned against me—her Rodolfo—and sang love songs from *La Bohème*. We embraced on a stone bench under some trees and then walked back to the hotel in the dark.

The next morning Renée and I lay next to each other and talked about that very moment with the intense gravity of youth. In a day or two we would separate. I ran my hand along her sleek purple nightdress, caressing her breast and the curve of her thigh, then whispered, "Renée, soon you'll go away and we'll probably never see each other again. But I want you to know that, no matter what, I will always remember the smoothness of this silk and the softness of you." She laughed at my earnest pronouncement, then brought her lips up to mine to stop me, as usual, from talking too much. Later that afternoon we wandered through the city, admired a sleek, low-slung Maserati parked near the Uffizi Museum, stopped at some open-air shopping stalls—I bought her a silk scarf, she found me a pair of thin leather driving gloves. "You can wear them when you drive your own Maserati," she told me in the sunshine of an outdoor café, as we sipped glasses of wine.

Two days later we tearfully said good-bye at the railway station. In the morning light of Tuscany, Renée looked so young, so infinitely desirable. Then the train pulled away and she was gone. Every so often since that summer I close my eyes and rub my fingers together and feel, just for second, her silken shift and her warm, sleepy flesh. "I have been faithful to thee, Cynara, in my fashion."

At Avignon's *Festival des Jeunes* the Obies joined students from around the world in a kind of international summer camp. We roomed in big dormitories, and were supposed to bond—in French—with kids from Germany, Italy, England and other parts of the world.

There must have been some kind of organized program, for I remember the excitement of Maurice Béjart's dance company performing my old favorite, *The Rite of Spring*, and a bus trip to Les Baux, the picturesque mountain village where we belted out songs in echoing caverns. On my own one afternoon I even made my way out to the encampment of the Living Theater. The troupe had created a mini-riot after some piece of experimental drama carried the performers and their audience out into the city streets. I wondered about how this Gypsy-like band of actors managed to live. And indeed they really seemed like Gypsies in their vans and tents. Mainly I recall conversing a while with cofounder Judith Malina as she rinsed out a dirty baby diaper and its user played naked in the pool of water beneath the pump.

Avignon's youth festival encouraged a wholesome Boy Scout Jamboree air, but one night a number of us escaped to a restaurant and enjoyed a riotous meal together. In the dark on the way back to the dormitories our little band sang bawdy French songs and I remembered my evening fiesta with the Mexican architectural students in Guanajuato. Then someone struck up "The International," the communist anthem: "*Cest la lutte finale/ Groupons nous et demain/ L'internationale sera le genre human.* (It is the final battle/ let us stand together and tomorrow/ The International will be all mankind.)" Such a stirring melody and this was 1968, after all—yet even that night I couldn't help but pay more attention to the young and blond Swiss schoolteacher in our midst.

At the beginning of August the Oberlin group finally returned to Paris. There we lodged at the *Foyer International d'Accueil de Paris*— the FIAP—and studied art history at the Louvre. I mourned Renée, and yet felt a swollen male pride that I had been found desirable by a captivating (and slightly older) woman. In the meantime, I peered intently at the paintings in the Louvre, listened to Madeleine Hours discuss art restoration—she directed the museum's scientific laboratory—and came to treasure the work of Poussin, Watteau, Fragonard, La Tour and Ingres. I would stare daily at Poussin's dark, traction-crackled painting *The Flood*, the remnants of mankind clinging to rocks and mountaintops as if they were trapped in a watery circle of Hell. And I quivered in awe and fear before Ingres' portrait of the overfed banker M. Bertin, the very embodiment of cold financial power and self-assurance. That unflinching gaze! But then I looked into the eyes of Watteau's clown, the Gilles, in which one felt an almost Christ-like sorrow for—what? Himself? All mankind? It was the saddest face in the world. Above all, I surrendered my heart to the wistful melancholy, the stillness and evanescent beauty of Watteau's *Embarkation for Cythera*, a landscape of happy couples intending to sail to the island of perfect love, seemingly unaware that no one ever arrives at Cythera. Oh, Renée!

And oh, Alexandra! For in the closing days of August I had to think more seriously about my real girlfriend, who was on her way to France for her junior year abroad. Her Middlebury-sponsored program would be stopping one night in Paris. I would be leaving the very next day to return to the United States and my own junior year at Oberlin. One night in Paris, only one night, but still . . .

I had saved money all summer by being frugal whenever possible and could now lay my hands on nearly $150. With this war chest I planned to underwrite the perfect romantic evening. Having already read a bit of Proust, I knew that the besotted Swann used to entertain the demimondaine Odette de Crécy at a restaurant called La Pérouse. According to the novelist, it provided mirrored private dining rooms for two with velvet banquettes. Rumor had it that Edward VII was wont to bring his mistresses to these plush closeted chambers and probably engage in lovemaking on the couches. La Pérouse still existed and one late summer afternoon a young American cousin to the urbane Count of Monte Cristo hesitantly opened the restaurant's door and asked to speak to the maître d'. I explained the romantic character of my planned evening, he agreed on a *prix fixe* meal and together we chose a champagne and reserved one of the private retreats.

Then I arranged for a horse-drawn carriage ride in the Bois de Boulogne after dinner. Finally, I engaged a pleasant room in the hotel where the Middlebury group was staying. I had thought of everything.

Except for what happened: Due to various travel delays, Alexandra's bus didn't pull up to the hotel until nine o'clock. Too late for dinner and the carriage ride. What's more, the entire program had stopped to eat earlier. So, after my tired sweetheart had gotten settled and changed, we sat in a nearby café, ordered dessert and awkwardly talked. We returned to the hotel together, but Alex—embarrassed, worried about my attentions—spent the night in her own assigned room.

The next morning we kissed and the tears flowed. Then the bus honked—"Take care of yourself." "You too"—and slowly pulled way. Alexandra was gone. I stood there stricken, and suddenly knew I had to see my darling just one more time. So I raced down into the Métro and arrived at the rail terminal, running and breathing hard, just before the train to Biarritz was scheduled to depart. I located Alexandra's railroad car and she cranked down the window. Above all the usual station clamor, I shouted that I adored her, and then leapt, grabbed the metal sill and pulled myself up to kiss her one last time. As I hung there on the side of the passenger car, so desperately in love, the train slowly began to pull out of the station. I let go and fell back onto the platform and stood there, waving and crying, until the caboose had disappeared. Little did I know that I would never kiss my Alexandra again, for during that year she gave her heart to someone else.

That morning, though, it struck me while walking sadly out of the station that I still carried most of $150 in my pocket. Pondering this unexpected financial windfall, I stopped at an outdoor café and ordered a bowl of *péche melba* and some coffee, then looked up an address in the phone book. Within the hour I had made my way to Guy Boussac's, the shop from which Bill Briola always purchased his

French books. It was austere, brightly lit and efficient, more clear-inghouse than bookstore. But they would ship for free or give you a ten percent discount.

I bought the Pléiade edition of Proust in three handsome flexi-leather volumes, a cheap seven-volume set of Balzac's *Comédie Humaine* in a red cloth binding and a half dozen yellow-backed Gar-nier editions of Racine, Voltaire, Flaubert, Stendhal, Musset and Baudelaire (who, no surprise, was soon my very favorite poet of all). The helpful sales agent packed everything into a compact but heavy carton, tied up in such a way that the loops of thick string made a handle. I passed over the equivalent of $125 and a few hours later boarded my plane for the trip back to Lorain, Oberlin and the rest of my life.

Epilogue

Against time and the damages of the brain
Sharpen and calibrate.

—*James Agee*

Over the next two years at Oberlin I continued to take a
good many classes in French, English and history. During
January winter term I studied Latin and learned enough to
read a few lyrics by Catullus and Horace, especially *"Diffigure nives,"*
which A. E. Housman regarded as the most beautiful poem of antiquity. It being the late sixties, I also signed petitions, occasionally joined
vigils around Tappan Square, worried about being drafted. One
semester I grew a beard and didn't bother to cut my hair for months.

Invited to join the honors seminar as a senior, I turned in a long
paper explicating four or five of William Empson's poems, essentially
performing Empsonian analyses on his twentieth-century recastings
of metaphysical verse: "My heart pumps yet the poison draught of
you." When I graduated in 1970 I was awarded Highest Honors in
English and the now-retired Bongiorno was proud of me. My father
never saw me receive my "diploma": The speech of our commence-
ment speaker, Jesse Jackson, and the armbands we wore so enraged
him he walked out in the middle of the ceremony.

In the years that followed I taught English in a Marseille lycée on
a Fulbright grant (my so-called gunrunning days), attended graduate

school at Cornell (medieval studies and European romanticism) and received a Ph.D. in comparative literature in 1977. I was offered teaching positions at various colleges, but, for reasons of my own, ended by refusing them all. Instead I drifted into freelance journalism, worked as a technical writer for a computer company, then started writing book reviews, first for the *Chronicle of Higher Education*, later for *The Washington Post Book World*, which in 1978 offered me a job as a writer and editor. I married, had children, grew older. One day I may recount these stories and others in greater detail, but my early life with books here comes to an end.

People sometimes ask me: "Did you have a happy childhood?" My instinctive reply is no. For I usually remember my father's anger and scorn, my early confusions at school, my painful awareness of being fat, nearsighted and inept at games, my several gut-wrenching fears (imagined monsters, public speaking), my sense of intellectual and social inferiority as a college freshman, my constant escape into the pleasures of the text.

Looking back in what I hope is roughly midlife, I see more clearly now how some of the crotchets and neuroses of my later years got started: my fear of making a mistake (Dad), my fear of doing wrong (Mom) and my consequent indecision at certain moments of crisis. But I also recognize what luck I had in my family, city, background. I may have slightly mythologized the past in these pages— all autobiographers do—and I may have presented what seems a Whiggish history, the unrelenting progress of a literary Horatio Alger hero, yet I cannot now look back at my early years with anything but gratitude and, as I hope these pages show, deep affection.

I do glimpse certain leitmotifs: the compulsion to succeed after initial failure; the periodic appearance of the revered mentor; the preference for certain kinds of stories (self-transformation, Secret History), the excited attachment to new writers, genres and literatures, a gradually expanding horizon—Lorain, Oberlin, Mexico, Europe. Sadly, I can hardly excuse the unrelenting earnestness and occasional sanctimony of my earliest romantic attachments. I truly wish I had been more playful and lighthearted. But obsessiveness and intensity are, for good or ill, part of my character. Still, that seriousness did allow certain interludes, such as the week I knew Renée Horvath, a glow they might not have otherwise enjoyed.

My taste in reading has continued to develop since those ancient days. I now find myself suspicious of the overblown, the gaudy, the excessive. No more tub-thumping. The art I prefer is cool, controlled and finely milled, witty instead of touching, artful or even artificial rather than realistic. History and biography often seem more attractive now than most fiction, classics beckon more seductively than contemporaries and Shaker plainness appeals to me. "*Surtout pas de zèle*," advised Talleyrand, and I tend to agree with him. Such austere tastes are, of course, an indisputable sign of middle age, the product of much, perhaps too much, reading and some weariness of the flesh.

In recent years I've started to return to favorite books, with disconcerting and ambivalent feelings: What could I have gotten out of *War and Peace* at age fourteen, from Proust at nineteen? Very little, I suspect. And then I wonder: How much am I getting from them now? I usually dismiss these notions—infinite regression looms therein—and concentrate on the ever-renewed pleasure of the story or on the various enticements of the author's style. I now read more often as an epicure than as an adventurer.

My father died in 1991, horribly, from cancer. But I still go back to Lorain three or four times a year, mainly to see my mother and my sisters. My own children spend part of their summers there with a swarm of cousins, wonderful days of baseball, swimming and hide-and-seek in the dark, and at the end of every visit they always say to me, "Dad, why can't we live in Lorain? Why do we always have to go back to stupid, dull Washington?" I never quite know what to tell them.

Long ago, my father used to warn me: "A writer writes. A reader reads." For most of my life, even that as a staff book reviewer and essayist for *The Washington Post*, I have thought of myself as primarily a reader. An enthusiastic, well-informed reader, to be sure, and one with a minor talent to evoke the particular excitement and quiddity of a novel, a collection of poems or a work of intellectual history. Nonetheless, I really should have listened to my dad and would give a lot to hear him yell at me just one more time: "Get your nose out of that book and go do something useful."

Yes, Dad. You may not, as you used to say, always be right, but you're never wrong. I now wish I had sat down with pen and paper more often than with an old paperback, had tilted my days more toward being a Writer than a Reader. Still, who knows? Perhaps even now it's not altogether too late.

Michael Dirda's Book List

What follows is the the book list I set down in my journal when I was sixteen. It lists, in no particular order, some of the more ambitious works I'd managed to finish by that age and, yes, it does seem at least a little pretentious. But I don't think any of these books is beyond the powers of a reasonably diligent teenager. The trick, of course, lies in actually wanting, in being eager, to read them.

Homer, *The Iliad, The Odyssey*
Plato, *The Republic* (parts)
Artistotle, *Ethics* (parts)
Francis Bacon, *Essays* (selections)
Will Durant, *The Story of Philosophy*
Jonathan Swift, *Gullivers Travels* (first two parts)
Bertrand Russell, *My Philosophical Development*
Immanuel Kant, *Preface to the Metaphysics of Ethics*
Lucretius, *On the Nature of Things* (parts)
Henry David Thoreau, *Walden, A Week on the Concord and
    Merrimack Rivers*
Aldous Huxley, *Brave New World*
J. D. Salinger, *The Catcher in the Rye, Nine Stories*
Voltaire, *Candide* and other works

Plutarch, *The Parallel Lives* (selected lives)

James Boswell, *Life of Johnson* (abridged)

Jean-Jacques Rousseau, *Confessions, Discourse on Inequality, The Social Contract, Reveries of a Solitary Walker, Profession of Faith of a Savoyard Vicar*

Ayn Rand, *Atlas Shrugged*

Marx and Engels, *The Communist Manifesto*

Herman Melville, *Moby-Dick*

Dante, *The Divine Comedy*

Bernard Shaw, *St. Joan, Man and Superman, The Devil's Disciple*

Arthur Miller, *Death of a Salesman*

Samuel Beckett, *Waiting for Godot*

Fyodor Dostoyevsky, *Crime and Punishment*

Leo Tolstoy, *War and Peace*

Walt Whitman, *Leaves of Grass* (parts)

Henry Adams, *The Education of Henry Adams*

William Golding, *Lord of the Flies*

James Michener, *Tales of the South Pacific*

James Hilton, *Lost Horizon*

Benjamin Franklin, *The Autobiography*

Henrik Ibsen, *An Enemy of the People*

Stephen Vincent Benet, *John Brown's Body*

Ernest Hemingway, *The Old Man and the Sea*

Ralph Waldo Emerson, "Self Reliance"

Rachel Carson, *The Sea Around Us*

Frank Gilbreth and Ernestine Carey, *Cheaper by the Dozen*

W. H. Hudson, *Green Mansions*

Sinclair Lewis, *Elmer Gantry, Arrowsmith, It Can't Happen Here*

George Orwell, *1984, Animal Farm*

Edgar Allan Poe, *Tales*
Guy de Maupassant, short stories
Oscar Williams (editor), *Immortal Poems of the English Language*
Many short stories

OTHER BOOKS READ BY END OF HIGH SCHOOL

Elsewhere in my journal I mention various other books I had read by the time of my graduation from Admiral King or that I'd somehow forgotten to include on my first list. These titles appear below. There were obviously scores of adventure stories and mysteries that never made either list.

In truth, I make no claims that I read any of these books "well," only that my eyes passed over the words and that, for the most part, I enjoyed nearly all of them. As a young reader I was humbly trying to stock my mind as fast as I could. Even now, I believe that anyone who aspires to understand books should first absorb a lot of them indiscriminately, then direct his or her critical attention to the intensive study of a handful of masterpieces.

Mark Twain, *Tom Sawyer*, *Huckleberry Finn*
Joseph Conrad, *Youth*, *The Nigger of the Narcissus*, *Heart of Darkness*
Stephen Crane, *The Open Boat*
Charles Dickens, *Great Expectations*, *A Tale of Two Cities*
Henry Fielding, *Tom Jones*
F. Scott Fitzgerald, *The Great Gatsby*
Nathaniel Hawthorne, *The Scarlet Letter*
William Faulkner, *The Unvanquished*, *The Bear*
Nikolai Gogol, *The Overcoat*
Katherine Anne Porter, *Noon Wine*

Glenway Wescott, *The Pilgrim Hawk*

James Joyce, *The Dead*

Henry James, *The Turn of the Screw*

Thomas Mann, *The Magic Mountain*

Somerset Maugham, *Cakes and Ale*

Stendhal, *The Red and the Black*

Ivan Turgenev, *Fathers and Sons*

Jacques Barzun, *God's Country and Mine*

Edith Hamilton, *The Greek Way*

Antoine de Saint-Exupéry, *Night Flight*

E. B. White, *One Man's Meat, The Second Tree from the Corner*

Hesketh Pearson, *George Bernard Shaw: A Full Length Portrait*

Aeschylus, *Prometheus Bound*

Andon Chekhov, *The Cherry Orchard, The Sea Gull, The Three Sisters*

Nikos Kazantzakis, *Zorba the Greek*

Sophocles, *Oedipus Rex*

J. M. Synge, *Riders to the Sea*

Oscar Wilde, *The Importance of Being Earnest*

Shakespeare, *Hamlet, Macbeth, Othello, King Lear, Julius Caesar, Antony and Cleopatra*

Will and Ariel Durant, *The Story of Civilization* (up to eighteenth century)

The Bible

Acknowledgments

Gratitude can be hard to express, even inadequately, but I'd like to thank all those mentioned in the preceding pages for being part of this story. In particular, I am grateful to my mother Christine Dirda and my sisters Sandra Dodson, Pamela Susanjar and Linda Gerhart, my aunts, uncles and cousins, and all my old Lorain and Oberlin friends, classmates and teachers. I hope their memories don't differ too much from mine.

Other people close to me must also be acknowledged, at least for their forbearance, and usually for much more: art conservator Marian Peck Dirda and our beloved sons Christopher, Michael and Nathaniel Dirda (hi, guys!), and my colleagues at *The Washington Post*, in particular those at *Book World*: Marie Arana, Jonathan Yardley, Francis Tanabe, Dennis Drabelle, Chris Lehmann, Jabari Asim, Jennifer Howard, Zofia Smardz, Nina King, Mary Morris and Chris Schoppa.

My tireless agents Glen Hartley and Lynn Chu stood patiently by me for years. My superb editor Robert Weil provided encouragement and thoughtful scrutiny of the manuscript, even as his multitalented assistants Jason Baskin and Brendan Curry, helped a neophyte author through the production process. In truth, I wish to thank the entire staff at W. W. Norton for ongoing kindness, thoughtfulness and counsel, as well as for this beautiful example of modern bookmaking. Let me mention in particular: Elizabeth Riley, Amanda Morrison, Andy Marasia, Georgia Liebman, Bill Rusin, Jeannie Luciano, Louise Brockett, Nancy Palmquist, and Dave Cole.

Not least: For quiet spaces in which to work on *An Open Book,* and often for much else, I am more deeply grateful than I can say to Dawn Trouard of the University of Central Florida in Orlando; the Atlantic Center for the Arts in New Smyrna Beach, Florida; Brian Jacomb of Washington, DC (and Puerto Vallarta, Mexico); my mother Christine Dirda of Lorain, Ohio; and Allen and Patricia Ahearn of Comus, Maryland. I also want to thank *The Washington Post* company for granting me a short leave in which to compose this reminiscence of my bookish youth.

Index

Aaron, Edward S., 138
ABC of Reading, The (Pound), 289–90
Abelard, Peter, 280
Abyss, The (Yourcenar), 300
Adams, Henry, 14, 164
Addison, Joseph, 168–69
Adler, Mortimer J., 195–98, 297
Adolphe (Constant), 140
Adonis, Attis, Osiris (Frazer), 257
Adventures in Time and Space (Healey and McComas), 167
Advise and Consent (Drury), 142
Agee, James, 303, 319
All's Well That Ends Well (Shakespeare), 302
Almagest (Ptolemy), 197
Ambassadors, The (James), 140, 282
Ambushers, The (Hamilton), 234
Anatomy of Criticism (Frye), 292–93
And Be a Villain (Stout), 121
Anderson, Sherwood, 282
And Then There Were None, 98
Annals of English Literature 1475–1950, 297
Anouilh, Jean, 233
Any Number Can Play (Fadiman), 139
Apology (Plato), 141
Appleton, Victor, II, 90, 91, 98
Aquinas, St. Thomas, 280
Arabian Nights, 168, 281
Aristotle, 139, 290
Armed Vision, The (Hyman), 294
Armour, Richard, 174
Around the World in Eighty Days (*Tour du Monde en 80 Jours*) (Verne), 229
Art of Courtly Love (Capellanus), 280
Assignment: Ankara (Aaron), 138
Atlas Shrugged (A. Rand), 221–24
Attlee, Philip, 234
Auden, W. H., 291–92, 297, 299, 300, 301
Auerbach, Erich, 293
Augustine, St., 13, 280
Aurelius, Marcus, 141
Austen, Jane, 140, 302

Babel, Isaac, 301–2
Bakunin, Mikhail, 280
Balzac, Honoré de, 83, 283, 318
Barefoot Boy with Cheek (Shulman), 112
Bartlett's Familiar Quotations, 174
Baudelaire, Charles, 274
Bear, The (Faulkner), 131
Beckett, Samuel, 128, 231, 307
Bede, 280
Behn, Aphra, 299–300
Bella-Vista (Colette), 301
Benjamin, Walter, 300
Berlin Stories (Isherwood), 301
Bester, Alfred, 120
Big Fisherman, The (Douglas), 142
Big Sister, 206
Big Sleep, The (Chandler), 292
Bit Between My Teeth (Wilson), 294
Black Mountain, The (Stout), 121
Blackmur, R. P., 286, 291
Black Rose, The (Costain), 142
Blatty, William Peter, 138
Bluest Eye, The (Morrison), 84
Bogan, Louise, 299, 303
Bomba, The Jungle Boy, 89
Book of the Damned, The (Fort), 52
Borges, Jorge Luis, 119
Bosco, Henri, 230
Boswell, James, 139
Bradbury, Ray, 55, 122, 195
Brave New World (Huxley), 164
Brideshead Revisited (Waugh), 256
Broch, Hermann, 278
Bromfield, Louis, 142
Brophy, Brigid, 299
Brothers Karamazov, The (Dostoyevsky), 140
Browne, Thomas, 169
Brown, Fredric, 140
Buck, Pearl S., 176
Buddenbrooks (Mann), 233
Bulwer Lytton, Edward, 120
Burgon, John William, 167
Burke, Kenneth, 291

Burning the Days (Salter), 299
Burroughs, Edgar Rice, 92, 116, 137, 193
Burton, Robert, 169
Byron, Lord, 143, 303

Caldwell, Taylor, 142
Caligula (Camus), 307
Call It Sleep (Roth), 166
Call of the Wild, The (London), 175
Camus, Albert, 230, 307
Candide (Voltaire), 205
Candy, 204–6, 207
Capellanus, Andreas, 280
Capote, Truman, 299
Captain From Castile (Shellabarger), 35
Captains Courageous (Kipling), 131
Carnegie, Dale, 132–33, 134–35, 174, 192, 212–13, 221
Carpetbaggers, The (Robbins), 142
Carr, John Dickson, 96
Case of Charles Dexter Ward, The (Lovecraft), 169
Case of the Careless Cupid, The (Gardner), 207
Case of the Curious Canary, The (Gardner), 207
Case of the Lucky Legs, The (Gardner), 140
Castelveltro on Poetry (Bongiorno), 272
Cather, Willa, 301
Catullus, 319
Cavafy, Constantine, 301
Caves of Fear, The, 91
Cellini, Benvenuto, 14, 35
Cerf, Bennett, 51
Certain World, A (Auden), 300
Cervantes, Miguel de, 32
Chandler, Raymond, 140, 172–73, 234, 292
Charlotte's Web (White), 59
Chaucer, Geoffrey, 187
Chekhov, Anton, 14–15, 289
Chesnut, Mary, 294
Chesterton, G. K., 96, 97, 166
Christie, Agatha, 97–98, 126, 166, 294
Churchill, Winston S., 174
Cicero, Marcus Tullius, 133, 171
Citizen of the Galaxy (Heinlein), 60
Clara Barton—Girl Nurse, 64
Classics and Commercials (Wilson), 294
Cleary, Beverly, 59, 93–94, 117
Cleghorn, Sarah N., 145
Cleland, John, 207, 208
Cocteau, Jean, 157, 295, 299, 303
Colette, 296, 299, 301, 302, 303
Collected Poems (Stevens), 256
Comédie Humaine, La (Balzac), 318
Comfortable Words (Evans), 171
Communist Manifesto, The (Marx and Engels), 163
Compton-Burnett, Ivy, 35, 300

Conan Doyle, Sir Arthur, 68–69, 100, 234
Confession of a Child of the Century (Musset), 306
Confessions (Augustine), 13
Confessions (Rousseau), 14, 191
Confessions of a Conservative (Wills), 299
Confidence Man (Melville), 299
Connecticut Yankee in King Arthur's Court, A (Twain), 56
Connell, Richard, 167
Connolly, Cyril, 299, 301–2, 304
Conquest of Plassans, The (La Conquête de Plassans) (Zola), 306
Conrad, Joseph, 140, 166, 221, 225, 226
Constant, Benjamin, 140
Cooper, Lane, 285
Costain, Thomas B., 142
Count of Monte Cristo, The (Dumas), 54, 97, 221, 223
Crabbe, George, 289
Crack-Up, The (Fitzgerald), 301–2
Craft, Robert, 299
Crane, Stephen, 282
Crashaw, Richard, 272, 287, 299
Crime and Punishment (Dostoyevsky), 126, 131, 166, 221, 226, 245
Crooked Hinge, The (Dickson Carr), 96
Crowley, John, 54
Curme, George O., 161
Curtius, E. R., 293

Danny Dunn and the Anti-Gravity Paint, 59
Dante Alighieri, 170, 272, 280
Davy Crockett—Boy Pioneer, 64
Dead, The (Joyce), 131
de Kruif, Paul, 188
Deeping, Warwick, 120
Deiro, Pietro, 79
Demolished Man, The (Bester), 120
Demosthenes, 133
Denby, Edwin, 301–2
Desire Under the Elms (O'Neill), 166
Devotions Upon Emergent Occasions (Donne), 191
Dialogues (Plato), 141
Dickens, Charles, 127, 264
Dickinson, Emily, 143
Discourses (Epictetus), 141
Divine Comedy (Dante), 280, 281
Don Juan in Hell (Shaw), 128
Donleavy, J. P., 163
Donne, John, 191, 254–55, 256, 272–73
Don Quixote (Cervantes), 32
Dooley, Tom, 162–63
Door into Summer, The (Heinlein), 125
Dostoyevsky, Fyodor, 126, 131, 140, 166, 221, 226, 245
Douglas, Gavin, 289

Douglas, Lloyd C., 142
Dowson, Ernest, 144
Dreiser, Theodore, 282
Drury, Allen, 142
Dryden, John, 144, 168–69
DuBois, W. E. B., 267
Duchess of Malfi, The, 257
Dumas, Alexandre, 54, 97, 221, 223
Dunsany, Lord, 167, 168, 169, 174, 224
Durant, Will, 159–60
Dyer's Hand, The (Auden), 291

Earthly Paradise (Colette), 296
Ecclesiastical History (Bede), 280
Eco, Umberto, 54
Education of Henry Adams, The (Adams), 14, 164
Edwards, Frank, 193
Eight Great Tragedies, 166
Eliot, T. S., 255–57, 288, 290, 300
Ellison, Ralph, 262
Emerson, Ralph Waldo, 195, 267, 272
Emperor Fu Manchu (Rohmer), 100
Empson, William, 286–87, 292, 293, 319
Enchafèd Flood, The (Auden), 292, 297
Engels, Friedrich, 163
Enzensberger, Hans Magnus, 282
Epictetus, 141
Essays on Elizabethan Dramatists (Eliot), 257
European Literature and the Latin Middle Ages (Curtius), 293
Exorcist, The (Blatty), 138

Fadiman, Clifton, 138–39
Fanny Hill (Memoirs of a Woman of Pleasure) (Cleland), 207–8
Fatal Skin, The (Balzac), 83
Father and His Fate, A (Compton-Burnett), 35
Father Brown Omnibus, The, 96
Fathers and Sons (Turgenev), 266
Faulkner, William, 131, 139, 202–3
Fer-de-Lance (Stout), 121
Fiedler, Leslie, 299
Final Deduction, The (Stout), 121
Firbank, Ronald, 169
Fisher, M. F. K., 306
Fitzgerald, F. Scott, 175, 301–2
Five Tragedies (Shakespeare), 35, 134
Flanner, Janet, 299, 301
Flaubert, Gustave, 220, 283, 307
Ford, Ford Madox, 301–2
Forster, E. M., 127, 128, 301
Fort, Charles, 52
For Whom the Bell Tolls (Hemingway), 191
Foucault's Pendulum (Eco), 54
Founders of the Middle Ages (E. K. Rand), 280
Frazer, J. G., 158, 257

Freud, Sigmund, 139, 265, 266
From Ritual to Romance (Weston), 257
Frost, Robert, 143, 287–88, 310
Frye, Northrop, 107, 292–93
Funk, Wilfred, 175

Gambit (Stout), 122
Gardner, Erle Stanley, 140, 207
Gault, William Campbell, 67
Genet, Jean, 301
George, Henry, 140
Géraldy, Paul, 308
Gide, André, 310
Ginger Man, The (Donleavy), 163
Ginsberg, Allen, 262
Giono, Jean, 230
Gogol, Nikolai, 131
Gold-Bug and Other Stories, The (Poe), 165
Golden, Harry, 131
Golden Argosy, The, 35, 225
Golding, Arthur, 289
Golding, William, 35
Goncharov, Ivan Aleksandrovich, 266
Goodbye, Mr. Chips (Hilton), 131
Grahame, Kenneth, 59
Graves, Robert, 289
Gray, Thomas, 188
Great Books of the Western World, The, 196–99
Great Tales of Terror and the Supernatural, 167
Green, Henry, 258, 266
Greene, Gerald, 258
Greene, Graham, 258
Guest, Edgar, 35

Haggard, H. Rider, 97
Haggins, B. H., 249
Halliburton, Richard, 60
Hamilton, Donald, 234
Hamilton, Edith, 165
Hamlet (Shakespeare), 134, 136, 226
Handful of Dust, A (Waugh), 264
Hardy, Thomas, 304
Haskins, Charles Homer, 280–81
Hawthorne, Nathaniel, 186–87
Heart of Darkness (Conrad), 166, 221, 225–26
Heart of Midlothian, The (Scott), 121
Hegel, Georg Friedrich Wilhelm, 108
Heinlein, Robert, 60, 92, 125, 188
Hemingway, Ernest, 175, 191, 282
Henry, O., 225
Henry Huggins (Cleary), 93–94, 117
Heppenstall, Rayner, 299
Herbert, George, 272
Heroes and Orators (Phelps), 299
Hero of Our Time, A (Lermontov), 266
Herrick, Robert, 272

Herzen, Aleksandr Ivanovich, 280
Heyer, Georgette, 201
Heywood, Thomas, 257
Hilton, James, 131, 142
Hitler, Adolf, 291
Homer, 198, 221
Hopkins, Gerard Manley, 145–46, 256
Horace, 319, 273
Hound of the Baskervilles, The (Conan Doyle), 68–69
Household, Geoffrey, 66
Housman, A. E., 144, 146, 256, 319
Howard, Richard, 299
Howe, Irving, 291
Howells, William Dean, 282
How to Make More Money (Small), 35
How to Pick Up Women, 203
How to Read a Book (Adler), 196
How to Stop Worrying and Start Living (Carnegie), 132, 221
Huckleberry Finn (Twain), 42, 199
Hume, David, 281
Hutchins, Robert M., 196, 198, 273
Huxley, Aldous, 164, 203
Hyman, Stanley Edgar, 294
Hypnotism Made Simple, 203

I, the Jury (Spillane), 170
Immortal Poems of the English Language, 143, 221
Inferno (Dante), 170
Insidious Dr. Fu Manchu, The (Rohmer), 54, 99–100
Interpretation of Dreams, The (Freud), 139
Isherwood, Christopher, 301, 304
Ivanhoe (Scott), 121

Jackson, Shirley, 127
Jacobs, W. W., 225
James, Henry, 140, 261, 282, 294, 299
James, M. R., 16
James, William, 134–35
Jarrell, Randall, 48, 287–89, 297
Jones, LeRoi (Amiri Baraka), 262
Jorkens Remembers Africa (Dunsany), 167
Jouhandeau, Marcel, 299
Journal (Renard), 300
Journey to the Center of the Earth, 92
Joyce, James, 121, 131, 226, 247
Julie de Carneilhan, 302

Kafka, Franz, 63, 282–83, 302
Kant, Immanuel, 160
Kazantzakis, Nikos, 221, 224–25
Keats, John, 35, 143, 287
Kent, Rockwell, 34
Keyes, Frances Parkinson, 35
Keys to Learning, 195

King Solomon's Mines (Haggard), 97
Kipling, Rudyard, 131, 132–33, 174, 289
Kjelgaard, Jim, 59
Krolow, Karl, 282
Krutch, Joseph Wood, 139

Laistner, M. L. W., 280
Lamartine, Alphonse de, 233
Landor, Walter Savage, 289
Language as Gesture (Blackmur), 291
Lanier, Sidney, 199
Laughton, Charles, 130, 171
Lawrence, D. H., 176, 301
League of Frightened Men, The (Stout), 121, 122
Lear, Edward, 193
Léautaud, Paul, 299
Le Diable et le Bon Dieu (Sartre), 307
Le May, Alan, 141
Leokum, Arkady, 50
Lermontov, Mikhail Iurevich, 266
Letters to Father Flye (Agee), 303
Lewis, Norman, 175
Life of Henry Brulard (Stendhal), 13–14
Life of Johnson (Boswell), 139
Lifetime Reading Plan, The (Fadiman), 138–39
Linguistics and Literary History (Spitzer), 293
Lion and the Honeycomb, The (Blackmur), 291
Literary Life, The: A Scrapbook Almanac of the Anglo-American Literary Scene, 1900–1950 (Phelps and Deane), 298, 301–2
Little, Big (Crowley), 54
Little Black Sambo (Bannerman), 22
Little Orphan Annie and the Ancient Treasure of Am, 53, 54
Lives (Plutarch), 170
London, Jack, 175
Long Goodbye, The (Chandler), 172–73
Lord Jim (Conrad), 140
Lord of the Flies (Golding), 35
Lord of the Rings, The (Tolkien), 280
Lord Weary's Castle (Lowell), 296
Lorenzaccio (Musset), 307
Lost Horizon (Hilton), 142
Lost World, The (Conan Doyle), 100, 234
Louis Agassiz as a Teacher (Cooper), 271
Love and Death in the American Novel (Fiedler), 299
Lovecraft, H. P., 52, 169–70, 174, 224, 233
Loving (Green), 266
Lowell, Robert, 296

Macbeth (Shakespeare), 70, 128–29
Magic Flute (Mozart; Da Ponte), 301
Magic Mountain, The (Mann), 190
Man and Superman (Shaw), 128
Mann, Thomas, 190, 233
Mansions of Philosophy, The (Adler), 196

Man Who Loved Children, The (Stead), 289
Map of Another Town (Fisher), 306
March of Literature, The (Ford), 301
Marquand, John P., 141
Martian Chronicles, The (Bradbury), 55
Marvell, Andrew, 249, 272
Marx, Karl, 163, 270
Mason, F. Van Wyck, 142
Mastering Judo, 203
Maugham, Somerset, 168
Maurice (Forster), 301
Medicine for Melancholy, A (Bradbury), 195
Meditations (Aurelius), 141
Mein Kampf (Hitler), 291
Melville, Herman, 34, 131, 161, 186–87,
     299–300
Memoirs (Cellini), 14
*Men of Good Will, The (Les hommes de bonne
     volonté)* (Romain), 230
Meredith, George, 144
Merry Wives of Windsor, The, 311
Metalious, Grace, 203
Metamorphoses (Ovid), 233
Mew, Charlotte, 21, 300, 304
Michener, James, 136–37, 142
Microbe Hunters, The (de Kruif), 188
Mike Mulligan and His Steam Shovel, 34
Miller, Henry, 231
Milton, John, 188, 281
*Mimesis: The Representation of Reality in West-
     ern Literature* (Auerbach), 293
Missing Chums, The, 90
Miss Pickerell Goes to Mars, 59
Moby-Dick (Melville), 34, 131, 161, 186–87
Montaigne, Michel, 195, 281
Moore, Marianne, 144
Morrison, Toni, 84
Mozart, Wolfgang Amadeus, 249, 301
Murder on Board (Christie), 98
Murder on the Orient Express (Christie), 98
Music for the Man Who Enjoys Hamlet
     (Haggins), 249
Musset, Alfred de, 306, 307
My Favorite Science Fiction Story, 121, 122
Mysterious Island, The (Verne), 97, 142
Mystery at Thunderbolt House, 67
Mystery of the Piper's Ghost, The, 66
Mythology (Hamilton), 165

Nabokov, Vladimir Vladimirovich, 169, 196
Necessary Angel, The (Stevens), 282
Neconomicon, 120
Newman, John Henry, 268
Nicholas Nickleby (Dickens), 234
Night Flight (Vol de nuit) (Saint-Exupéry),
     229
Night of the Jabberwock (Brown), 140

Night They Burned the Mountain, The (Doo-
     ley), 162–63
1984 (Orwell), 131, 161
Noble Voice, The (Van Doren), 172
Noon Wine (Porter), 131
Norris, Frank, 282
Norton, Charles Eliot, 196
Nourritures Terrestres (Gide), 310
Nympho, 203

Oath of a Freeman, 121
Oblomov (Goncharov), 266
Octopus, The (Norris), 282
Odyssey, The (Homer), 198, 221
Oedipus the King, 188
Oeuvres Intimes (Stendhal), 300
Of Time and the River (Wolfe), 175
Omnibus of Crime (Sayers), 167
On Baile's Strand (Yeats), 166
O'Neill, Eugene, 166
One Writer's Beginnings (Welty), 14
Only in America (Golden), 131
On the Nature of Man (Aristotle), 141
Orwell, George, 131, 161
Osler, William, 132
Our Lady of the Flowers (Genet), 301
Our Oriental Heritage (Durant), 159
Outline of History (Wells), 121
Overcoat, The (Gogol), 131
Ovid, 233, 289

Packard, Vance, 131
Pagnol, Marcel, 230
Panofsky, Erwin, 267
Paper Pistol Contract, The (Attlee), 234
Parker, Dorothy, 143
Party of One (Fadiman), 139
Pasternak, Boris, 294
Pater, Walter, 169
Pease, Howard, 59
Perfect Wagnerite, The (Shaw), 249
Persius, 294
Persuasion (Austen), 140, 302
Peyton Place (Metalious), 203
Phelps, Robert, 296–304
Philosophy of Literary Form (Burke), 291
Pilgrim Hawk, The (Wescott), 131
Pirandello, 302
Plato, 141, 197, 247
Plutarch, 170
Poe, Edgar Allan, 32, 121, 165
Poetics, The (Aristotle), 139
Poetry and the Age (Jarrell), 287–89
Poison Belt, The (Doyle), 234
Pope, Alexander, 144, 188, 272
Porter, Katherine Anne, 70, 131
Portrait of the Artist as a Young Man (Joyce), 247

Pound, Ezra, 289–90
Pratt, Fletcher, 97
Preface and Introduction to the Metaphysical Elements of Ethics (Kant), 160
President Fu Manchu (Rohmer), 100
Prisoner's Base (Stout), 121
Pritchett, V. S., 305
Professional Secrets (Cocteau), 303
Profession of Faith of a Savoyard Vicar (Rousseau), 191–92
Progress and Poverty (George), 140
Proust, Marcel, 226, 281, 316, 318, 321
Ptolemy, Claudius, 197

Queen, Ellery, 98

Rabelais, François, 195
Raleigh, Sir Walter, 143
Rand, Ayn, 221–24, 231
Rand, E. K., 280
Rapids Ahead, 117
Red and the Black, The (Stendhal), 215
Remembrance of Things Past (À la recherche du temps perdu) (Proust), 281
Renaissance of the Twelfth Century (Haskins), 280–81
Renard, Jules, 300
Revolt on Alpha C (Silverberg), 92
Richard III (Shakespeare), 129–30
Riders to the Sea (Synge), 128
Rilke, Rainer Maria, 202, 282–83
Rise and Fall of the Third Reich, The (Shirer), 142
Robbins, Harold, 142
Robe, The (Douglas), 142
Robeson, Kenneth, 100
Robinson, Edwin Arlington, 23
Roche, Mazo de la, 35
Roethke, Theodore, 287
Rogue Male (Household), 66
Rohmer, Sax, 54, 99, 100
Rolling Stones, The (Heinlein), 92
Romains, Jules, 230, 239
Rorem, Ned, 299, 303
Roth, Henry, 166
Rousseau, Jean-Jacques, 14, 160, 191–92, 196, 199, 220, 292
Roy Rogers and the River of Peril, 116
Ruskin, John, 169

Sacred Wood, The (Eliot), 257
Saint-Exupéry, Antoine de, 229
Saki, 225
Salter, James, 254, 299, 304
Santayana, George, 195
Sartre, Jean-Paul, 290, 307
Sayers, Dorothy, 167
Scarlet Letter, The (Hawthorne), 186–87

Scott, Sir Walter, 121
Searchers, The (LeMay), 141
Second Confession, The (Stout), 121
Secret and Urgent (Pratt), 97
Secret of Skeleton Island, The, 90–91
Secret Sea, 117
Seven Types of Ambiguity (Empson), 286–87
Sex Slave, 203
Shakespeare, William, 35, 68–69, 70, 128–30, 133–34, 136, 144, 171, 174, 181, 226, 270, 272, 282, 287, 300, 302
Shaw, George Bernard, 128, 140, 249
Shellabarger, Samuel, 35
Shelley, Percy Bysshe, 129, 143
Shiel, M. P., 169
Shirer, William L., 142
Shropshire Lad, A (Housman), 144
Shulman, Max, 112
Silverberg, Robert, 92
Sinclair, Upton, 194
Sin of Father Mouret, The (La Faute de L'Abbé Mouret) (Zola), 306, 310–11
Sisler on Baseball, 35
Six Great Modern Short Novels, 131
Slaughter, Frank G., 35
Sleep No More, 169
Small, Marvin, 35
Snow Treasure, 66
Sontag, Susan, 299
Sophocles, 188
Sound and Sense (Perrine), 164
Spanish Cave Mystery, The, 66
Spillane, Mickey, 170
Spin and Marty, 117
Spitzer, Leo, 293
Sport and Pastime, A (Salter), 304
Sportsman's Sketches (Turgenev), 289
Status Seekers, The (Packard), 131
Stead, Christina, 289
Steel Square Handbook, The, 35
Stein, Gertrude, 161
Steiner, George, 196
Stendhal, 13–14, 215, 226, 300
Stevens, Wallace, 33, 228, 255–56, 282
Stockton, Frank R., 225
Stopover: Tokyo (Marquand), 141
Story of Civilization, The (Durant), 159–60
Story of Philosophy (Durant), 159
Stout, Rex, 121, 122
Stranger, The (L'Étranger) (Camus), 230
Stranger in a Strange Land (Heinlein), 188
Streetfighting with Razors, 203
Summing Up, The (Maugham), 168
Sun Also Rises, The (Hemingway), 175
Susann, Jacqueline, 203
Sweet Lorain! (Weigl), 88
Swift, Jonathan, 168–69

Synge, I. M., 128
Syntopicon, The (Adler), 197

Tale of Two Cities, A (Dickens), 127
Tales of the South Pacific (Michener), 136–37,
   142
Talleyrand-Périgord, Charles Maurice de, 321
Tamerlane (Poe), 121
Tarzan and the City of Gold (Burroughs), 92
Tarzan and the Lost Safari (Burroughs), 116
Tarzan the Untamed (Burroughs), 137
Taylor, Jeremy, 169
Tell Me a Story (Laughton), 130
Temptation of St. Anthony (Flaubert), 307
Tender Is the Night (Fitzgerald), 175
Tennyson, Alfred Lord, 145, 222
Thackeray, William Makepeace, 139
Third Book of Criticism (Jarrell), 297
30 Days to a More Powerful Vocabulary (Funk
   and Lewis), 175
Thomas, Dylan, 145, 288
Thomas, Lowell, 35
Thomson, Virgil, 249
Thoreau, Henry David, 132, 135–36, 171,
   174, 195, 221, 222, 269
Those Barren Leaves (Huxley), 203
Thought and Letters in Western Europe, A.D.
   500–900 (Laistner), 280
Three Musketeers, The (Dumas), 97
Thurber, James, 269
Time Machine, The (Wells), 56
Tolkien, J. R. R., 280
Toi et Moi (Géraldy), 308
Tolstoy, Leo, 162, 266, 321
Tom Swift and His Jetmarine (Appleton), 91
Tom Swift in the Caves of Nuclear Fire (Apple-
   ton), 98
To the Finland Station (Wilson), 294
Tourneur, Cyril, 257
Treasure at First Base, 66
Trial, The (Kafka), 63
Trilling, Lionel, 291
Triple Thinkers, The (Wilson), 294
Trollope, Anthony, 272
Tropic of Cancer (Miller), 231
Troyes, Chrétien de, 280
Tunis, John R., 60
Turgenev, Ivan Sergeyevich, 289, 294
Twain, Mark, 42, 56, 199, 282
Twentieth-Century Culture: The Breaking Up
   (Phelps, ed.), 299
Twenty Thousand Leagues Under the Sea
   (Verne), 97
Tynan, Kenneth, 304

Ulysses (Joyce), 121

Unquiet Grave, The (Connolly), 301–2
Unvanquished, The (Faulkner), 131
Updike, John, 174

Valéry, Paul, 249, 275, 292, 302
Valley of the Dolls (Susann), 203
Van Doren, Mark, 172
Vanity Fair (Thackeray), 139
Vaughan, Henry, 272
Verne, Jules, 92, 97, 142, 229
Vidal, Gore, 299
Villon, François, 274
Virtue of Selfishness, The (A. Rand), 224
Vision, A (Yeats), 282
Voltaire, François-Marie Arouet, 160, 205

Waiting for Godot (En Attendant Godot) (Beck-
   ett), 128, 307
Walden (Thoreau), 132, 135–63, 174, 221, 222
War and Peace (Tolstoy), 162, 321
Waste Land, The (Eliot), 290
Waugh, Evelyn, 256, 264
Waverley, 121
Waves, The (Woolf), 300
Webster, John, 257
Weigl, Bruce, 88
Weil, Simone, 302
Wells, H. G., 56, 121
Welty, Eudora, 14, 243
Wescott, Glenway, 131, 297, 299, 303
Weston, Jesse, 257
What Is Literature? (Sartre), 290–91
Which Way to Mecca, Jack? (Blatty), 138
White, E. B., 59, 127
Whitman, Walt, 140, 150–51, 289
Wilde, Oscar, 90
Wilder, Thornton, 126
Williams, Oscar, 143, 144, 145, 289
Wills, Gary, 299
Wilson, Edmund, 293–94
Wind in the Willows, The (Grahame), 59
With Lawrence in Arabia (Thomas), 35
Wodehouse, P. G., 51
Wolfe, Thomas, 175
Woolf, Virginia, 300, 302
Words for the Wind (Roethke), 287
Wordsworth, William, 89, 144

Yeats, W. B., 145, 166, 255–56, 282
Yerby, Frank, 120
Yourcenar, Marguerite, 300
Yours Till Niagara Falls, 49

Zeb Pike—Boy Mountaineer, 64
Zola, Émile, 306, 310–11
Zorba the Greek (Kazantzakis), 221, 224

About the Author

Michael Dirda, longtime staff writer and senior editor for *The Washington Post Book World*, received the Pulitzer Prize for Distinguished Criticism in 1993. His major interests include intellectual and literary history, innovative or neglected writing of all sorts and classics in translation. His previous book, *Readings: Essays and Literary Entertainments*, gathers some of his more personal and lighthearted Sunday pieces.